Lee Soltow and Edward Stevens

The Rise of Literacy and the Common School in the United States

A Socioeconomic Analysis to 1870

Chicago
Originals

The Rise of Literacy

and the Common School

in the United States

The Rise of Literacy

and the Common School

in the United States

A Socioeconomic Analysis to 1870

Lee Soltow and Edward Stevens

The University of Chicago Press

Chicago & London

Lee Soltow is professor of economics at Ohio University
and author of *Men and Wealth in the United States,
1850–1870; Patterns of Wealthholding in Wisconsin since
1850;* and *Toward Income Equality in Norway.*

Edward Stevens is professor of education at Ohio
University and the author of numerous articles.

The University of Chicago Press, Chicago 60637
The University of Chicago Press, Ltd., London

© 1981 by The University of Chicago
All rights reserved. Published 1981
Printed in the United States of America
85 84 83 82 81   5 4 3 2 1

Library of Congress Cataloging in Publication Data

Soltow, Lee.
  The rise of literacy and the common school
in the United States.

  Bibliography: p.
  Includes index.
  1. Illiteracy—United States—History—19th
century.   2.   Public school—United States—History
—19th century.   I.   Stevens, Edward, 1938–
II.   Title.
LC151.S64   428.4   81-7464
ISBN 0-226-76812-0   AACR2

Contents

List of Illustrations

List of Tables

One

Introduction

It is always dangerous to speculate about the motivations of historians and the climate of opinion which helps to provoke their commentaries, yet it seems that the recent historical work on the development of literacy owes its emergence, in part, to a worldwide concern with the relationships between "modernization," literacy, and social policy. At the international level, efforts to eradicate illiteracy have been most visible in the UNESCO Experimental World Literacy Programme, the target populations for which have been primarily nonindustrial, third-world countries. In a 1973 appraisal of UN efforts to increase literacy, Mason has noted that there appears to be broad agreement among adult educators, planners, policymakers, and politicians that "illiteracy is one of the inhibitors in the process of the diffusion of innovation and a brake on the pace of 'modernization.'"[1] Aside from the difficulties in using the concept of "modernization" to address a cross-cultural phenomenon, recent attempts to combat worldwide adult illiteracy have for the most part been unsuccessful in confronting the problems of causation and of the linkages between literacy and socioeconomic development. The problem undoubtedly demands an approach that would be called interactionist, which is to say that any simplistic causal model must be replaced by a model emphasizing the reciprocal causal relations between literacy and social and economic institutions.

The problems encountered by post–World War II attempts to wage war on illiteracy, that is, problems of causation, definition, meaning, and context, seem to invoke a historical perspective and historiographical skills. Unfortunately, however, the historical study of such a fundamental process as the development of literacy in the making of modern civilizations is still in its infancy—a result, in part, of the traditional reluctance of historians to accept and apply the quantitative techniques capable of

1

generating a comprehensive selecting and weighing of those factors which determine the rise and perpetuation of literacy. In this study, quantitative techniques are employed, in conjunction with a descriptive context for developing social institutions, in order that the place of demographic and socioeconomic factors in the rise of literacy might be defined with greater accuracy. The extent of illiteracy and the processes whereby illiteracy was perpetuated and literacy maintained are our foci throughout. The precise estimation of the impact of socioeconomic and demographic factors, particularly population density, on the extent and distribution of illiteracy has been our major concern.

Certainly the most sophisticated of quantitative techniques cannot give meaning to numbers, nor can they be taken as a substitute for identifying the concepts and choosing the "right" questions to ask in a historical study. Nonetheless, they can be powerful tools with which to generate the basic evidence necessary to undertake such studies. The basic data for this study have been drawn from federal census manuscripts, local school attendance records from Ohio and New York, military records, petitions, deeds, wills, estate inventories, newspapers, textbooks, and children's literature. Data from manuscript censuses from the period 1840–70 provide an opportunity to examine county and regional variations in illiteracy rates as well as relationships among literacy, occupation, nativity, ethnicity, and wealth. The comprehensiveness of the censuses, that is, the fact that they provide information for an entire population and allow examination of changes in literacy rates over time, make them a valuable tool for the student of literacy.[2] While the army enlistee records we used extend from 1798 to 1894, their chief value for this study lies in the systematic data they provide for the first thirty years of the nineteenth century. This formative period for the new republic would otherwise be extremely difficult to study because the United States census did not gather literacy data before 1840. The use of census data in conjunction with local school records has enabled us to overcome some of the problems associated with data on aggregate school attendance published by state school officials— problems relating to length of attendance during the year and accuracy of data.[3] The particular uses to which we put these various records will be evident in succeeding chapters. At the outset, however, it should be pointed out that in a number of cases, the use of more than one source strengthens assertions which, if based upon one source only, would be open to question. In many instances we direct our comments to the development of literacy and schooling in Ohio because its rapid growth from a wilderness frontier in 1790 to a well-settled state by 1870 enables us to measure the impact of population density and rapid economic expansion on literacy. Thus, in addition to its larger, national focus, the study provides a monographic treatment of Ohio.

One of our first concerns is to bring together a number of sources from colonial America in order that the level of literacy by 1800 might be more precisely defined and the participation of illiterates in the economic and political lives of their respective communities might be assessed at a cultural stage when illiteracy rates were relatively high. We then examine three major vehicles for cultural transmission—the newspaper, the library, and the book trade—as they relate to (1) raising the consciousness of a people toward literacy (developing an ideology of literacy), (2) the achievement of literacy itself, and (3) the major upsurge in common schooling after 1830. Relationships between the common school and literacy are then discussed. Levels of study in reading, writing, spelling, and grammar are approximated from school attendance records, and school attendance itself is studied. The latter is treated within the context of school and work patterns of youth and by examining the special effects of wealth, nativity, and ethnicity on school enrollments. Finally, the level and distribution of illiteracy between 1840 and 1870 are examined by studying state, county, and regional variations and by assessing the extremes of illiteracy for clues which they might provide concerning the perpetuation of illiteracy. Demographic factors, including fertility, population density, urbanity, and intergenerational ties, are discussed in relation to the possible counterfactual case of a laissez-faire (noninterventionist) approach to the elimination of illiteracy.

The Problem of Definition

There is considerable difficulty in defining levels of literacy in a way that will be both operational and suitable for comparative analysis.[4] More often than not, students of literacy have viewed the achievement of literacy either as a way for the individual to cope with the uncertainties of his social or economic environment or as a way to achieve some ulterior community or national purpose, or as both. These aims often translate into the function-nonfunction distinction which is common when discussing and defining levels of literacy.[5] Such a distinction, however, is not so precise as one would like, for accompanying the distinction are always the questions, functional for whom, where, and at what time? It is certainly conceivable that literacy is functional for one individual at one time and place, but not at another for the same individual. As Graff has noted, "Without the specification of a context in which literacy is to serve either the individual or society, attempts to establish a valid concept of functional literacy cannot succeed."[6] Functional literacy was defined by the United States Army in World War II, for instance, when it defined illiterates as "persons who were incapable of understanding the kinds of written instructions that are needed for carrying out basic military functions or tasks.''[7] The understanding of nonmilitary tasks, on the other hand, might present quite a different problem and quite a different standard for functionality. In an earlier period, a rude trader of the Tennessee frontier might have found his basic literacy adequate for dealing with merchants and river boatmen in the mid–Ohio River. Such a man, had he decided to improve his economic well-being by moving to Pittsburgh or Cincinnati and becoming a merchant, might well have found his basic literacy inadequate in conducting a city business, and socially inadequate as well among the more literate merchants of the city. It is not likely that this study will settle the functionality issue as applied to nineteenth-century America. We do, however, offer some valuable insights into the distribution of literacy relative to the distribution of wealth, and are thus in a position to interpret for the period under study the functionality of literacy as it related to economic mobility and success.

In a monograph published by UNESCO in 1956, Gray offered a general definition of the literate person as one who ''has acquired the knowledge and skills in reading and writing which enable him to engage effectively in all those activities in which literacy is normally assumed in his culture or group.''[8] Within such a definition, however, literacy is a very flexible concept and can be interpreted as covering a range from an ''absolute minimum to an undetermined maximum'' of ability:

> At any minimum level, literacy may be vaguely defined as 'ability to read and write in a language.' This definition may be modified by specifying a certain level above the absolute minimum, as for example, by excluding the mere ability to write and read one's own name, or by adding to the definition some such words as 'a simple message' or 'a letter from (or to) a friend.' This is the relative minimum level of ability generally implied in questions on literacy included in population censuses.[9]

Defining literacy in an operational manner has remained a difficult process for historians and current reformers alike. One of the most common attempts to define literacy has been the assignment of school grade level as an indicator of reading ability. Few educators today, however, would argue that this measure has any virtue other than simplicity. More recently, the ability to follow directions on a traffic ticket and accuracy in interpreting an insurance policy have been more successfully employed as measures of functional literacy.[10] One interesting assessment of literacy was carried out in accordance with school law by teachers in the state of Ohio in 1853. In this attempt to assess accurately the numbers of school children who could be classified as literate, teachers were requested to judge whether or not a child could read and write and to specify the academic subjects in which the child was enrolled. These reports were returned to township clerks and published in aggregate form in 1854. An analysis of these statistics shows that enrollment in the subject of grammar was decisive in determining whether or not children were judged to be literate. The inference certainly is that in the best judgment of teachers taken collectively, literacy was achieved with the taking of grammar. Thus, in this important instance, we have judgments about literacy given by people who closely observed the process of becoming schooled in literacy. We also have a more refined measure than the simple grade-level measure. Moreover, the data, when combined with school attendance figures, enable us to estimate the age at which literacy was expected to be achieved in the school setting.

Historically, the problems of definition are similar, although greater in degree, to those encountered by present-day reformers; that is, the twin difficulties of comparability of data and defining literacy operationally remain much the same. In the use of census figures on illiteracy there are major obstacles to comparability of data even within a single country. As Clammer notes in his study *Literacy and Social Change,* the level of literacy is "self-defined" in many censuses and "the accuracy of this clearly depends on the ability of the respondent to assess his own competence and on his honesty." Moreover, "these factors are likely to be highly fluid," notes Clammer, "especially where the literacy is low," and the problem is "analogous to that of testing the intelligence of non-literate children."[11]

In the United States in 1840, census enumerators simply asked the heads of families how many white persons in their families over twenty years of age were unable to read or write. For 1850 and 1860, enumerators recorded the same data on the basis of *individual responses* for those over twenty. Beginning in 1870, however, census takers included ages ten to nineteen in their inquiry and asked, "Can you read and can you write?" The assumptions underlying the change in the 1870 census are significant and point to another problem in determining actual levels of illiteracy:

> great numbers of persons, rather than admit their ignorance, will claim to read, who will not pretend that they can write. . . . If a man cannot write, it is fair to assume that he cannot read well; that is, that he really comes within the illiterate class. . . . Taking the whole country together, hundreds of thousands of persons appear in the class 'Cannot write' over and above those who confess that they cannot read. This is the true number of the illiterate of the country.[12]

Despite these limitations, census data have much to recommend them. In his essay "Towards a Meaning of Literacy," Graff has argued, using the 1861 Ontario, Canada, census, that census data give us a minimum standard of literacy and, when administered in a standardized format, enable the researcher to make intergroup comparisons, which are valuable in studying the dispersion of literacy among various occupational and ethnic groups. Moreover, in the case of the Ontario census, the measure of literacy was direct in the sense that the respondents' signatures were required on completed forms, thus making signature counts possible.[13] Such counts are not possible with United States censuses, where the burden for accuracy was placed totally on the shoulders of the enumerators. (We do not discuss here the actual meaning and reliability of signatures as a measure of literacy since, with the exception of chapter 2, they do not form the basis of our study. We do note, however, that Lockridge in his study *Literacy in Colonial New England* assumes that the level for signatures "runs below but closely parallels reading skills and runs above but roughly parallels writing skills." He concludes that "the most precise *absolute* definition which could be placed on signatures is that they correspond to the actual level of fluent reading.")[14] Finally, the comprehensiveness of census data has much to recommend it. Because federal censuses, for example, were administered so broadly, their figures lend themselves to interregional and intergroup comparisons as well as comparisons over time. Thus, in a study which makes comparisons over an eighty-year period during which data from four federal censuses are available, the use of the census is a most valuable tool.

The Problem of Purpose and Meaning

A critical assessment of the UNESCO Experimental World Literacy Programme in 1976 noted the importance of the notion of stewardship among governments and nongovernmental agencies which promoted literacy programs. To put it differently, "Illiterates were defined and interpreted by literates," and there accompanied this the view that illiterates were "marginal" men unable to participate in the "life of the national community." The implication, it was noted, "is that the illiterate's life has somehow less human value than that of the literate." The concept of the marginal man is closely tied to the presumption that illiteracy is a form of isolation and that the "illiterate is unable to communicate with his fellows in written symbols and hence is largely restricted to his immediate social groups for many forms of social stimuli."[15] The assumption that the illiterate is a marginal person and a threat to social stability in a democracy is summed up (not endorsed) by Graff:

> Their dire position leaves the illiterates outside the dominant social processes ... exacerbating their own disadvantages and enlarging the loss they represent to the society and the economy. ... Moreover, their existence threatens the function of internalized controls and the successful operation of a democratic, participatory social order. Comprising either a real or a symbolic threat, or both, to social progress, they are targets of abuse and denigration which can in many cases

become attacks upon their social existence—in rhetoric, in policy, or in action.[16]

The presumption that illiteracy is an obstacle to communication and thus a deterrent to social interaction carries with it the judgment that literacy itself is a mind-expanding skill, that it is valuable in information processing and aids the individual in the making of decisions and the sharing of power. Illiteracy, on the other hand, contributes to powerlessness and a relative lack of autonomy. Thus, learning to read, as Brown suggests, is a "political act," and the inability to read may be seen as an obstacle to participation in the life of the political community.[17] The question remains, however, a "political act" by whom?

The degree to which illiteracy was an obstacle to political participation, for instance, certainly was not of the magnitude from the sixteenth to the eighteenth centuries that it has come to be in the Western industrialized democracies of the twentieth century. As we note in chapter 2, the seventeenth-century American colonist apparently did not find illiteracy an obstacle to political activity. During the Lutheran Reformation a century earlier, the illiterate was also able to participate in one of the most decisive political events of that period—the Peasants' Revolt. Literacy surely was an influential factor in the spread of that uprising, as Febvre and Martin have pointed out. They note that Zwingli had testified at the outset of the revolt that "the home of every peasant had become a school where he studied both Old and New Testaments." Equally important is their observation that "even those who were illiterate had the text read and explained to them by better educated friends."[18]

In Great Britain in the late eighteenth century, the vital link between literacy and political activity under different circumstances has also been noted. The extensive circulation of Thomas Paine's *The Rights of Man* is a case in point: the total circulation of part 2 of *The Rights of Man* was reputed to be 1.5 million copies at the time of Paine's death. While such a figure seems "incredible" to Altick, the circulation of the work was extensive enough to result in the Royal Proclamation of 1792 prohibiting the selling of " 'divers wicked and seditious writings.' "[19] Educationally, the result was an attack by conservatives on the thousands of Sunday schools which they perceived to be at the root of the problem because they were facilitating the reading habit among working-class people. The advocates of Sunday schools were unjustly blamed for their failure to anticipate the coming of Tom Paine, but they were quite rightly judged to have provided the opportunity for consciousness raising. That Sunday schools had sought to provide only education consonant with conservative political views and traditional morality simply made the situation more ironic.[20]

In the foregoing cases the act of becoming literate was presumed to be an act of consciousness raising for the individual, whether the emergent consciousness ultimately resulted in greater social control, in political exploitation, or in the enhancement of private thought and the exercise of greater choice among attitudes, beliefs, and values. Yet, in these cases also, there is the implication that illiterates do not understand what is in their best interests, indeed, that illiteracy is an obstacle to the development of higher cognitive powers. Berger has noted that literacy is often a form of cognitive imperialism no matter what the "ideological or political coloration." He argues, moreover, that apart from moral offensiveness, cognitive imperialism commits the philosophical error of assuming a "hierarchical view of consciousness."[21] Nineteenth-century reformers, as we shall see, implicitly accepted such a hierarchical view as they sought to establish links between intelligence, virtue, and literateness in an ideology of literacy.

In a recent review of literature bearing upon the psychology of literacy, Scribner and Cole have observed a similar stance taken by developmentalists (Bruner, Greenfield, and Olsen) and have noted that "from this [developmental] perspective the capacities generated by literacy are seen not merely as different, but as higher-order capacities because they resemble the abilities that psychological theories attribute to later stages in development."[22] Our interviews with contemporary illiterates, however, reinforce the finding that it is a mistake to attribute greater intellectual capacity to literates by virtue of their being literate. Three individuals, one a coal miner, one a certified welder, and one a mould maker, serve as examples from the twelve illiterate individuals interviewed by us. All are dependent as a result of their illiteracy. The eldest of these three—the coal miner—relies upon a trustworthy friend when the signing of documents is necessitated. The certified welder entrusts much to his banker and lawyer when confronted with legal and financial documents, and the forty-five-year-old mould maker finds that his consumer patterns are restricted, for he must purchase items from salespeople he can fully trust. Thus, each of the three finds it necessary to rely upon others to compensate for his inability to read and to express himself in standard writing.

All three of our interviewees, however, showed a desire to gain access to printed information, and all had devised ways to accomplish this. The miner, who wished to keep abreast of mining laws, relied upon his wife to read the newspaper to him. When it came to the performance of mining operations themselves, however, he felt no inadequacies. Similarly, the welder's performance was not affected, as he had acquired the ability to read blueprints despite his general inability to read. In the case of the mould maker, his trust in a friend combined with ingenuity enabled him to decipher his first love letters from his wife-to-be by having one friend read one word and another friend read the second and so on, so that only he knew the entire substance of the missive. In return letters, however, he was forced to rely upon one friend. Perhaps his most startling achievement was that of being secretary of his church. He was able to record some notes as pictures—for example, a wolf's head for Pastor Wolfe's name and a plate and knife picture representing a banquet. After a church meeting his wife would write out the notes as he dictated them, leaving enough space for pictures for his rereading. The pastor adeptly helped with the subterfuge in unexpected situations.

The perceptions of the coal miner and the certified welder are particularly interesting for their bearing on the question of intellectual superiority (higher-order cognitive functioning) and literateness. Both the certified welder and the elderly coal miner believed (whether rightly or wrongly) that their intellectual processes were more lucid and superior for the fact of their being illiterate. The welder explained that in an important sense his thought processes are superior to those of a literate individual because he may take more time than a literate individual to ponder or reflect upon a problem. The inference is that a literate individual often thinks in an automatic and restrictive fashion based upon his past experiences of reading and writing. The coal miner volunteered several times that unlettered people are more contemplative, observant, and imaginative than people whose minds are occupied with reading the thoughts of others; that is, he felt that people who read are often considering two views simultaneously—the author's and their own—to the neglect of clear thinking. Thus, literate individuals were perceived as captives of their words, while these illiterates saw themselves as experiencing greater freedom by not relying on print.

The developmental model, Scribner and Cole point out, conveys the impression that the components of literacy, whether an alphabetic script or essay, "are likely to have the same psychological consequences in all cultures irrespective of the contexts of use or of the social institutions in which literacy is embedded." "In reality," they conclude, "the developmental model has been elaborated in terms of institutions and technologies specific to our own society."[23] The point, for our purposes, is that the "hierarchical view of consciousness" implicit in developmental models is easily translated into an attitude of cultural imperialism.[24] While the developmental model was not clearly articulated for cognitive processes in the first half of the nineteenth century, it is clear (as is evident in chapter 3) that literateness was perceived by some to be associated with higher intellectual capacity and that the illiterate individual was seen as the less able one in intellectual matters. Within the school, then, becoming literate may be seen as a link between the cognitive (academic achievement) and the affective (socialization) dimensions of education. In turn, higher performance on a scale of accomplishment in literacy could have been interpreted not only as evidence of the development of higher cognitive powers, but as an indicator of having been more thoroughly socialized. Thus, it was possible for literacy to become part of "education as intrusion," as Finklestein calls it, that is, to become a tool to facilitate such functions of the school as the selecting and sorting of individuals for manpower allocation or social stratification, and the socialization of individuals to prescribed norms.[25] The moral didactic of nineteenth-century schoolbooks, in turn, may be seen to serve as part of the larger purpose to carry the "word" to unsullied and delinquent youth alike in hopes that many might be brought to an acceptable level of socialization.

What is evident (regardless of one's judgments about nineteenth-century moral didactic) is that literacy as consciousness raising carries with it the implication that literacy and the act of becoming literate are an expression of a system of values. If literacy is perceived as an apt way to the efficient socialization of the young, for instance, then we would expect that, substantively, literacy would include norms in accord with the established political community. Likewise, literacy might serve the interests of revolutionary power as it has in Cuba. Literacy thus becomes a way of "linking meaning to the conditions of concrete behavior" and a way of "organizing human action."[26] We may say then, by way of explanation, that the meaning of being literate is manifest in the system of values carried by the condition of being literate and in the behaviors which are linked to that condition. It would not be feasible in a single study to consider all the behaviors which are linked to the condition of literacy, but we do treat the role of the school in helping to transmit a value system accompanying literacy. The role of the newspaper in the promotion of literacy is seen in the same light, and we note that an ideology of literacy is evidenced in both newspapers and schoolbooks.

Finally, the meaning and purpose of literacy take on added significance if we consider literacy as a form of social control, that is, as a way to impose the values of one group upon another. Recent literature on this dimension of literacy takes as its point of departure the assumption that in a nonliterate society alternative solutions to social problems "are quickly forgotten and excluded from the [social] body of knowledge because, among other things, the system of recording such alternatives [depends upon] memory and oral transmission."[27] In a nonliterate society, Goody and Watt argue, "every social situation cannot but bring the individual into contact with the group's patterns of thought, feeling and action: the choice is between the cultural tradition—or solitude."[28] But the forcefulness of the oral tradition, it might be argued, eliminates alternatives to traditional behaviors and beliefs. Heyman argues that literacy "allows the amassing of cultural tradition in a fashion different, both in kind and degree, from the possibilities inherent in a nonliterate society."[29] To put it differently, literacy allows members of a culture to depart from traditional modes of thought and to seek alternative ways of addressing social problems. In recent years the most dramatic example of the impact of literacy as social control has been in revolutionary Cuba.

Historically, the concept of literacy as social control is forcefully illustrated in a different way in the work of Griffith Jones in eighteenth-century Wales, in that of Hannah More among the Mendip peasants, in the Sunday school movement of early nineteenth-century America, and in the move to state control of education. All illustrate the particularity of literacy, that is, the necessity for interpreting the meaning of literacy within a particular context, and all demonstrate the use of literacy to impose the values of one social group upon another, that is, its use as a form of social control. We turn now to a consideration of these examples in order to explore some of the ways in which reformers (both British and American) linked literacy to the imposition of established values.

Literacy, Religion, and Social Control

From the seventeenth through the nineteenth centuries, religious leaders in America and Great Britain often spoke of the need for literacy within the context of spiritual salvation. In their commitment to lay literacy through Bible reading they followed the precedents so forcefully established by Protestant leaders during the Reformation. Their concerns were both social and individual; both the salutary effects of Bible reading on individual souls and the preservation of social order were their objectives. The process of becoming literate, circumscribed as it was by religious instruction, served as an efficient means for the imposition of social and spiritual values. In short, literacy for social control was a guiding principle in the period which forms a prolegomenon to the major thrust of our study.

Before examining the links among religion, literacy, and social control, some qualifications are in order. It is possible that the imposition of control by organized religion could be achieved by an oral tradition among an essentially illiterate population. A multiplier effect, however, would be produced with printed materials which would reach those not hearing the words of the churched. In the United States, the cogency of having a literate society achieved its thrust not only from individuals and groups dominated by religious fervor, but also from the spirit of general cultural enlightenment conveyed by men like Benjamin Franklin, Benjamin Rush, and Thomas Jefferson. In addition, families themselves may have seen the need for literacy in their daily economic activities. The desire to understand legal documents, particularly those dealing with land titles and other property, also could have provided a strong thrust in establishing a literate society.

A statistician dealing with literacy in America in the seventeenth and eighteenth centuries might crave an adequate data set where literacy could be related to religious, economic, legal, and family activities as well as to demographic variables. A comprehensive set of measures might show that religious or economic activity explained relatively small portions of the total variance in literacy levels. Unfortunately, we are lacking the ideal data set, although we do, in the succeeding chapters, deal with all the factors mentioned above. Our purpose in this section, however, is to outline the social and ideological contexts for the achievement of literacy in the eighteenth century. It is not our purpose to explain differentials in literacy rates on the basis of religious convictions.

In his *Evangelical Religion and Popular Education* McLeish notes that after many frustrating years of attempting to propagate the Gospel among illiterate Welsh peasants, Griffith Jones, an eighteenth-century clergyman of the Anglican Church and the founder of Welsh primary education, became convinced that children and adults alike must be taught to read and that preaching and catechizing without basic literacy was doomed to failure.[30] According to Altick, Jones shared the conviction of the Society for Promoting Christian Knowledge that schools were necessary to inculcate among the masses the values of piety, morality, industry, and, in general, a commitment to the Protestant faith.[31] For Jones, "reading was valuable only insofar as it [would] fix the truths communicated by catechizing firmly in the mind."[32] Instruction sufficient to understand the Bible and catechism took only three months, and thus it was possible to make rapid progress in eradicating Welsh illiteracy through the establishment of circulating schools for the Welsh peasantry.

Jones did not strive for the broadening of literacy to writing and calculating, since they were of no use in conveying fixed moral precepts. (It is interesting to note that later the Reverend Andrew Bell in his monitorial schools still limited literacy among the poor to Bible reading in order to avoid the risk of elevating the poor "above their condition.")[33] Today, we are accustomed to think of reading in terms of "information processing," in terms, that is, of a skill which could and should be extended to all dimensions of understanding. For Jones, however, "any idea that education [and literacy] could be an agent for the liberation of the imagination, or a training of the reason [was] completely alien."[34] That education and literacy were particularized in the context of the Welsh peasantry's relationship to established religion is clear from Jones's experience. Literacy was in no way designed to serve the aims of modernization, as it was with Victorian culture less than a century later. The carefully circumscribed world of literacy, as designed by Jones, is apparent in the three conditions he laid down for the operation of the Welsh circulating schools:

The sole Design of this Undertaking is to promote their spiritual and everlasting Welfare, and to make them more conscientiously useful in the Rank they are in. . . . It is by no means the Design of this Spiritual Kind of Charity to make them Gentlemen, but Christians and Heirs of eternal life. . . . We do not meddle with teaching any of them Writing or Cyphering, which would require more Time than their Circumstances and more Expense than my little Cash can afford.[35]

In his attempt to systematically "impose the ideology of the middle classes on the Welsh peasantry," Jones typified what may be called "charismatic innovation." Compared with Hannah More,' his awareness of social class, says McLeish, was marginal relative to his concern with saving souls.[36] This, however, does not negate the importance of his work to social control. Rather, it simply testifies to the persistent link between literacy for piety and education for discipline in eighteenth-century schooling.

For Hannah More, and for those who supported adult schools in England, "the preservation of the hierarchical social structure was central to their whole conception of the need for literacy education."[37] More, whom McLeish calls a "Pillar of the Establishment," was solidly opposed to any change in the structure of society or government, yet her work may surely be considered social innovation even though she, like others of her day, perceived social causality "in the form of an inscrutable Providence which meted out some kind of rough justice in so far as social classes . . . were concerned."[38] Thus, the poor were the depraved, and their misfortunes followed directly from their condition of depravity. Bible literacy for the poor, however, would allow them to do their religious duty, and in the achievement of literacy itself they would be taught habits of industry and thrift. Of her work among the poor of Cheddar, More wrote the following:

My plan of instruction is extremely simple and limited. They learn, on week-days, such coarse works as may fit them for servants. I allow of no writing for the poor. My object is not to make them fanatics, but to train up the lower classes in habits of industry and piety. I know no way of teaching morals but by teaching principles; or inculcating Christian principles without imparting a good knowledge of scripture.[39]

For More, the operation of Sunday schools and the attempt to combat adult illiteracy became part of a larger concern with community rehabilitation, the aim of which, notes McLeish, "was to give *everyone* in the community the idea of an ordered life" by reconstructing the fallen cottage and village economy of the past. The aim was to encourage the poor to help themselves; the methods were Bible literacy and the formation of women's "benefit" societies. Special incentives were established and rewards for proper behavior given:

on marriage a girl who had attended school and who was a member of a club was presented with five shillings, a pair of white stockings knitted by Hannah, and with a Bible. Bibles, prayer books, cheap Repository Tracts, money, clothing and other tangible rewards were carefully allocated according to a graduated incentive scheme to club members and their children.[40]

The penny press had, according to More, "brought down to the pockets and capacities of the poor" a "speculative infidelity" which "forms a new era in our history." The antidote was to capture the popular literature "for the greater glory of God and the security of the nation." Drawing upon prior Methodist experiments with religious tracts, and a tradition which dated back to the production of "cheap pamphlets and propagandist tracts" successfully used by German printers in behalf of the Lutheran Reformation, More and her sympathizers produced the "cheap Repository Tracts." These tracts, with their moral tales and ballads, attempted to combat "seditious" and "anti-Christian" literature in the latter part of the eighteenth century. The price of one halfpenny, one penny, or one and one-half pennies, made the tracts competitive with other popular literature, and by 1796, one year after their issue, 2 million had been sold wholesale.[41] While the threat of Jacobinism had receded by the time that the tracts were officially discontinued in 1798, the possibilities for future political unrest remained and the *perceived* link between literacy and dissent continued in the minds of conservatives. The Evangelicals believed they had found the right formula for transmitting correct morality: "Sound religious and political doctrine" "embedded in wholesomely entertaining tales and songs."[42]

The tract tradition was in the making, and more important, it had been proved that a mass audience lay waiting for the moral didactic of this popular literature. The methods of More, however, were apparently too successful for political and clerical conservatives alike. In the late years of the eighteenth century the publication of Price's *Observations on the Nature of Civil Liberty* and Paine's *Rights of Man,* the formation of numerous "Jacobin" societies, and the flourishing of radical bookshops brought an outburst of protest by British conservatives against the "seditious" press and an angered reaction to Sunday schools, which were seen as harbingers of a potentially dangerous reading public.[43] Much of the conservative reaction, however unjustly, focused upon Hannah More and her "Evangelical friends," who, in her words, "stood charged with 'sedition, disaffection, and a general aim to corrupt the principles of the community.'"[44]

The tract tradition, which had become well-established by the end of the eighteenth century, remained strong in the nineteenth century, writes Webb.[45] The lessons learned from the mass publication of tracts were of inestimable benefit to both tractarian societies and Sunday schools in the United States. The difficulties of Hannah More and other Evangelicals, however, did not go unobserved by future tract writers. Thus, the question which emerged from their efforts and which occupied the "best minds of England," notes Altick, was, "How could the people's reading be made safe?"[46] Among the Evangelicals, he continues, the "reading habit" was "indispensable as a daily program of prayer and observance of a strict moral code":

> With the Bible always at the center, there grew up a huge literature of admonition, guidance and assurance.
> So insistently did the evangelicals emphasize the spiritual necessity of reading that the old seventeenth-century bibliolatry revived. Wherever their influence reached, Bible-reading was practiced less as a conscious exercise of the intellect than as a ritual which was an end in itself. . . .
> One who knew his letters, regardless of any further education, was sufficiently equipped to perform the sacred rite which lay at the very heart of religion.[47]

In the United States, the tract tradition was equally strong and reflected the indebtedness of American proselytizers to their British counterparts. The most observable of the tractarian efforts were among the Methodists, and their impact was particularly apparent in frontier areas of low population density. Thus, notes Miyakawa, "a significant Methodist contribution to western education was the mass circulation of its low-priced books and pamphlets. . . . Methodists introduced books and pamphlets into areas almost destitute of reading matter, and they helped many westerners to develop the reading habit."[48]

As we have suggested previously, the use of literacy for social control was frequent in America in the early years of the new republic. Here, as in Great Britain, the most notable examples occurred as part of the sweeping missionary activities of evangelical Protestantism and the "experience and sense of common purpose shared by the transatlantic evangelicals."[49] Over the protestations of the many churchmen who objected to the work of learning to read as a profanation of the Sabbath, Sunday schools nonetheless applied themselves not only to saving the unconverted but to the teaching of basic literacy.[50] The two objectives, in fact, were perfectly complementary, and between 1815 and 1826 interdenominational efforts among Presbyterians, Congregationalists, Methodists, Baptists, and Episcopalians succeeded in founding the American Education Society, American Home Missionary Society, American Bible Society, American Tract Society, and American Sunday School Union. All, says Griffin, "worked outside regular church organizations to convert the nation to God."[51] In the process of conversion,

Sunday schools, modified but still deeply indebted to British forerunners, served an important function in promoting the sanctity of property rights, the ideal of social stability, and the prevention of crime and delinquency through Bible literacy and the reading of Christian tracts.[52]

Perhaps the best example of a concerted drive to teach basic literacy and Bible literacy along with the general tenets of Christian belief and behavior was that undertaken in Sunday school activities prior to the establishment of the American Sunday School Union. In the early years of the nineteenth century particularly, the teaching of basic reading skills and Bible literacy was an important element in the overall Christian education offered by these schools. Christian education, moreover, went beyond increasing the probability of personal salvation. It was, as Kaestle has noted, ''an effort by reformers to solve social problems through moral education sactioned by the Bible.''[53]

The First Day Society of Philadelphia, led by Benjamin Rush and Bishop William White among others, is an excellent example of the way in which voluntarism and philanthropy brought to young scholars an integrated mode of instruction which included basic literacy, moral didactic, and character formation. All reading lessons, generally for the poor, were from the Bible, and the content of primers and spelling books approved by the society ''consisted of words and short sentences from the Scriptures.'' The total molding of character was the aim of instruction, and premiums rewarding good behavior were standard practice. The 2,127 scholars who received free instruction in the first ten years of the society's existence were given as premiums for good behavior such volumes as *Beauties of Creation, Catechism of Nature, Doaley's Fables,* and *Fruits of the Father's Love.* Control of student behavior both in and out of school was a principal objective and was codified in the rules of government for schools. Teachers, for example, were required ''to see that pupils committed to their charge attended the places of public worship to which they severally belonged.''[54] A rule regulating cleanliness also stipulated the following for scholars:

> if guilty of lying, swearing, pilfering, indecent talking, or any other misbehavior, the teacher shall point out the evil of such conduct, and if that should prove unavailing, notify the visiting committee who, if they see cause, are to expel such delinquent from the school, in the presence of the other scholars.[55]

The close relationship among basic literacy, Bible literacy, and the formation of Christian character continued to be widespread until the mid-1820s wherever Sunday schools flourished. Rice has noted that American Sunday schools adapted graded plans of instruction from Raike's schools and the London Sunday-School Union but that in the early American schools the six grades common in English Sunday schools were reduced to four. The alphabet and monosyllabic words were taught first, and these were followed by instruction in the spelling of words with two or more syllables in the next grade. The third grade was composed of scholars who could read, albeit imperfectly, while the fourth and highest grade included those "who could readily read in the New Testament." Throughout, instruction was accompanied by a system of rewards and punishments based upon red tickets (worth one-half cent) and blue tickets (worth one-twelfth cent) which could be redeemed every three months for religious books and tracts. Penalties involved the forfeiture of such tickets and were assessed for absenteeism, neglect of recitation, and improper behavior in church.[56]

The close relationship between instruction in basic literacy and Christian character formation gradually gave way to a specialization of labor whereby the American Sunday School Union, formed from the Sunday and Adult School Union in 1824, came to rely more heavily upon the common schools to provide basic literacy and reserved for its own objectives Bible literacy and Christian training. The energies of the union as they still pertained to literacy in general, however, continued to be devoted to the development of proper instructional strategies, the preparation of dictionaries, commentaries, manuals, and primers, the publication of periodicals for teachers and juvenile religious literature, and the establishment of libraries for public use. By mid-century, Sunday schools (which were cheap and boasted of a good record in providing basic literacy) were used as substitutes only for the few public schools "which failed to arrive."[57] This institutional division of labor did not mean that basic literacy, Bible literacy, and Christian training were experientially separate for the many scholars who attended both common and Sunday schools. In the Protestant consensus which dominated the common school prior to the Civil War, children still were expected to acquire the "comprehensive life orientation" which accompanied a Protestant world view and which would suit them for success in American culture.[58]

Throughout the eighteenth century the close link between Protestantism, literacy, and socialization was very much in evidence. In some cases, voluntarism was the characteristic mode of imposition, but in others, as Lockridge notes, state intervention appears to have been decisive. In Calvinist Scotland, where the overwhelming majority of people adhered to the Church of Scotland, cooperation between Church and state resulted in the establishment of parish and burgh schools. The moral and spiritual culture of the children was clearly at stake, and the heritage of John Knox had strength enough to link religion, schooling, and literacy in a moral imperative.[59] Under these conditions the male literacy rate of 33 percent in 1675 rose to nearly 90 percent by 1800.[60] The impact of Protestantism is even more dramatic in Sweden, where the State Church oversaw the reading skills and catechetical knowledge of each parish member from 1650 forward.[61] The quality of literacy, however, was uneven under these best of conditions. Using the parish catechetical examination records, Johansson has noted that the discrepancy between oral reading and comprehension was considerable, and that about 75 percent of those who were high achievers in oral ability comprehended "partially at best."[62] The point is an important one for those who would attempt to judge the quality of literacy in the seventeenth and eighteenth centuries, for literacy in many instances was limited to recitation and memorization of familiar passages and did not include the interpretation of "new" reading matter. The problem persists when judging the quality of literacy in the nineteenth century; "subsequent pedagogic efforts in literacy," notes Resnick, "were heavily influenced by early religious activities," and the same gaps between word recognition and comprehension might be expected to persist in the century of common school reform.[63] But perhaps in these cases, as well as in colonial New England, the gap between recognition and comprehension, while present, was not significant, since the direction of Protestant concern was not toward the creation of alternative patterns of behavior to adjust to changing economic conditions. Rather, social innovation operated within a socially conservative context where ritual in the form of reading recitation was functional in terms of a moral imperative and proper socialization. The purpose and method of achieving literacy were interpreted within the existing social structure, and the type of literacy achieved was closely linked to the goals of established institutions and the imposition of values associated with these institutions. Literacy thus was never given more than a utilitarian value to serve greater spiritual and social ends, and this was nowhere more evident than in Puritan (and, later, Congregationalist) New England.

The development of literacy in the late eighteenth and the first half of the nineteenth centuries remained very much tied to Protestantism. Prior to (but not terminating with) the era of Victorian cultural influence in America, political leaders and those reformers interested in solving the political problems of an emerging republic gave a great deal of thought to the relationship of education to the process of nation building and cultural integration. Nation and culture were certainly not coterminous in early nineteenth-century America, but efforts to make them so were found in proposals for the reform of the English language and in enthusiastic proposals for a national system of higher education. One may easily conceive of the impact of Victorian culture in terms of Kuhn's paradigmatic explanation for scientific discovery. If we follow the lead of Pratte in applying Kuhn's model to the examination of ideology, it is clear that the first quarter of the nineteenth century in the United States witnessed the beginning of a shift from a religious-literacy framework for education to a nation building–literacy framework.[64] The two emphases were not incompatible, and, in fact, the former was quite capable of accommodating the nation building–literacy model for some time. The very conception of nationality, itself, was Protestant, notes Timothy Smith, and leading citizens by mid-century "assumed that Americanism and Protestantism were synonyms and that education and Protestantism were allies."[65] This was true particularly in the early years of the nineteenth century, when economic changes had not yet made their full impact on the social structure of the family and when evangelical Protestantism effectively laid claim to newly settled regions of the American West. Nonetheless, the intrusion of the "civic-national" model for literacy, as Resnick calls it, signaled the more general, but gradual, modernization of American culture. By the late 1820s, in turn, educational reformers were able to *begin* the systematization of the common school, a process carried on with missionary zeal and the faith that state-supported schooling would find a middle ground between the secularism of nation building and economic expansion and the sectarianism of the evangelical Protestant tradition.[66]

Ironically, the pan-Protestantism of the common school made the wedding of secular and religious instruction possible. The historical and conceptual link between Protestantism and worldly success provided a foundation for the broad-based but essentially Protestant values taught in public schools, where moral training was a standard feature of instruction. For reformers, the public school was to become "all things to all children": "a classroom, a family room, a church house," as Schultz has noted.[67] The impression should not be given, however, that opposition was absent. H. Harbaugh, writing for the *Mercersburg Quarterly Review,* criticized the public school system of Pennsylvania for making "no provision whatever for the religious wants of children."[68] By the late nineteenth century, however, the following compromise solution to secular versus religious instruction could be proposed by a Protestant religious spokesman:

> The State is . . . pretty generally regarded as acting entirely within its own proper sphere when it provides for the education of the young by the establishment of free common schools. But it is also pretty generally conceded that mere secular knowledge is not enough even for the purposes of good citizenship. . . . Education to be of any real, practical value, must help a man to solve the problem of his own life . . . , to unfold the thought of the divine mind as revealed in his own creation.[69]

No doubt there were remnants of bitterness over the tendency to exclude sectarian teaching from the common schools. Yet, as Tyack has noted of Oregon ministers and schoolmen, there was a belief that a "middle ground" could be reached "between secularism and sectarianism: a Protestant common denominator."[70] In the nineteenth century literacy itself became a favored vehicle for cultural and political integration, and we see in efforts to develop a literate public the dilemma of nineteenth-century American nation building itself—the plight, that is, of liberal democracy with its political concern for social integration necessitating a shared community of values, but its socioeconomic concern with the value of competitiveness and the provision for upward social mobility through some system of social differentiation. The moral consensus assumed by nineteenth-century public school reformers made it possible for them to see in literacy a vehicle for both social integration and social differentiation. As we demonstrate in chapter 3, the ideology of literacy developed in schoolbooks and newspapers enabled reformers to link morality and intellect: literacy could be an instrument for moral consensus, yet a convenient measure of social selection. This was feasible because it was possible (1) to distinguish the literate from the illiterate and thus reward the former accordingly, and (2) to convey literacy in such a form that the values necessary to social and political cohesion would be transmitted.

From 1830 forward in Great Britain and the United States, literacy became an important element in the social transformation associated with Victorian culture. Howe has noted that Victorianism is not easily interpreted in terms of class conflict, rural-urban divisions, or even a particular brand of Protestantism. Nonetheless, Howe continues, while the "social base of American Victorianism was broader than the urban middle class" with which it is often associated, "the origins of most of its spokesmen were narrower" and came from what has been described as the American gentry.[71] Within this context, the Whig-Republican reform efforts in the North in behalf of the common school link that reform and its impact on basic literacy to the larger cultural developments of the period. The efforts of this vocal element of American Victorianism, whose membership included many literary men and women, editors of northern newspapers, and common school reformers, may be seen as part of a "communications system," an essential feature of which was the popularization of literacy and the use of literacy to promote cultural reform. This is clearly apparent in the ideology of literacy developed by newspapermen and school text authors treated at length in chapter 3. Apart from the journals of common school reformers, the excising of moral distemper is nowhere more evident than in the newspapers of the North, where editors (not all Whig) promoted the value of education, schooling, and literacy within the context of moral reform, economic self-improvement, and nation building. Indeed, the evangelical element which persisted in Victorian thought functioned to help internalize the Puritan values of hard work, self-reliance, and an obligation to social betterment through duty to established institutions. Access to Victorian culture and the accompanying values of modernization was predicated on the assumption of literacy, just as access to New England Puritanism depended so much on Bible literacy. In America and Great Britain "the socializing functions of print were fully realized," to use Harrison's phrase, and the "'whip of the word' was a most powerful agent in shaping the new society."[72] The literate culture, as Goody and Watt have noted, is more easily avoided than the oral one, and it may be observed that in their emphasis upon the "whip of the word" evangelical Protestantism and Victorianism alike implicitly recognized the ease with which the word might be avoided.[73] The developing industrial context for social experience, in turn, was to dramatize the obsolescence of the oral tradition by mid-century, thus underscoring the necessity for mass literacy in order to maintain social stability through moral intrusion in the face of the destabilizing conditions of industrial expansion. The major focus of this essay—namely, determination of the social and economic variables which fostered or deterred literacy—thus should enable, in the future, a closer scrutiny of the conditions which facilitated or impeded the impact of Victorian culture and its values (hard work, competitiveness, deferred gratification, sexual repression, self-improvement, and sobriety) in America.

Because the common school was so intimately involved with the transmission of culture and literacy, it became the focal point of major policymaking decisions and represented for educational reformers a historical alternative of cultural intervention in the affairs of local communities. The other alternative—a laissez-faire attitude toward the achievement of literacy—would have depended upon demographic factors and economic development to solve the problem of illiteracy. It is within the context of the victory of imposition over laissez-faire that we treat in chapter 5 the economic and demographic factors which affected the distribution of literacy in nineteenth-century United States.

As with their immediate intellectual predecessors of the Enlightenment, leaders of Victorian culture in America were promoters of an educated public. Their concern with systematizing the educative process, combined with the popular morality of Protestantism, made excellent rhetorical ammunition for common school reformers. If, as Howe has concluded, "the intended product of Victorian didacticism was a person who would no longer need reminding of his duties, who would have internalized a powerful sense of obligation and could then safely be left to his own volition," then the common school was an excellent institution for transmitting that type of literacy characterized by moral didactic which would then ensure proper socialization.[74]

Within the framework of literacy for social control and the context of Victorian culture in the United States, the common school itself was seen as the guarantor of a particular cultural system—that is, as the institution which could guarantee that a particular cultural outlook would be perpetuated through literate future generations. The potentially increased variety of choice offered by a literate public compounded for reformer and educator alike the problem of transmitting established norms, and forced them to confront the twofold problem of extending literacy to all and controlling the substance of that literacy. Thus, the literacy guaranteed by the common school was of necessity a *particular* literacy as well as a general mastery of the symbols underlying the ability to read. Reading, as a phrase would have it, was not just reading; it was the reading of something. Thus, even at the level of basic literacy one should not unreservedly make the claim that the mastery of words, sentence structure, and diction will open vistas of the imagination for the reader. This could ultimately be so, if one were speaking of literary culture and the imaginative, creative powers of the artist. For most, however, the long-range impact of literacy would more than likely be determined by the peculiar nature of the literacy learned in childhood, that is, literacy designed to instill proper beliefs and codes of conduct. The opportunity to read as facilitated by the common school (or any other school) would not, then, be an unlimited opportunity, but, rather, an opportunity to have access to a particular way of viewing the world and to a particular system of values. These values, as we discuss in chapter 3, came to be part of an ideology of literacy.

Social and Economic Variables

The tradition of evangelical Protestantism, the emergence of an ideology of literacy, and the interpretation of literacy within the context of a Victorian commitment to modernization all help to define the meaning and purpose of literacy as it developed in American culture. These dimensions of literacy, however, do not specify the actual variables which intervened between purpose and impact, and it is the latter to which we now turn in our introductory discussion of social and economic variables.

Recent scholarship, including that of Lockridge and Johansson, testifies to the importance of population density in the spread of literacy. The findings of Furet and Ozouf point to extremely large regional disparities in literacy rates in early nineteenth-century France which, as they note, correlate with differences in population density and degree of industrialization.[75] Throughout our work we stress the importance of population density in the development of literacy, since areas of low population density more often than not have lower literacy levels than those of high population density. Regional distinctions—that is, North-South, East-West differences—in literacy levels accompany variations in population density, as would be expected in an era of rapid frontier development and national expansion. The basic condition of population density, while it should be viewed as a primary causative factor in literacy rates, is operative only through numerous intervening variables. These variables themselves can often be used as indicators of literacy levels. Such is the case with the building of churches, schools, and libraries, for example, because they accompanied increasing population density and resulted in what can be called "social concentration." The same is true with increasing commercial and manufacturing activity, including that specifically associated with printed materials such as publishing, the printing of books and newspapers, and the manufacture of paper. Increasing aggregate wealth, also, certainly was an intervening variable.

The absence of schooling in areas of low population density presumably was an intermediate variable affecting levels of literacy. Where schooling was restricted or altogether absent, the responsibility for teaching the young to read and write would undoubtedly fall to parents and siblings. The major question which must be raised in this respect is, What was the extent of intergenerational illiteracy in the absence of formal education? To put it differently, what we need to know is whether illiteracy was a condition which commonly persisted from generation to generation and whether schooling was the only viable method for reducing the number of illiterates. The point is well made by Johansson when he suggests that literacy through home education might be an alternative for "developing" countries in the twentieth century. This approach to the illiteracy problem would seem to be plausible if one assumes strong direction from a central or state-based authority. In the absence of such authority, however, intergenerational illiteracy poses a rather different problem. The Appalachian region–border-state area of settlement is a case in point in nineteenth-century United States. This region represents the extremes of illiteracy, an absence of centralized authority, and a lack of social concentration. Without the intervening variables strongly associated with literacy, intergenerational illiteracy was high in this region. Nonetheless, it is possible to argue that higher fertility rates among illiterates could eventually result in the greater population density needed to attract commercial enterprise (for example, newspapers and paper production) and would eventually lead to a print-oriented communications network. Thus, part of the institutional structure necessary for the promotion of literacy—paper production and newspapers—could develop without direct government intervention. In this region of high intergenerational illiteracy, however, it is questionable whether printing and publishing activity could be profitable without the schooling, whether by clergymen or common school teachers, to produce literate consumers. The problem is most difficult because it is possible that the probability of becoming literate in this region was such that illiteracy would gradually diminish primarily as a result of age and fertility factors. In our treatment of literacy using 1870 census data, we demonstrate that it was possible, given the presence of some literate individuals, to increase literacy levels despite the absence of state intervention through schooling. This, however, would have been a slow process, and the interventionist methods of school reformers considerably lessened the time needed to raise literacy, in the aggregate, to an acceptable level. Thus, we find that schooling was a critical variable in raising the level of literacy in nineteenth-century America.

In a number of studies, occupational status and level of literacy have been found to be positively related. At one level, these associations are related to population itself, particularly when one is using a dichotomous variable such as farm-nonfarm workers. At a more refined level of analysis, however, occupation can be seen to be operating independently; that is, when occupational categories become more refined differences in literacy levels still appear. Schofield, in his study "Illiteracy in Pre-Industrial England," for instance, notes that the occupational hierarchy evident in marriage registers is "one of the most consistent features of illiteracy in the past."[76] He interprets this as evidence that "literacy had a different functional value in each of the occupational groups" and that some occupational groups need to be literate to perform their economic roles. Cressy's work on seventeenth- and eighteenth-century Britain has also highlighted the occupational-social stratification of literacy. "The ability or inability to sign one's name," he notes, "was more closely correlated with social and occupational status than with anything else."[77] Furet and Ozouf attribute the rise in literacy levels in eighteenth-century France ("les gains spectaculaires") to the emergence of new economic conditions which brought with them a division of labor necessitating higher literacy skills.[78] Lockridge, in dealing with colonial New England, also stresses the point that certain groups, particularly those who had to deal with merchandizing or other commercial activities, needed literacy. Literacy, then, may be viewed as a precondition for certain occupations, for example, those of the skilled artisan or craftsman.[79] This latter point is stressed by Graff for the skilled sector of the economy. "Skilled work may not always have required literacy," he notes, "but literacy facilitated opportunities for entry to it and, consequently, commensurate remuneration."[80] Yet the question of causation remains, as does the question of the relationship of economic mobility to literacy. It would seem that if literacy were a precondition to higher skilled or higher status occupations, then literacy itself would be an important determinant of economic mobility. But the relationship here is tenuous, since it does not answer the question of whether a person was successful in a certain occupation because he was literate rather than illiterate. Graff, in his study of mid-nineteenth-century Ontario, Canada, has played down the importance of literacy to social stratification in general, noting that "most rewards were based on ethnicity, age and sex. The resulting disparity between promise of achievement and social processes shows literacy to be a mediating and reinforcing factor, not an autonomous or determining one."[81] The issue of literacy and socioeconomic mobility, then, is far from a settled one with perhaps the most important question being whether illiteracy impedes upward mobility. In chapter 5 we treat in detail the link between literacy and mobility, not in terms of occupation, however, but in terms of wealth. Suffice it to say at this point that we find the positive relationship between wealth and literacy a strong one, one that argues substantially for the importance of literacy in upward economic mobility.

The problem of the relationship between wealth and literacy is a similar one to that between occupation and literacy, and once again the direction of causation is at the heart of the issue. Wealth and literacy were certainly related if we are to judge by the American experience in both the eighteenth and nineteenth centuries. Lockridge has suggested that "wealth was more a product than a pre-condition of literacy."[82] For the late eighteenth and early nineteenth centuries, however, there is some evidence to support the contention that the direction of causation was reversed. In a study of estate inventories for early Ohio, book ownership on the developing frontier was found to be a determinant of the quality of literacy if not a precondition to basic literacy. Ownership of the classics was found to be strongly associated with wealth as was the number of books owned. In the case of the latter, presumably the extent of an individual's reading would be affected by his ability to purchase more than one book. Large libraries, of course, were the privilege of the wealthy, but even when one is speaking of fewer numbers of books (for example, three), those below the median wealth line were less likely to own books than those above it. If exposure to different titles indicates broader reading and hence a likelihood of improved comprehension, then, on the basis of estate data, wealth and quality of literacy exhibit a positive relationship.[83]

Questions of the relationship among wealth, occupation, and literacy are particularly important in determining the role of schooling in literacy, since the factors of parental occupation and wealth affect school attendance itself, and it is assumed that the level of literacy was a function of the length of time spent in school.[84] Literacy, if it were to affect economic mobility via the intermediate variable of the school, would be strategically related to school attendance and the quality of literacy associated with formal education. An occupational hierarchy was a common feature of school attendance in the nineteenth century and was commonly discussed in the annual reports of city and state superintendents of education. Troen, in his study of St. Louis schools, has observed that the occupational structure of school attendance, as measured by parental occupational status, mirrored the society in general. "Class," he notes, "became the most important parameter and, in effect, controlled the length of childhood and the nature of the options available to the young."[85] Under these conditions we would expect parental illiteracy to be an important factor in the literacy levels of their offspring unless the effect of the school on literacy was so decisive as to overturn previous social restrictions associated with economic class and family life. In regard to the relationship of literacy to economic mobility it is possible, of course, that literacy itself had little to do with mobility but that the length of school experience did. It may have been that the level of literacy skills needed for entry into occupational roles that led to upward mobility was low enough to be insignificant for economic selection. In this case, years of schooling could serve as a convenient measure for selection even though the *level* of literacy commonly associated with various lengths of time spent in school was irrelevant to the economic sorting process.

The question of who could finance the education of their young has been dealt with in the recent literature on the economics of public education by conceptualizing the problem in terms of opportunity costs. Most notable in this respect have been the works of Fishlow and Solmon, who have dealt with differences in rural and urban schooling by examining differences in earnings foregone by children attending school. For the most part, these studies have been interested in aggregate levels of spending and comparisons among different states. We have dealt with the problem of opportunity costs, also, in a previous essay using 1870 census data. In the present work we have emphasized the positive relationship between parental wealth and school attendance while taking into account occupational differences, differences in nativity, and ethnic distinctions.[86]

Concerns with nonattendance and irregular attendance were frequently expressed in the surveys and statistical reports of mid-nineteenth-century school reformers. Kaestle and Vinovskis have remarked of the attendance problem that it was quite different in rural and urban areas. Reformers interested in rural school attendance, they note, were preoccupied with regularity of attendance, and figures on rural attendance suggest "the limited but firmly established role of school attendance for children in the community." When school reformers attacked the problem in urban areas, however, they focused on nonattendance, and their concerns suggest that they were interested in using the school "to *create* cohesion" in areas characterized by greater ethnic diversity and mobility.[87] In fact, the relationship of wealth and school attendance in general was confounded by the demographic changes related to ethnic diversity in mid-nineteenth-century United States. These changes, in turn, made their mark on the ideology of common school reform (an ideology which stressed social cohesion through assimilation of diverse ethnic groups) and led mid-century reformers to emphasize the importance of re-creating consensus and preserving the civic religion of the common schools.[88] In a recent paper we have dealt with the quantitative dimensions of the acculturation of immigrant children and have examined the interrelated effects of ethnicity and wealth on school attendance.[89] The interaction is admittedly complex, but we hope to have demonstrated that the impact of wealth on school attendance, while mediated by ethnicity and age, was still significant and hence that, in the long run, wealth was an important determinant of the quality of literacy as well as of the achievement of basic literacy itself.

A few remaining remarks should be made with respect to this study of literacy in nineteenth-century United States. As with most studies of literacy, our ultimate concern has been to clarify the relations of literacy to individual and collective behavior. In attempting this, we have stressed the social and economic variables associated with the extent and dispersion of literacy in American culture. The relations of these variables to the ideological foundations of literacy, in turn, provide us with a broader context for interpreting the purpose of literacy within a particular historical epoch. The extent to which we may generalize our findings from this epoch to contemporary problems of illiteracy is restricted, of course, by the particulars of the historical situation. Nonetheless, it is hoped that from the historical model itself, some useful guidelines for the study of contemporary issues in literacy will be forthcoming.

Two

The Extent of Illiteracy
before 1840

Introduction

The close relationship between religious instruction and the achievement of literacy was manifest in the concern of the early New England colonists that their children learn to read the Scriptures. This fact alone has become legendary in works dealing with the development of American culture. It has become axiomatic that Puritan divines and magistrates waged their war on the devil and illiteracy in the belief that ignorance was the way to hell, and enlightenment the way to order and social stability, if not to heaven. The importance of the household as the "primary agency of human association and education," moreover, assured that parents themselves would stress Bible literacy and view the object of education as the religious salvation of their offspring.[1]

Given this purpose, the teaching of reading and the acquisition of Bible literacy were activities primarily concerned with the learning of propositional ("knowing that") knowledge as contrasted with performative ("knowing how") or dispositional ("knowing to") knowledge. For example, knowing *that* the individual was to make a covenant with God was a first lesson to be learned from Bible literacy. This lesson, in turn, would be followed by learning the skills to establish such a covenant and finally by its actual establishment, the latter requiring the right formation of attitudes disposing one to enter into the covenant with God. Bible literacy, then, was but a *first step* in an educational process which ultimately *did* attempt to teach performative and dispositional knowledge, both of which were necessary to personal salvation and social stability. Thus, literacy was not conceived to be simply a recital of the more significant Scriptural passages, albeit recital itself might function as a ritual to ensure proper religious training. Rather, literacy was conceived in broader behavioral terms, that is, as knowledge which would guarantee proper behavior. If we are to judge by magisterial and clerical concern over disobedience among the young, Bible literacy did not always lead to proper behavior. The fact that such a link was perceived as an ideal, however, set an important precedent for future theorizing about the nature of a pedagogical science, that is, theorizing which conceived of instruction as leading to a change in behavior (on the part of immigrants' children, for example) rather than simply a recitation of selected passages from readers.

Hornbook and primer were brought to the aid of suffering children and were usually sufficient to do the triple duty of teaching children to read, to point their reading toward a proper interpretation of the Scriptures, and to believe in a way that would be rewarded by Church and God alike. If these were not enough (and they often were not), encouragement in the form of exhortations from an eminent clergyman might be needed. Thus, in 1656, John Cotton urged parents to educate their children by "learn[ing] them to read the Scriptures," and, nearly fifty years later, Benjamin Wadsworth declared, "If we are not able to *Read,* we should use all regular means, and imploy all opportunities for our learning; but if we can *read,* we should not (unless some extraordinary matter prevents) suffer one day to pass, without reading some portion of the Word of God."[2]

But, of course, not all New England children received the education of a saint, and perseverance and commitment notwithstanding, it soon became evident that the task of education could not be left to the family alone. As Bernard Bailyn has observed, "Within a remarkably short time after the beginnings of settlement it was realized that the family was failing in its more obvious educational functions."[3] Thus it was that Massachusetts began a long series of legislative enactments which recognized the extent to which families had neglected the education of the young, and attempted to hold both masters and parents accountable for children's abilities to read and understand religious principles. The colonies of Connecticut and New Haven passed similar legislation. In the seventeenth century, Rhode Island, unlike other New England colonies, did not pass any compulsory education law.[4] It is interesting within this context to note the observations of La Rochefoucault Liancourt in 1795 that "the people of Rhode Island are singularly illiterate" and that "scarcely ... the whole island [has] a single well conducted free school."[5] His contrasting observations of Connecticut and Massachusetts are equally as suggestive, even if his appraisal of the extent of literacy is inflated: "Hardly a person can be met with in Connecticut, any more than in Massachusetts, who is not qualified to read, write and perform the common operations of arithmetic."[6] If we are to judge by the syntax of his continuing remarks, he, like school reformers of the nineteenth century, observed a close relationship between education and the prevention of crime. In Massachusetts and Connecticut, he noted, "the laws are more faithfully observed, and crimes more rare, here, than in other places."[7]

There was unquestionably a sizable gap between legislative efforts and judicial enforcement of compulsory school laws. One historian of provincial society in early eighteenth-century New England has remarked that the "old picture of every village with its free school and a population athirst for learning is a pure figment of the imagination."[8] Such an appraisal is particularly appropriate if the focus is on the plight of poverty-stricken Rhode Island farmers or the poor of New Hampshire who, as a 1766 enactment declares, "neglect the care and Education of their Children."[9]

In the seventeenth and the eighteenth centuries, both the quantity and quality of schooling seem to have been associated with urbanity. In Pennsylvania, "the situation of rural churches and rural schools is similar," noted a clergyman by the name of Gottlieb Mittelberger: "In general, churches and school houses are located only in those places where several neighbors or church members live close together." Insufficient numbers of preachers and schoolteachers "for whose support the inhabitants do not have the means" was said to have been the reason.[10] It is interesting that where schools did exist in mid-eighteenth-century Pennsylvania, parents, hesitant to permit their young to master the tenets of evangelical Christian doctrines, sent their children to school not in order to absorb religious beliefs, "but only to acquire the necessary ability to read and write."[11]

Not all children developed a passion for reading as did Benjamin Franklin in his youth, but many undoubtedly shared his belief that education ought to make some contribution to worldly success. To aid in the negotiation of the upward path of Mr. Franklin's open-ended universe, some might expect to find a useful education in the many academies of the middle and late eighteenth century or in writing schools like those in the city of Boston. In the case of the latter schools, one could expect to find children seven to fourteen years of age pursuing the tasks of writing and ciphering.[12] For the poor or orphaned lad, however, it is unlikely that these avenues for advancement were available. Instead, the more likely road to success in the eighteenth century lay in apprenticeship, where a boy might learn his vocational skills and his basic literacy simultaneously. At the same time, his indigency and that of others like him was prevented, thus helping to ensure greater economic and social stability. Mittelberger spoke highly of the apprenticeship system, stating that in America "many have the ability to produce even the most elaborate objects in a short span of time." "When these young people have attended school for half a year," he continued, "they are generally able to read anything."[13] It must be assumed that Mittelberger was here referring to young teenage apprentices who, having received the rudiments of instruction at seven or eight, then returned to an evening school as part of their contractual agreement with a master.

The entire subject of apprenticeship and its contribution to the education of the poor in basic literacy is one deserving of further study. Few historians fail to mention the subject, but few elaborate upon the extent to which the clauses in apprentices' contracts were fulfilled. That many contracts were not honored is evidenced by cases appearing in New York City's Mayor's Court and quarter sessions, where cruel treatment of the apprentice, lack of necessary provisions, and refusal to instruct in trade were grounds for complaint.[14] In their quest for a ready supply of skilled labor, merchants, artisans, and shopkeepers "transplanted the English system of apprenticeship" as early as 1631 to Boston and by 1675 to New York. The motives for apprenticeship, however, were not simply economic. As early as 1648, Massachusetts law explicitly provided for the teaching of reading to apprentices upon penalty to masters who were "too indulgent and negligent of their duty." In doing so, the law also took care to provide for an education that would ensure social and political stability:

> It is therefore ordered that the Select men of everie town, in the severall precincts and quarters where they dwell, shall have a vigilant eye over their brethern and neighbours, to see first that none of them shall suffer so much barbarism in any of their families as not to endeavour to teach by themselves or others, their children and apprentices so much learning as may inable them perfectly to read the english tongue, and knowledge of the Capital lawes; upon penaltie of twentie shillings for each neglect therein.[15]

Even with the extent of enforcement unknown, the fact remains that an acute awareness of the need for literacy among the underprivileged existed. That awareness was translated into legislative action in Massachusetts, for instance, which gave selectmen and overseers of the poor the power to "bind" poor children as apprentices. Between 1692 and 1771, Massachusetts and the town of Boston passed eight laws dealing with the problem of apprenticeship for the poor.[16] The tradition was sufficiently strong to be perpetuated in new states. An 1806 Ohio act concerning apprentices and servants stated that

> all indentures made by overseers of the poor, by and with the consent of a justice of the peace in any township in this state, or by any parents or guardians for binding or putting out any child as an apprentice or servant, shall among the covenants in such indenture made and agreed upon between the parties, always have a clause to the following effect, that every master or mistress to whom such child shall be bound as aforesaid, shall at least cause such child to be taught and instructed to read and write.[17]

It was common for apprentice contracts to provide for instruction in reading, writing, and ciphering, and, in a number of cases, attendance at an evening school. There is some evidence, also, that educational provisions were a more common feature of eighteenth-century indentures than seventeenth-century ones. An examination of indentures for apprentices in New York City between 1694 and 1727 indicates that provision for education increased substantially from the late seventeenth to the third decade of the eighteenth century. Between 1694 and 1708, only 39 percent of the indentures provided for education. Most of these (68 percent) specified the subjects in which the apprentice was to become proficient. During the period from 1718 to 1727 the percentage of indentures providing for education increased markedly to 58 percent. Moreover, approximately 44 percent of these provided for evening school attendance. Forty-nine percent specified the subjects to be taught, and these seldom went beyond reading, writing and ciphering. The remainder of the indentures having educational provisions usually designated the number of quarters of schooling the child would receive.[18] By the end of the eighteenth century the percentage of indentures specifying the number of school quarters to be attended probably increased. The fifty-eight of sixty-one indentures of managers of the House of Employment in Philadelphia County in 1798 specifying the number of school quarters to be attended indicate the extent to which the school, rather than the master, had become responsible for education and literacy.[19]

For the poor child who was a ward of the state, apprenticeship may have been the only practical means to literacy. Thus, in New York City in 1701, for instance, "John Reade a poor fatherless and motherless child aged eight years and a halfe or thereabouts" was bound over by the church wardens and overseers of the poor to William Jackson, a cordwainer. In addition to the usual provisions for learning of a trade and for sustenance, the lad was to be taught "perfectly to Reade and write the English tongue." Similar provisions were made for Ann Skreen, aged ten years, whose parents were deceased. She was to be taught housewifery. Her academic education did not include learning to write, but only "to Reade the English tongue."[20] A poor youth of the late eighteenth century might expect a similar indenture. The contract below, administered under the Form of the Act of Assembly for the Relief of the Poor in Philadelphia (1798), required instruction in ciphering as well as in reading and writing:

Thomas Milikin with consent of his father Philip Milikin bound an apprentice to William Scull of Philadelphia chaise maker, 7 years 2 months and 2 weeks, to be taught the art, trade and mystery of a chaisemaker, read, write, and cypher as far as through the rule of three, found all necessaries, and at the expiration have 2 complete suits apparel one whereof is to be new.[21]

In many respects the legislation designed to ensure the literacy and proper religious convictions of children and apprentices was legislation for citizenship, but it is well known that citizenship itself was set within a religious context. Even when speaking of legislative enactments dealing with the vocational capabilities of apprentices, it must be kept in mind that the economic and social citizenship encouraged by the apprenticeship system operated within a moral and spiritual context. The close relationship between work and religious obligation, particularly in intensely Protestant New England, remained evident in American culture for some time to come. Clearly, the well-being of commonwealths was assumed to be at stake, and literacy through family, school, and apprenticeship was a necessary item on the agenda for social stability, social justice, and spiritual welfare.

The question of effectiveness and enforcement must be raised with respect to legislative enactments. What we have considered thus far in the colonial period has been both a statement of awareness and a declaration of social policy, but neither awareness of social problems nor legislative action carries with it any guarantee that social policy will come to pass. From the historian's point of view, what is needed is some measure of the extent to which social policy contributed to cultural growth within colonial society. Examination of both the extent of literacy and its configuration gives us at least a beginning in this respect. To look at patterns of literacy, we may say, is to look at one dimension of the efficacy of social policy. In a larger sense, it is also to look at the way in which social policy contributed to the achievement of cultural goals.

Information relating to literacy and illiteracy in the colonial and early republican periods comes from diverse documents that may or may not be representative of the society-at-large. Thus, while an estimate of the extent of illiteracy during these early periods is not too difficult to make, the distribution of illiteracy among different socioeconomic groups is very problematic. With the exception of military enlistment records (of which more will be said shortly), perhaps the most important sources for the study of illiteracy in America before 1840 are the colonial records for each state. Here, petitions and probate records provide basic data from which signature/marker ratios may be calculated.

Our comments regarding the extent and configuration of literacy in early America are necessarily brief since the period itself is not the focus of this study. (Figures which estimate the extent and distribution of illiteracy are generally for males. The only exceptions to this are the data from wills in Essex and Hartford counties and New Hampshire, where females constituted from 5 to 10 percent of the sample [see figure 2.1].) Nevertheless, some statements are in order regarding the extent of literacy, the relationships between illiteracy and urbanity, and the participation of the unlettered in the economic and political life of their communities. These considerations constitute, as it were, a necessary point of departure for the more intensive study of literacy in the nineteenth century.

The Colonial Period

The student of literacy in seventeenth-century America usually finds that he must rely upon the evidence left by testators' signatures or marks. This type of data was the basis of Lockridge's study of literacy in colonial New England, where he found, with some variations in slope, a continuous rise in literacy from 1650 to 1795. For male signatures alone, Lockridge found an increase in literacy rates of approximately 30 percent (from 60 to 90 percent) over this 145-year period. For the much smaller number of women in the sample, the increase itself was less, as were the absolute levels of literacy of 30 to 45 percent.[22] Our findings for the colonial period, with some exceptions, are consonant with those of Lockridge, but before citing the former, we should make some mention of the problems associated with the use of wills.

Four criticisms of data collected from testator's signatures and marks are readily apparent. First, as Stone has remarked, "we do not know now, and may never know, the precise relationship between the capacity to sign one's name . . . and true literacy, that is the ability to use the written word as a means of communication."[23] To some extent, this problem may be addressed by pointing to the fact that children were commonly taught to read before they were taught to write. Thus, it may be inferred that, for those who were schooled, the ability to sign one's name is likely testimony, also, to the ability to read. The level of mastery, whether for reading or writing, would remain unknown, however.

Second, some very old persons who were weak or sickly when they drew their wills may not have been able to produce signatures. Cressy has observed a positive association between illiteracy and senility from a comparison of wills with depositions of the Consistory Court of the diocese of Norwich under Elizabeth and the Stuarts.[24] It is a fact that illiteracy does seem to increase among the elderly for physiological reasons, in part because of a loss in manual dexterity. The extent of the age factor, determined statistically by randomly creating a distribution for the deceased from that of the living based upon the probabilities of dying, shows that the illiteracy rate associated with the expected age at death was 10 percent greater than that associated with the expected age of the adult living.[25] It is probable, however, that little of the 10 percent differential is attributable to physiological deterioration. Rather, in the higher illiteracy rates for the elderly, we are more likely capturing a long-run decline in illiteracy, since older people are representative of an earlier period. We have no literacy data for intestate cases.

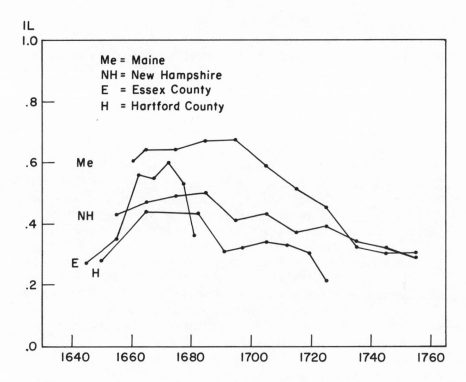

Figure 2.1
Illiteracy rates (IL) in Essex County, Massachusetts (1640–81), Hartford County, Con-
necticut (1635–1729), and New Hampshire and Maine (1641–1750). (Source: *The Probate
Records of Essex County, Massachusetts*, vols. 1–3 [Salem, 1916]; *A Digest of the Early
Connecticut Probate Records*, comp. Charles Manwaring [Hartford, 1904]; *Probate Rec-
ords of the Province of New Hampshire*, vol. 1 [1635–1717], ed. Albert Stillman Batchellor
[Concord, 1907]; *Probate Records of the Province of New Hampshire*, vol. 2 [1718–40], ed.
Henry Harrison Metcalf [Bristol, 1914]; *Probate Records of the Province of New Hampshire*, vol. 3 [1741–49], ed. Henry Harrison Metcalf [Concord, 1915]; *Probate Records of
the Province of New Hampshire*, vol. 4 [1750–53], ed. Otis G. Hammond [State of New
Hampshire, 1933]; *Probate Records of the Province of New Hampshire*, vol. 5 [1754–56],
ed. Otis G. Hammond [State of New Hampshire, 1936]; *Probate Records of the Province
of New Hampshire*, vol. 6 [1757–60], ed. Otis G. Hammond [State of New Hampshire,
1938]; John T. Hull, *York Deeds*, vols. 1–13 [Portland, Me., 1887]. Maine and New Hampshire points are averages of three decadal periods.)

Third, there is the problem that those with little or no wealth were more
likely to die intestate and less likely to be literate.[26] This is probably the
case despite the fact that some wills were written by men with little or no
property who wished to dispose of a few cherished items such as a sword,
a little book, or a cheese in a closet. The probable motivation of such
people was simply that such items were symbols of earthly wealth other
than cash or other assets, and might, for the living, serve as a reminder

that other forms of wealth could also constitute success. We do know, in the case of New Hampshire, that the average size of estates of testates was double that of intestates. Illiteracy rates in a general population are slightly lower for groups having twice the wealth of others. Thirty-five percent of testate illiterates had estates larger than the testate median value. It may be inferred, then, that data from testators will bias literacy rates upwards.

Finally, there is the fact that many propertied men probably chose not to make a will. This would surely have been the case for those who wished the eldest son to receive a double portion of the estate.[27] Also, those with few or no children might have felt less need to have wills. It is very difficult to predict what distortions might arise within this context, for the very level of literacy of the population at one point might produce a greater proportion of persons with wills in the next generation.

The four basic samples which we use to examine the extent of illiteracy in colonial New England came from Connecticut, Massachusetts, New Hampshire, and Maine. The sources for these data make it possible to present intercentury comparisons, as we see in figure 2.1, which gives the illiteracy rates (IL) for specified periods of time for Essex County, Massachusetts; Hartford County, Connecticut; the Province of New Hampshire; and Maine.[28] Although the periods of time are unavoidably different for each sample because of the way in which the sources recorded the data, this should not prove to be a difficulty in interpretation.

The data taken together make it apparent that between 1650 and 1680 illiteracy was on the rise in New England. While the specific illiteracy levels are not identical, the trend in each sample is the same and tends to support other research claims that the level was in the range of 40 to 60 percent in the fifth, sixth, and seventh decades of the seventeenth century. The one period for Essex County (1680-81) and the several periods for Hartford County and the Province of New Hampshire indicate a rather dramatic drop in illiteracy rates following 1680, a trend continuing well into the eighteenth century. The peak in Maine appears to last until almost 1700.

Certainly one would expect to find local variations within these trends. Because schools had not yet attained the prominence and significance in the education of the young that they were to have a century later, early school laws passed in Massachusetts, New Hampshire, and Connecticut were often ignored by local communities and the dispersion of the population to frontier settlements made enforcement difficult. No doubt, schooling did "advance literacy," as Lawrence Cremin remarks, but the great variation in local support of schooling probably affected illiteracy rates from community to community. Andover, Woburn, Watertown, Middleboro, Dedham, Haverhill, Groton, and Framingham in Massachusetts, for instance, were all indicted for having no schools.[29]

How political and economic factors affected the curvilinear pattern of illiteracy requires some interpretation, but it may be suggested that changing patterns of land ownership, the settling of new towns by a relatively youthful population, and an initially high rate of literacy were important in affecting the shape of the illiteracy pattern. In the compact villages of New England described by Powell in his *Puritan Village,* the open field system of medieval England had been adapted to the irregular terrain of New England, and the cooperative arrangements necessary to regulate the system helped preserve a matrix of institutions which, at least initially, required able, literate leadership. (Impressionistic evidence indicates that literacy rates among the first New Englanders were fairly high.)[30] The factor of population density was a most important determinant of literacy rates and is closely associated with the building of schools. It is suggested, then, that the schooling provided in the tightly knit New England village was considerably more stable and continuous than that provided in isolated farm areas.

By 1650, a centrifugal movement generated by changing patterns of land ownership had begun. The trend toward individual farm management which *eventually* made the autonomous farmstead "the most common form of settlement"[31] was accompanied by the phenomena of greater population dispersion and the rapid formation of new towns. The illiteracy rate proceeded upward in the first phase of this development, between 1650 and 1680. It is certainly possible that if the rate of formation of new towns was greater than would normally be expected, given the increase in population, then illiteracy would be expected to increase with the greater population dispersion. The relatively youthful population of newly formed towns would not have had the necessary accumulation of wealth to build and maintain schools. Moreover, apprenticeship—which was the equal of schooling as an institution for transmitting literacy—would have been less common in newly formed towns. Following 1680, if the rate at which new towns were formed relative to the population increase lessened compared with previous years, a steady rise in literacy might be predicted.

Although a concerned Connecticut legislature reported in 1690 that there were many people who were "unable to read the English tongue,"[32] it is evident from our samples of wills in Essex County, Hartford County, and New Hampshire and Maine that illiteracy had decreased by the late seventeenth century; moreover, the trend toward greater literacy persisted at least until the mid-eighteenth century. Additional evidence affirms the finding. A 1701 petition by New York City Protestants objecting to the way in which former officeholders had been "turned out of places in the Government" yielded a 70/350 ratio (20 percent) of illiterates to literates among all signers.[33] In a similar case of selective representation in 1702 in which 346 of the "Chiefest Inhabitants and Freeholders of the Province of New York" affixed their marks and signatures to a letter welcoming His Majesty's Governor, 16 percent (56 of the 346) were un-lettered.[34] Hence, the figures calculated from our samples of wills—34 and 39 percent—appear to be quite realistic.

A case from the late colonial period in Baltimore confirms the previous estimate and those estimates made from a study of wills. In 1768, petitions for removal of the county seat of Baltimore County from Joppa to the town of Baltimore provide us with an extensive list (2,030 petitioners) of signers. This is our most elaborate list thus far to have been published on one specific issue. In the petitions, criticisms were made of the high level of expenditures of the present court and prison, and charges leveled that criminals and other prisoners had escaped. The petitions were posted on the door of the court house in Joppa, on the doors of one church in each of four parishes, on the doors of the chapels of three, and presumably in other places. In all, there were thirty-seven separate petitions in favor of the transfer of the county seat, six of which were printed in both English and German. In the case of the latter, there was an 11 percent illiteracy rate. For all thirty-seven petitions, 407 of the 2,030 petitioners were mark-ers, about 20 percent. Several of the petitions had illiteracy rates of .30 to .50, while the rates of others were as low as .01—a sizable variation within the area.[35] Given such variation and the overall figure of 20 percent, it is likely that the level of illiteracy for the entire colony of Maryland was somewhat higher, but still within the range of our other eighteenth-century samples.

Illiteracy rates from the late eighteenth century are considerably less consistent than those found for the previous fifty to one hundred years. We have evidence from the New Hampshire Association Test—an ex-pression of loyalty in opposing British fleets and armies against the united American colonies—that very few colonists were unlettered at the onset of the War for Independence. Of the 8,199 signatures in favor of opposing the British and the 733 who refused such opposition, only 4 percent can be attributed to markers, but many of the names appear to be in the hand-writing of copiers.[36] On the other hand, North Carolinians, who in 1778 signed oaths of allegiance to defend against the King, showed illiteracy rates which varied from 2 to 52 percent and averaged 10 percent.[37]

Evidence from a petition circulated twenty years later and unrelated to wartime endeavors suggests that the frequency of illiteracy at this later date was considerably higher than at the beginning wartime period. The case cited here involves 207 signatures and arises from a petition of the inhabitants of the town of Livingston, New York, to the New York legis-lature in 1795 demanding an investigation into the Robert Livingston land title:

> And your petitioners further represent that a great part of your Peti-tioners are Tenants holding under the Descendent of the said Robert

Livingston upon Terms and Conditions oppressive and burdensome to the last degree, unfriendly to all great exertions of Industry and tending to degrade your Petitioners from the Rank the God of Nature destined all mankind to move in, to be SLAVES AND VASSALS.[38]

Here we find that the illiteracy ratio was 97/207, a rate of 47 percent. Supposing that this group of petitioners represented only the lower half of the wealth distribution of the labor force, the rate is sufficiently high to suggest that a state-wide rate of .25 would be a realistic figure. As we shall see in our examination of military enlistment records for the early republican period, a 25 percent illiteracy rate at the opening of the nineteenth century is quite likely.

Toward a Mathematical Formulation

We have already suggested that population density affected literacy rates substantially, and we may now hypothesize that the illiteracy rate prior to 1800 and perhaps prior to 1850 was inversely related to population density. With a greater number of people in a given area, the institutions needed to support literacy would be more readily available. A county with twice as many people as another would presumably be less occupied with clearing land, building log cabins, and fighting Indians, so that it could give more attention to teaching its children.

Let us assume that illiteracy is inversely related to the logarithm of population density in the form $IL = a + b/(\log D)$, where IL is the illiteracy rate, D is the number of people per square mile, and a and b are constants. For purposes of illustration, let us assume that $a = 0$ and $b = 10$. Then, for $D = 2$, 4, and 8, $IL = 10/(\log D) = .33$, .17, and .11, respectively. The first doubling of density would cut illiteracy in half; the second doubling would cut it by less than half in this particular case. As density in a given area became quite substantial, illiteracy might become insignificantly related to density or perhaps, as in the case of major cities, adversely affected. The hypothesis of the inverse relationship will be examined in chapter 5 using actual statistical data.

It is known that density of population in most areas of the country increased in a methodical fashion after initial settlement. The number of urban areas increased, but not as rapidly as did the population. The experience in Connecticut for 1670–1770, for example, can be described quite adequately by the equation $T = .32P^{.44}$, where T is the number of towns and P is the total population of the province. This means roughly that the average size of towns, P/T, increased about 47 percent each time the population doubled.[39] From 1670 to 1770 the number of towns increased from twenty-one to sixty-nine, the population multiplied 15 times, and the average size of a town increased to 4.4 times the initial value. If we assumed that the illiteracy rate and population density were related as in our numerical example above, we would find that illiteracy would have dropped to less than a third of its former value. The data of figure 2.1 demonstrate that it was quite possible for illiteracy to decrease from a range of .5–.6 to a range of .2–.4.

An alternative calculation might be made from simulating the growth of population of specific areas commencing in a given year. The distribution of cities in the United States with a population above 2,500 is known for the decennial years from 1790.[40] The relative dispersion of these distributions is essentially constant from 1790–1880 so that there is evidence of consistent and methodical growth. The distribution of town size in Connecticut in 1700, for example, varied between 48 and 330 polls. Supposing that each town quadrupled in size and that the illiteracy rate was inversely related as in our example, a calculation can then be made of the drop in illiteracy using the number of people as an index of literacy and also as a population weight in determining the relative importance of each town.

A more comprehensive formula would also consider the effect of time aside from population growth and particularly the possibility of economic growth over time. Such a formula would also include such factors as occupation, nativity, residence, and wealth. Figure 2.2, which plots population against number of American imprints, gives us a glimpse at the possibilities for a more comprehensive formula. It is seen from the data plotted in the figure that the number of distinct titles of publications or imprints in the colonies increased more rapidly than did the population as a whole and that the per capita growth from 1660 to 1831 was about .7 percent a year—a substantial change. The number of imprints, like illiteracy itself, might be explained solely in terms of increasing urbanization or population density, if it were assumed that printing and publishing activity was concentrated in areas of higher population density where there were ready markets. It is more likely, however, that the number of imprints is also a reflection of some general increase in well-being which could be measured as income or wealth. While the exact nature of this growth in the seventeenth and eighteenth centuries is very difficult to measure, we offer the equation $IL = \alpha\,(1/Y)^m\,[b/(\log D)]^n$, where Y is per capita income (or possibly wealth or annual increase in wealth per capita), m and n are constants, and α is a constant representing any specific subset of occupation, nativity, residence, and wealth.

The mathematical formulation expresses a theory of gradualism. Because population density is given a central place in determining literacy rates and because population increases rather slowly, the net effect on illiteracy is gradual but steady. Under frontier conditions we would expect greater illiteracy to accompany sparseness of population, while in

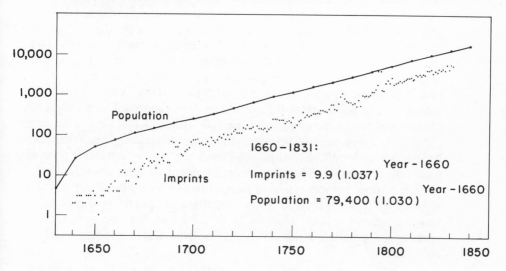

Figure 2.2
The total population and the number of books, pamphlets, and periodicals published each year in America from 1639 to 1831. (Source: Charles Evans, *American Bibliography,* 14 vols. [publisher varies: vols. 13 and 14, by American Antiquarian Society, Worcester, Massachusetts], and Roger P. Bristol, *Supplement to Charles Evans' American Bibliography* [University Press of Virginia, Charlottesville, Bibliographical Society of America, and Bibliographical Society of the University of Virginia, 1970]; *American Bibliography, a Preliminary Checklist,* compiled by Ralph R. Shaw and Richard H. Shoemaker [New York: Scarecrow Press, various issues, 1958–68], and *A Checklist of American Imprints,* compiled by Richard H. Shoemaker et al. [New York: Scarecrow Press, various issues to 1975]; United States Department of Commerce, *Historical Statistics of the United States,* Series Z1 and A7.)

areas no longer having a frontier illiteracy would decline. It is ironic that within the context of an emerging agrarian republic, that is, the Jeffersonian ideal, we would expect illiteracy to be high and that without the concentrations of population (which threatened the purity of Jefferson's virtuous agrarian polity) illiteracy would remain a problem.

Educational reformers and religious leaders were aware of the difficulties in the spreading of a literate culture in frontier areas. An individual settler, said Edward Everett, " 'can fell the forest, build his log house, reap his crops, and raise up his family . . . but, he cannot, of himself, found or support a school, far less a college; nor can he do as much toward it, as a single individual, in older states, where ampler resources and a denser population afford means, cooperation, and encouragement, at every turn.'"[41] Efforts to reduce illiteracy through the expansion of common school education, including Jefferson's own plan for common school education in Virginia, were forced to contend with the fundamental demographic fact of sparse frontier populations. Even when the frontier, per se, ceased to be an obstacle to the spread of literacy, there remained large areas of relatively low population density which, in the eyes of mid-nineteenth-century school reformers, became the "rural problem" in education. The Appalachian region of the mid-Ohio Valley provides a salient case in point and will be discussed more thoroughly in chapter 5. Common school reformers from the late 1830s to the Civil War were aware that sparseness of population and the consequent inadequate tax base to support educational institutions were serious obstacles to common school reforms. The Ohio superintendent of common schools frequently expressed concern over inequalities of educational opportunity, some of which were created by the long distances pupils were required to travel to attend school. Inadequate funding was likewise a concern in areas of low population density. Thus, the commissioner noted as late as 1867 that

> in sparsely settled townships, where the territory of the sub-districts is large, in proportion to the number of youth of school age and the amount of taxable property, it was impossible, with the funds available, even when the maximum levy was made, to meet the requirements of the law.[42]

It had become apparent by the mid-nineteenth century that rhetoric and legislation alone were unable to solve the problem to the satisfaction of school officials.

Political and Economic Participation of the Unlettered in Colonial America

It will be remembered that our interviewees were not "marginal" men, alienated from the mainstream of society because of their illiteracy. It was equally evident that they were "dependent" upon literates for some of their basic social interaction. The dependency did not necessarily extend to all dimensions of their social lives in every case. Rather, their abilities to interact depended upon the roles or tasks they were expected to perform. When we turn to the political and economic participation of the unlettered in colonial America, again the marginality of the illiterate is absent, but the dependency is apparent. One of the earliest documentary indications of the participation of the unlettered in the local political processes of the new England colonies comes from a Rhode Island petition dated August 1636. The petitioners, who may have been part of Williams's following when he fled Massachusetts Bay, were participants in the common practice of establishing a new town. The petition, like so many which characterized the fashioning of a new town, committed its signers to a corporate way of life including obedience to rules and regulations enacted for the public good.

> We whose names are hereunder, desirous to inhabit in the town of Providence, do promise to subject ourselves in active and passive obedience to all such orders or agreements as shall be made for public good of the body in an orderly way, by the major consent of the present inhabitants, masters of families-incorporated together in Towne fellowship, and others whom they shall admit unto them only in civil things.[43]

Five of the thirteen men who signed the above were markers, and presumed to be unlettered. Four years later in a report with many of the same signatures affixed containing proposals for a form of government to be instituted, seven of the thirty-nine signers were markers.[44] In neighboring Massachusetts in the towns of Black Point, Bleu Point, Casco Bay, and Spurwincke, illiteracy was somewhat higher if we may judge by a 1658 agreement of Falmouth (Casco Bay and Spurwincke) and Scarborow (Black Point and Bleu Point) townspeople to be subject to the government of Massachusetts Bay. Among the twenty-eight signers were fourteen markers.[45]

Equally as important to a consideration of political participation by the unlettered are instances in which the power of political representation was given through the signing of an agreement. The first instance which we cite was that occurring in the New York province in 1643. The case involved forty-four signers of a "resolution adopted by the commonality of the Manhattans" who, as a group, had been invited to a fort to express their opinions on a proposition and procedure for electing representatives to review and render judgment upon regulations passed and representatives chosen by the director and council of the Fort. The list, which was probably representative of all white male adults in the colony, included nineteen markers.[46]

The second case involved a 1638 Maryland procedure giving the power of representation to a Henry Bishop:

> (We) chose for the Burgess of the hundred of Mattapanient Henry Bishop and have Given unto him full and free Power for (us) and for every of them to be present in their names at the next Assembly as their Burgess or deputy and in witness thereof have hereto sett (our) hands.
>
> The mark of Richard × Garnett
> The mark of Richard × Lusthead

The mark of Joseph × Edlo
Robert Wiseman
The mark of Anum × Benum
The mark of Lewis × Freeman[47]

Similar situations in the Maryland colony yield ratios of the unlettered to the total signers of 7/12, 7/15, 8/19, 0/24, and 0/24 in addition to the above ratio of 5/6. The overall illiteracy rate approximates 27 percent and ranges from a high of 83 percent to a low of zero.[48] This is somewhat lower than the rate for the New York colony.

Unlike the previous situations in which *power was invested* through signature, the loyalty oaths of seventeenth-century America simply requested that allegiance to established authority be forthcoming from those affixing their signatures or marks. The extent of "marksmanship" is startlingly consistent from state to state in these oaths. On a New York oath of 1639, four of eight Englishmen who pledged to follow the director or Council of Manhattan Island and to defend the local inhabitants were markers.[49] A Rhode Island oath of loyalty to the king in 1639 showed fifteen of twenty-nine signers were markers, while a Kent County, Maryland, oath of 1652 promising to "engage ourselves to be true and faithful to the Commonwealth of England, without King or House of Lords," was marked by thirty-two individuals and signed by thirty-one others who could write their names.[50] Thus, some 50 percent of the men signing these familiar adjuncts to seventeenth-century political authority were unlettered, a situation filled with greater irony for the fact that a written instrument was employed to police them.

Much of the evidence relating to the participation of markers in the economic life of seventeenth-century communities comes from court records for the colonies. The Provincial Court at St. Mary's in Maryland, a court for all matters civil, criminal, and testamentary for the city and county as well as for the appellate jurisdiction for larger areas, may serve as a case in point. In 1636 the court had twenty-five cases in which the principal signers were markers. For the most part, these cases dealt with indebtedness, although some involved the freedom of indentured servants to earn what they could in a year in return for payment of 1,000 pounds of tobacco. For the three-year period 1637–39, the total cases indicated an illiteracy ratio of 21/60, or 35 percent. For the 1649–50 period the rate was approximately the same. Cases dealing with land values thirty-five years later show a somewhat higher level of 47 percent, or an illiteracy ratio of 28/60. Similarly, proceedings in the court in Charles County from 1658 to 1662 involving notes, depositions, powers of attorney, bills of sale, patents, and so on, produced 76 markers (53 percent) among 142 signers.[51]

In New York our first two cases deal with the signing of leases and involve only seven people. They are cited because they illustrate dramatically the enormous gap in literacy which could exist between members of different socioeconomic groups—a gap, however, which did not prevent the unlettered from participating in detailed financial arrangements. The first lease was between the director general of New Netherland, on one hand, and the former director, on the other. They naturally signed the agreement with their own hands.[52] The second lease had four marks among five names; the three principal parties and one witness were illiterate. Yet this lease of a bowery by a baker to two brothers is very detailed as to the terms of payment for six consecutive years. The baker delivered four "milch" cows, two heifers, one heifer calf, three bull calves, one mare, two stallions, a yearling sow, two wagons, and a new and serviceable harrow and plough, for which the brothers agreed to pay each year 150 pounds of butter (one-half before and one-half after the harvest) and fifty schepels of grain (either wheat, rye, or barley).[53] The agreement continues with specific payments of cattle that were to be made at the end of the six years. The lease demonstrates that two illiterate groups could be parties to an elaborate agreement, given the help of local authorities who were accustomed to such arrangements and who presumably would be available to enforce them.

Two additional but brief cases from New York will be cited. The first is a general list from the Town of Hempstead in 1656. In this instance we are dealing with a charter of 1645 which had stated that at the end of ten years, a tenth of the revenue arising from "the Ground manured by the plough or hoe" was to be paid. By 1656, however, the inhabitants of the town felt that the immediate damages by Indians to their property should mitigate against the full payment of the "tenths." The forty petitioners, who could probably be considered a cross section of the labor force, included eighteen markers, for an illiteracy rate of 45 percent. A few years later, in 1663, the inhabitants of Breuckelen wished to settle a new village in a woodland area where there would be room for twenty to thirty families. The petition in this case has nine men using symbols or signs among its list of thirty-three.[54]

Clearly, illiterates participated in the civic and economic life of colonial communities. They settled townships, agreed to be obedient subjects of a particular local government, elected political representatives, and pledged loyalty to a higher political authority. The rate at which illiterates participated in such activities of the body politic varied between .20 and .50. Moreover, we may observe in such participation the several uses of literacy: the expressing of the will of the body politic, the selecting of political servants, and sometimes (in the case of loyalty oaths) the exploitation of the illiterate by the literate. What should be stressed here, however, is the fact that the illiterate individual, dependent as he was upon the literate, shared in these uses of literacy. On some occasions, the role of dependency might even be reversed as in cases of grand jury investigations and juries of inquiry. Court records, regardless of location, generally show active participation by illiterates in these matters. Jurors themselves were often illiterate, and evidence was generally accepted from illiterates. Eleven percent of some twenty-five New Plymouth Colony juries in 1652 consisted of markers.[55] A Kent County, Delaware, jury hearing a case on land disposition in 1705 was 58 percent (7/12) illiterate.[56] In 1676 a jury of inquiry from Talbot County, Maryland, investigating the value of the land of the deceased was 67 percent illiterate.[57] Finally, in Suffolk County, Massachusetts, in 1673, we find the interesting situation of two illiterates giving evidence in a case involving the unjust "selling and disposeing of severall parcells of goods." The illiterates, ironically, testified to the accuracy of an accounting of goods.[58]

For the unlettered individual's participation in the economic life of the community, the story is much the same. Obtaining titles to land, obtaining loans, signing leases, and negotiating for retrieval of financial losses were activities open to the unlettered. Once again the rate of illiteracy in such situations varied considerably, from 25 to 50 percent and, on occasion, to 80 percent. The fact that the unlettered were involved in large numbers in the economic life of their communities argues against any suspicion that illiteracy itself was a serious obstacle to upward economic mobility in the seventeenth century. Moreover, it sustains the argument that in this period "the gap between the literacy of the population and the functional demands of the society was not great."[59]

However much the religion-literacy linkage might have helped to stabilize the dominion of the spirit in the American colonies, its relevancy to the dominion of the secular is not readily apparent. In terms of explaining individual economic and political participation, the utility of the linkage must be questioned, for certainly the unlettered were very politically and economically active. This is not to say in the case of the latter that the level of activity was unrelated to wealth. Wealth, as Lockridge has noted, was probably a function of literacy in these early years in New England, and one would expect that the level of economic activity, in general, would be higher among the literate than among the illiterate.[60] Any assertion regarding the political and economic activity of the unlettered, however, should be qualified by pointing to the dependency of the unlettered on the literate. In turn, it might be argued that because of the religion-literacy bond, which became institutionalized in school laws and apprentice contracts, enough men acquired the skills necessary to the drawing of contractual agreements, petitions, and settlements, and that economic and political stability was ensured. Moreover, it is clearly a possibility that the nature of literacy provided by this bond, a literacy which resulted in the ability to recite verbatim but not necessarily with transfer of meaning, was such that it was inapplicable outside the context for which it was intended. It is quite plausible that, because it was unnecessary in the economic and political life of the seventeenth century, no transfer of meaning to economic and political contexts was anticipated. The increasing complexity of economic and political life a century and a half later, however, necessitated a reevaluation of the adequacy of the unlettered to contend with new social conditions. By the nineteenth century, an ideology of literacy itself had reinterpreted the uses of literacy in response to changing social conditions. To put it differently, the ideology of literacy had begun to be secularized. The idea of literacy for social and economic mobility was beginning to take its place beside literacy for salvation and literacy for citizenship. While the potential for conflict was great among these three elements, they, in fact (as we observe in chapter 3), existed side by side with little observable difficulty.

The Early Republican Period

There is little question that in 1800 political and religious leaders were fearful of the increasing illiteracy. The fear had been common among colonial magistrates and clergymen as well, but following the War for Independence anxiety seemed greater than usual—anxiety no doubt occasioned by observations that educational institutions had noticeably suffered during the war. In 1798 the Reverend Samuel Knox, then president of Frederick Academy, asked the following rhetorical question of the Maryland legislature: "In every corner or portion of the state how many hundreds of our youth are deprived of the means of instruction suitable to the offspring of free and independent citizens?"[61] The question, not an unusual one for educational reformers in the new republic, was one that would be repeated many times over with variations stemming from different motivations in the next seventy years.

The sentiment that education was too often neglected at the peril of a strong republican government was widespread among orators and political leaders in this early period, although the presence of the same sentiment among the poor and illiterate is not certain. In 1797, "Academicus" had noted in a letter to Jefferson that it was "a matter of the highest importance to republican government to disseminate knowledge and to keep the evenness of access to it open to all, and especially to the middle, or even the lower class of people."[62] And we may read in Samuel Harrison Smith's prize-winning essay of 1798 that prior to "any prospect of success" of a stable society and government, "society must establish the right to educate and acknowledge the duty of having educated, all children." He continues thus:

> it is the duty of a nation to superintend and even to coerce the education of children, and . . . high considerations of expediency not only justify, but dictate the establishment of a system, which shall place under a control, independent of, and superior to, parental authority, the education of children.[63]

Such challenges to the traditional prerogatives of the family were actually few in this early period, although they did provide an important link to the later systematization of common school reforms. Motivations for the establishment of both national and state systems of public schooling varied from outright commitment to Enlightenment ideas of progress to a concern with education as a conservative force in curbing "an excess of popular liberty."[64] Generally, however, all agreed that a basic literacy among the poor and a system for guaranteeing the emergence of capable political leadership were requisites to the stability and perpetuity of the American republic. Some, such as Knox, shared the view of Protestant leadership in the several states that a general system of education ought to cater to those "who are most likely to be deprived of the advantage of such an institution."[65] The level of education suggested for the poor varied widely, but it always included basic literacy and usually Bible literacy; it was assumed that moral discipline would accompany literacy and that the former would contribute substantially to the prevention of crime and, on an individual level, the simple avoidance of improper behavior and degeneracy.

Early republican sentiments which testify to the emergence of a civic-national model for literacy should not obscure the influence that a well-established Protestant tradition had on shaping attitudes toward literacy and education. Churchmen themselves, notes Humphrey, were conscious of their place in the emergent republic and approached the civil life of the nation by emphasizing their role in the maintenance of religion and morality.[66] This concern with the proper place of religion and morality in government, of course, had a strong basis in New England Puritanism as well as in the resurgence of pietism which accompanied the great awakening of the eighteenth century. In the case of both, it was assumed that "America was the center of God's interest in the world."[67] The "new lights" of the eighteenth-century evangelical tradition, notes Cowing, tended "to ignore religious and political boundaries and press for a continental union" which emerged as a "deep and pious nationalism" on the eve of the War for Independence. Following the war, pietists in the same tradition pressed for a "'sweet harmony' between church and state," and despite the theories of Jefferson and Madison, says Cowing, "they got sub-stantially what they wanted."[68] Bible reading in the local schoolhouse was a natural state of affairs, just as the tradition of voluntarism in Chris-tian charity for the basic education of the poor was a self-imposed obliga-tion for the sake of spirit and nation alike.

Evangelical Protestantism and a republican theory of government came together at the psychological level to provide a basis for republican-Protestant pedagogy. Benjamin Rush believed that the Bible was the preferred vehicle for teaching youth to read, despite "its division into chapters and verses and its improper punctuation, which renders it a more difficult book to read *well*."[69] Proof of its effectiveness as a pedagogical instrument was to be inferred by observing the delight which the elderly took in reading the Bible. Rush himself was convinced that the histories and precepts of the Bible "*associated* with the events of childhood and youth" were responsible for the pleasures given to the aged through Bible reading. In his plan for the establishment of public schools in Penn-sylvania he concluded that "a Christian cannot fail of being a re-publican," "for every precept of the Gospel inculcates those degrees of humility, self-denial, and brotherly kindness, which are directly opposed to the pride of monarchy and the pageantry of a court." "A Christian cannot fail of being useful to the republic," he continued, "for his religion teacheth him that no man 'liveth to himself.'"[70] This premise was implicit in De Witt Clinton's address to the trustees of the Free School Society in New York in 1805 when he told them that public duty (and presumably a larger public good) demanded that they undertake the education of the poor and the neglected. "It is in vain," he continued, "that laws are made for the punishment of crimes, or that good men attempt to stem the torrent of irreligion and vice, if the evil is not checked at its source; and the means of prevention, by the salutary discipline of early education, seasonably applied."[71] Four years later, Clinton championed the Lancasterian (monitorial) plan of instruction on the basis not only that it was efficient, but that "it comprehends reading, writing, arithmetic, and the knowledge of the Holy Scriptures." He spoke of Lancaster as the "benefactor of the human race" and acknowledged his system as a "blessing sent down from heaven to redeem the poor and distressed of this world from the power and dominion of ignorance."[72]

In the educational mix of public, quasi-public, and private schools of the late eighteenth and early nineteenth centuries, Protestant educational activities, Smith has noted, helped to shape the American concept of nationality and "stamped upon neighborhoods, states and nation an inter-denominational Protestant ideology which nurtured dreams of personal and social progress."[73] Americanism and Protestantism were linked to-gether in the education of children for basic and Bible literacy. Education in the classics, however, was usually reserved for the wealthy as was ownership of such works. (In fact, an analysis of estate data for Ohio demonstrates that among various types of books, including religious books, classical books, schoolbooks, and practical aids, only ownership of classical books was clearly associated with wealth levels. In the case of classical authors, one finds that the mean estate value of those owning classical works was more than twice that of the mean value for all book owners.)[74] The effects of the "mixed" system of schools in this period are not easily judged, since we are probably dealing with large numbers of individuals who attended no school at all but nonetheless learned to read with the aid of a peer, parent, or neighbor. Assumed causal relationships between schooling and literacy, then, must be approached with caution. We can, however, examine the extent of illiteracy in the early republican period and observe illiteracy rates as they relate to nativity, occupation, and region of birth.

The early republican period gives us our first chance to examine extensive lists of signatures compiled over periods exceeding forty years. The first such list (1798–1840) is a result of a 1796 act for the relief and protection of American seamen in which registration procedures were established requiring the name, nativity, and signature of beginning merchant seamen. The second list, a much more comprehensive one, derives from the army enlistment files for 1799–1894. Differences in the absolute levels of literacy are evident from comparison of the data from merchant seaman registrations with those taken from army enlistee records. Army enlistees probably represent a broader socioeconomic spectrum of the population and may, in fact, be biased downward in terms of wealth. Within the enlistee data, however, there are important differences in literacy rates when the data are cross-classified by occupation, region of birth, and nativity.

The total sample for American seamen was taken from complete enumerations of the seaman records for Philadelphia for 1798 and 1830–31 and smaller samples for other years.[75] The results are tabulated in table 2.1.

Table 2.1   The Illiteracy Rate (IL) among Merchant Seamen Registered in Philadelphia, 1798-1840

| | IL | | | |
	Whites	Nonwhites	All	Number in Sample
1798	.28	.71	.32	306
1810-20	.32	.67	.42	210
1830-31	.25	.81	.41	282
1840	.33	.74	.42	105
All	.28	.74	.38	903

Source: National Archives, Record Group 36, Stack 10 E-3.

For nonwhites, the illiteracy rate of nearly .75 reflects an educative experience bordering upon total neglect. The figures for white males indicate that about three of every ten could not write and that this percentage remained rather constant over a forty-two-year period. The overall rate for whites is somewhat below that derived from the Livingston petition, mentioned previously, but in line with our statewide estimate for New York at the turn of the century. Thus, the figures, in a general way, confirm our estimate of approximately 25 percent illiteracy at the turn of the century.

The military enlistments from 1799 to 1894 provide continuous data for a century during which an almost unaltered enlistment form was employed. The average year of enlistment for the group was 1812, and the average enlistee age was twenty-six. This means we are dealing with men who most likely would have been twelve-year-old school lads in the year 1798 and that they were born just after the formation of the union. The fact that the average age and height of enlistees remain essentially constant indicates that our sample is stable and that its reliability is good. The routine and systematic nature of the evidence enables us to begin to answer questions regarding regional disparities in illiteracy rates, possible urban-rural differences, and, most important, the relationship between illiteracy and socioeconomic position.

The printed form employed for army enlistment remained essentially the same for the years 1799–1894. It was a statement signed by the individual, acknowledging that he was voluntarily enlisting as a soldier in the Army of the United States; further, the form asked for both the state of birth and the state of enlistment, the enlistee's age, complexion, color of eyes, color of hair, height, and, importantly, occupation. The form bore the name of a witness to the enlistee's signature and often the bounty amount received at the time of enlistment. Because each enlistee either signed his name or made his mark, we can establish continuous data for characteristics that can be related to the attribute of illiteracy as determined by whether or not an individual was a marker.

From table 2.2 it is readily apparent that the illiteracy rate for enlistees remains constant from 1799 to 1849. Three major reductions in illiteracy occur in the continuum, the first following a decade of intense social reform, including common school reform (1850–59), the second (more modest) appearing in the decade following the Civil War, when a number of states enacted compulsory education laws (1870–79), and the third appearing in the decade following the passage of compulsory school attendance laws in most states and their enforcement in some (1880–89). It is the discontinuity at the end of the 1850s which provides evidence of renewed efforts to wage war on illiteracy—a crusade, whether dictated by a reformist elite or not, that permeated the population as a whole.

Table 2.2   The Illiteracy Rate (IL) among Army Enlistees in the United
                 States, 1799-1894

	Number in Sample	IL	Average Age	Proportion Foreign Born	Average Height
1799-1809	102	.42	25.1	.18	68.3
1810-19	1,656	.42	26.6	.15	67.7
1820-39	120	.39	25.0	.36	67.3
1840-49	120	.35	24.8	.40	67.3
1850-59	100	.25	23.6	.66	66.9
1860-69	306	.24	23.8	.44	67.0
1870-79	171	.17	24.6	.33	67.0
1880-89	130	.07	24.1	.38	66.9
1890-94	57	.07	23.7	.33	67.4

Source: National Archives, Record Group 94, various boxes. The records
are essentially in two groups, those for 1792-1820 and those for after 1820.
A procedure was devised for selecting boxes at regular intervals and papers
within the boxes selected. Roughly half the men chosen were from the
earlier period, where there are 8 boxes, and half were chosen from the
latter, where there are 851 boxes.

Table 2.3   Illiteracy Rates (IL) among Army Enlistees in the United
                 States, Classified by Occupation and Cross-Classified by
                 Region of Birth, 1799-1829 and 1830-95

	Number in Sample	IL All	Farmers	Laborers	Artisan-Craftsmen (skilled)
All					
1799-1829	1,802	.42	.46	.54	.35
1830-95	960	.21	.28	.30	.15
North					
1799-1829	969	.34	.39	.43	.28
1830-95	427	.17	.24	.24	.11
South					
1799-1829	555	.50	.60	.66	.40
1830-95	127	.31	.38	.27	.30
Foreign Born					
1799-1829	278	.53	.44	.64	.49
1830-95	406	.22	.30	.36	.14
New England					
1799-1829	395	.25	.33	.24	.15
1830-95	94	.12	.22	.18	.07
Other North					
1799-1829	574	.40	.46	.54	.34
1830-95	333	.19	.24	.26	.13

Source: The sample of 2,762 men. The minimum cell sizes are in the
1830-95 category: for foreign-born farmers (N = 30), New England
farmers (N = 18), and New England nonfarmers (N = 17).

Table 2.4   Rates of Illiteracy (IL) among Army Enlistees in the United
                 States, Classified by Nativity and Occupation, 1799-1894

	Native Born	Foreign Born	Farmers	Laborers
1799-1829	.40	.53	.46	.54
1830-49	.30	.38	.41	.46
1850-69	.25	.22	.28	.34
1870-94	.12	.12	.16	.18

Source: Same as table 2.2.

The region of birth for army enlistees is of interest because it provides us with some rough estimates of the levels of illiteracy which existed in various parts of the country a generation before the availability of the more complete data of the 1840 census. From table 2.3 it is apparent that in New England illiteracy rates were clearly lower than in the remainder of the North, a fact which reflects the frontier conditions and low population density of the western states at the time as well as the firmly established religion-literacy bond which had been written into New England law concerning education. Within New England, illiteracy rates from 1799 to 1829 varied only slightly—from .21 to .26 in Massachusetts and Connecticut taken separately, and New Hampshire, Vermont, and Maine taken together. In the Middle States ("Other North") of New York and New Jersey, illiteracy rates were .36 and .41, respectively, while Pennsylvania was higher at .46. Thus, there was an East-West and a North-South gradient in the northern states. New York held an intermediate position between the New England states and Pennsylvania on one hand, and between New England, and New Jersey and Maryland on the other. The southern illiteracy rate was similar to that of the foreign born in general, but it was within the southern rural sector that illiteracy was rampant in the early nineteenth century. The .58 illiteracy rate of enrollees from North Carolina is indicative of this. The statistics before 1830 clearly show the disparity in the array of state illiteracy rates from New England to New York to Pennsylvania and south.[76]

Table 2.3 shows that the illiteracy rate overall dropped one-half from 1799–1829 to 1830–95. Standardization for occupation and nativity increases the overall 1830–95 rate of .21 to only .23. By far the largest occupational groups which enlisted in the army were farmers and laborers, constituting approximately 50 percent. Each group had an illiteracy rate higher than average, but each followed the downtrend after 1830, as shown in table 2.4. The fact that both these groups shared in the expansion of literacy makes it seem unlikely that any rural-urban shift occurring after 1820 would explain the decline of illiteracy. Standardizing the

1830–95 data by using the farm-nonfarm populations of 1799–1829, as in table 2.4, raises the illiteracy rate for nonfarmers from .21 to only .22.

It will be recalled that one of the major problems in dealing with the illiteracy data from colonial America was the difficulty in determining the relationship between illiteracy and wealth. While we are not yet in a position to address this question fully, the occupational data from military enlistments, most of which are included in tables 2.3 and 2.4, help us to make an initial effort. It would be expected from table 2.3, and is verified by table 2.4, that illiteracy decreased substantially for all occupational groups between 1800 and 1870. Farmers and laborers, the native born and the foreign born—all participated in this widespread upsurge in literacy. For the foreign born, among whom illiteracy was more prevalent than among the native born until 1850, the shift downward in illiteracy was more dramatic until 1870. If we compare the occupational groups of farmers and laborers, we observe a shift downard in illiteracy of approximately the same magnitude in the crucial 1850 to 1870 period. Laborers overall, however, were from 5 to 8 percent more illiterate than farmers during the period from 1800 to 1870. The occupational class of artisan-craftsman includes most of those who were neither farmers nor laborers. The illiteracy levels of these skilled men (see table 2.3) were substantially lower than those of the farmers and laborers, except in the South for the period 1830–95. Most of the skilled craftsmen in the North, of course, were likely to have come from urban areas or at least from more densely populated areas with greater numbers of schools and more publishing activity. Also, many had been apprentices with contracts obligating their masters to provide for their instruction in the basic skills of reading and writing. Nonetheless, it is apparent from table 2.3 that the possession of occupational skills did not ensure literacy. Rather, it is evident that region of birth, urbanity, and occupation combined to account for lower illiteracy.

Further breakdowns by occupation show that the conditions affecting the decrease in illiteracy were selective, although all groups participated in the downward trend. Farmers and laborers, for instance, who were the two groups exhibiting the highest rates of illiteracy between 1799 and 1829, underwent rapid declines of .18 and .24 by the end of the century. Illiteracy among shoemakers, one of the most literate of the occupational groups listed for 1800, was practically eradicated by 1895. Other occupational groups such as musicians and hatters also showed low illiteracy rates. Among clerks, the literacy rate was zero as might be expected.[77]

Conclusion

In this chapter we have set out some of the fundamental considerations for the study of literacy in nineteenth-century America. As was the case with other intensely Protestant countries, concern with literacy became a matter for social policy in early America, particularly in New England. This fact provides us with a baseline for interpreting the extent, quality, and institutionalization of literacy in the nineteenth century. In the social structure of colonial America all things important in the matter of educating future generations were to be attended to (if not controlled) by the family. In areas where "social concentration" (the term is from Lockridge) was not sufficient to provide for churches and schools, the entire burden for transmitting literacy from one generation to the next lay with the family. As we have noted, however, the number and size of towns increased methodically with increases in population. The "civilizing" influence of Church and school came quickly following initial town formation in sparsely populated regions. Protestant churches and, to a lesser extent, schools in the colonial period were able to assume some of the burden for teaching youth to read and write. Thus, in the early nineteenth century when an emergent industrial economy was altering the work patterns and patterns of socializing the young within the family, Church and school were able to facilitate the spread of a literacy heritage by building upon precedents established in colonial America. The passage of numerous legal provisions for schooling throughout the colonial period, moreover, set a precedent for state intervention in educational matters. By the late eighteenth century, an increasing number of indentures specifying the number of years of schooling rather than the level of knowledge to be attained foreshadowed an age in which years of schooling would become a standard measure of educational achievement and the achievement of literacy.[78]

For colonial leaders committed to the preservation of the spiritual foundations of culture as well as to the maintenance of social order and stability, literacy for the poor and apprenticed was of gravest concern. In short, the religious-literacy model taught that Bible literacy ought to be guaranteed to these youth in order to prevent behavior which, if left unchecked, would lead to social disintegration. The emergence of the civic model for literacy following the War for Independence did not alter the commitment to Bible literacy. It did, however, signal the beginning of a reevaluation of the functionality of the religious-literacy linkage in the face of new economic conditions. Common school reform itself was one dimension of that reevaluation. Both civic and religious models for literacy were linked in complementary fashion for some time, thus making it possible for a developing ideology of literacy to serve conservative and progressive interests alike. It is true that the secularization of literacy had become increasingly apparent among educational reformers by mid-nineteenth century, but the synthesis of an evangelical Protestant tradition with a republican theory of government was still very much in evidence in the pedagogy and rhetoric of common school reformers for the first seventy years of the nineteenth century. Moreover, reformers themselves were able to bring together the tradition of evangelical Protestantism with the Victorian commitment to modernization. This, as will become evident, was an important ideological accomplishment in the promotion of literacy in the nineteenth century.

Studies by Johansson, Graff, and Lockridge have established that selected variables intervened to affect the rate at which certain subpopulations became literate. While we will have a great deal more to say of these variables later, we note here that there is ample evidence that levels of literacy were affected by age, sex, nativity, region of birth, occupation, and level of wealth. In the matter of age, the interventionist posture of the Church is reflected best in the data from Johansson's study of literacy in Sweden during the seventeenth and eighteenth centuries. In his studies, Johansson has noted that ability to read (as differentiated from ability to recite catechetical knowledge) was far more prevalent among adolescents than among older adults. The ascribed variable of sex was found by Lockridge to determine literacy levels in the earlier colonial period of America, although this was to change considerably among the young as common school reform made its impact by mid-nineteenth century. Nonetheless, at the opening of the nineteenth century, a persistent discrimination against women was evident. Our own analysis of army enlistment records also reveals a persistent relationship between level of literacy and the ascribed variable of nativity, a finding which is reinforced by our census data from a later period and that of Graff for Ontario, Canada. By mid-nineteenth century, however, the greater systematization of schooling was to help reduce the literacy differential among the native born and foreign born.[79]

Our examination of army enlistment records indicates rather large regional disparities in illiteracy rates on the eve of the nineteenth century. Illiteracy in the South was certainly greater than in the North and was particularly rampant in the southern rural sector. As one moves from East to West, illiteracy rates rise. Surely population density was a major factor in these regional differences in illiteracy rates, so much so that we may say (and our mathematical model suggests) that urbanity was a major factor in increased levels of literacy. We would expect that areas with greater population density would provide "social concentration" and that this, in turn, would lead to an increase in the intensity of institution building. The building of schools, churches, and libraries which accompanied greater population density undoubtedly contributed to a rise of literacy rates in urban areas at least to some optimal limit, so long as these areas remained dominated by what we call, in the next chapter, an "ideology of literacy." The relationship between urbanity and an ideology of literacy itself would depend upon a concentration of population and a communications network (such as that created by newspapers) which could overcome the difficulties of transmitting literacy among culturally diverse groups. The same communications network would be a prerequisite to the promotion of literacy in sparsely populated areas.

Finally, preliminary analyses of the occupational structure of literacy and the relationship of wealth to literacy give us further insight into the uneven diffusion of literacy within a culture. In England and in colonial America, literacy was definitely related to occupation and wealth, with those of higher occupational status and greater wealth being generally more literate. Our findings for army enlistees in the early nineteenth century reinforce this appraisal and show that skilled laborers (artisan-craftsmen) were generally more literate than farmers, while unskilled laborers were less literate than both farmers and skilled laborers. Within the skilled laborer category, carpenters (an occupation which would seem to have demanded enough reading skill to follow blueprints) had the lowest illiteracy rate. Nonetheless, the possible causal relationships between literacy and occupation are most tenuous and, in all likelihood, reciprocal. As Lockridge has noted, "The correlation of wealth and occupation with literacy was not entirely causal, since there can be little doubt that literacy also led to greater wealth and to certain occupations."[80] A most obvious example of this would be the case of clerks who, we found, had an illiteracy rate of zero. In the matter of wealth itself, the problem persists, and we cannot, with any certainty assign causal relations among levels of literacy and levels of wealth in the colonial period. The impact of industrialization upon the lives of individuals as the nineteenth century progressed gradually altered the relationship of wealth and occupation to literacy, and fortunately our data from a later period will help clarify this problem. What is of major importance with respect to the occupational and wealth structure of literacy is the fact that the condition of being illiterate did not seem to deter participation in the economic life of the community, nor did it deter political participation. Viewed in this manner, literacy itself should not be construed to be a survival skill in either political or economic terms in the colonial and early republican periods. Rather, the value of literacy in this early period should be seen primarily in terms of a concern with proper socialization.

Three

An Ideology of Literacy and the Spread of Reading Materials
Ohio as a Case Study, 1800–1870

> "When *I* use a word," Humpty Dumpty said, in rather a scornful tone, "it means just what I choose it to mean—neither more nor less."
>
> "The question is," said Alice, "whether you *can* make words mean so many different things."
>
> "The question is," said Humpty Dumpty, "which is tó be master—that's all."
>
> Lewis Carrol, *Through the Looking-Glass*

In this chapter we discuss the ideological dimension of the spread of literacy and the institutions instrumental in effecting that ideology. A detailed account of schooling itself is left to chapter 4, and the effect of other institutions such as libraries and newspapers on actual levels of literacy is left to chapter 5. In his study of the spread of literacy in Sweden, Johansson has noted that the achievement of literacy in a population "requires some form of organized instruction or a number of literacy campaigns." He has characterized this thrust toward literacy in Sweden as a "campaign" carried out for political and religious reasons.[1] The concept of a campaign for literacy, while useful for studying the spread of literacy in early nineteenth-century United States, must be applied with caution. First, the concept of a campaign generally connotes a centrally orchestrated attempt to achieve something. Authority for promoting an ideology of literacy in nineteenth-century United States was diffuse, however, and early efforts were characterized by voluntarism. Second, in the presence of diffuse authority there was no effective way (without the aid of schools) to guarantee implementation of the legislative victories of a campaign for literacy. (Even with the aid of schools, legislative action for schools was often unenforceable.) In addition, the newly formed state superintendencies were not really centralized authorities. Third, lacking enforcement capabilities, literacy advocates were forced to rely on per-suasive tactics—tactics in which newspapermen, booksellers, and print-ers had become highly skilled, tactics which were often a matter of survi-val in the day-to-day fiscal uncertainties of the printing business. Diffuse authority and voluntarism, enforcement difficulties, and the dominance of persuasive over compulsory tactics helped to shape the impact of the ideology which emerged in the early nineteenth century. In the remaining chapters, we assess this impact more closely as we examine the effective-ness of the common school revival. The levels of literacy achieved with schooling and the inequalities of schooling themselves are studied with their implications for the meritocratic system in the United States. The social, economic, and demographic variables which determined literacy rates are analyzed in detail.

In our discussion of ideology and literacy we hope to avoid most of the entanglements which have plagued usage of the term "ideology," with respect to both its historical development and its use among ideologues. A good measure of the debate surrounding the term has been set within a political context, and perhaps the Marxian reinterpretation of the concept of ideology is justification enough for this. More recently, however, the discussion of ideology has received greater attention by students of cul-ture, and the function of ideology has been seen in broader terms by culturologists and political scientists alike. Seliger defines ideology as a belief system serving a group of people "on a relatively permanent basis." As a belief system, he notes, it functions by an appeal to moral norms and a "modicum of factual evidence" to justify the "legitimacy of the implements and technical prescriptions which are to ensure concerted action for the preservation, reform, destruction or reconstruction of a given order."[2]

Most studies of ideology acknowledge its importance as a means for dealing with social and political discontent. Thus, Pratte notes that "the function of ideology is to link up discontent with behavior," and Geertz comments that ideologies attempt "to render otherwise incomprehensible social situations meaningful, to so construe them as to make it possible to act purposefully within them."[3] Psychosocially, he notes, they are "maps of problematic social reality," and this accounts for the higly figurative nature of ideological language and for the intensity with which ideologies are held once they are accepted.[4] The concept of ideology, it is acknowl-edged, is a useful tool to examine the way in which reformers and non-reformers alike handle rapid and unsettling social change. One of the new social roles of education in nineteenth-century western Ontario, Graff has observed, "was the resurrection of restraint and control in times of rapid and disruptive social change."[5] In mid-nineteenth-century United States, what we term an "ideology of literacy" had the potential not simply to restrain and control but to communicate to children and adults a code for success when the ways for success were becoming increasingly uncertain.

Preoccupation with the "falsifying" aspects of ideology has recently been replaced with a trend toward interpreting ideology as part of a cultural imperative in mass societies. This is to say that ideology has been conceived to function as part of a cultural system in which it is seen as a link between the mandates (or prerogatives) of the culture and individual behavior. This shift in attention has been accompanied, in turn, by a concern with the moral dimension of ideologies. Although his concern is with politics and ideology, Seliger has noted that "whether or not moral commitment has . . . a 'falsifying' influence (since it is not necessarily cut off from factual analysis and description), it must be accorded a good measure of centrality [in the concept of ideology]."[6] Pratte has accorded to moral commitment a similar degree of importance. Ideology, he notes, "capitalizes on a kind of moral enterprise."[7] The moral and prescriptive nature of ideologies—that is, the fact that they offer moral and value prescriptions for the conservation or reconstruction of social institutions—makes them links between beliefs and actions. That ideologies are also elements in more comprehensive "language systems" allows us to examine their functions and the function of language in promoting social and cultural reform or reconstruction. Generally, then, we employ the term "ideology" to denote a system of beliefs and values which have been given the force of action. It is important that such beliefs are shared, that they constitute a collective opinion and not simply the private and isolated convictions of an individual. Thus, when we speak of ideology, we are not speaking of contemplation, but of a social phenomenon that is characterized by the goal of action. It is important to reiterate Pratte's analysis in this respect and note, again, that ideologies are moral and prescriptive in nature, thus making them links between beliefs and actions.

Literacy, as most modern reformers recognize, is a double-edged sword, and the reformers of late eighteenth- and early nineteenth-century America were acutely aware of the "good" and "evil" potential of mass literacy. The imposition of literacy on an entire population is fraught with difficulties for the reformer—not merely difficulties of a technical nature but, rather, difficulties associated with the nature of print itself. Bantock, among others, has observed that the implications of printed words, that is, the experiences which they attempt to convey and to link to future behavior, become private and idiosyncratic compared with the impact of oral communication. "A print culture," he notes, "offers a multiplicity of identities [and] the rapid growth in the number of books was an essential preamble to that personal psychic mobility and acceptance of change which have almost come to be the defining characteristics of modern man."[8] While they were not faced with the same degree of psychic mobility as participants in twentieth-century Western cultures, nineteenth-century educational reformers who spoke to the problem of literacy and who helped establish an ideology of literacy were clearly aware of the possibility that, in the absence of control over reading habits, literacy might not achieve its intended goal. In fact, they faced the same problem with which More and the British Evangelicals had to contend: that literacy itself had the potential to be counterproductive to their efforts. The *concern* of American reformers, likewise, was not substantially different, for instance, from that of Swedish churchmen and officials whose edicts and efforts to record in detail the level of reading and the type of individual knowledge possessed by children and adults testify to their intense interest in controlling the type of knowledge conveyed by print.[9] Finally, what must be emphasized in this respect is that a faith in literacy to do the job of proper socialization (a faith which made of literacy a virtue) was accompanied by a realistic appraisal of the dangers of literacy. One could not take for granted the outcome of exposing children and adults to the magic of print. The use to which a newly literate individual might put his recently acquired skills was too problematic. Thus, it was imperative that an ideology of literacy speak directly to the moral consequences of literacy and that pedagogues carefully select that reading most suited to their perceptions of proper socialization.

It is not our purpose here to engage in an extensive treatment of the psychosocial linkages—the role of ideology in the organization of role personalities and in individual emotional health—of ideology.[10] It is sufficient to note that ideology may be broadly considered as a mechanism for the individual's structuring of reality, that ideology thus may be seen as a device for socializing the young and consequently as a means of explaining how social relations are structured and how they constitute reality. This legitimizing function of ideology and its relationship to literacy will be one concern in our discussion as we examine the role of ideology in bringing stability to uncertain social realities. Our focus is not on the way in which print itself was a formative feature of ideological development, although that topic would certainly be deserving of detailed study. Rather, we wish to demonstrate that in the northern states, attitudes toward reading, as evidenced in schoolbooks and newspapers, took on certain ideological characteristics and, in effect, constituted an ideological view of literacy. This view of literacy shared by common school reformers (an "assertive" group, as Vaughn and Archer would label them)[11] thus laid the basis for the assertion and eventual domination of Whiggish interventionist policies in public schooling. Moreover, literacy conceived of from an ideological standpoint fitted nicely with the reformist policies of the public school movement and the diffusion of evangelical Protestantism as it moved toward a reconciliation with the Victorian commitment to modernization.

A final word of introduction is perhaps necessary regarding an ideology of literacy. The logic of dialectic obliges us to consider the possibility of an ideology of illiteracy, however unlikely this prospect might seem within the culture of late eighteenth- and early nineteenth-century America. Documentary evidence attesting to a commitment to illiteracy is not readily forthcoming for obvious reasons, and the only type of evidence which might be used to demonstrate the existence of such an ideology would be left to us by literates. Most of this, unfortunately, does not actually testify to an ideology of illiteracy but, rather, to a state of deprivation among the ignorant and unlettered as judged by the literate. The devaluation of the intellect which was manifest in the political rhetoric of Jacksonian Democrats *could* be interpreted as an expression of antiliteracy, for example. This, however, was probably not the case. To the proponents of popular culture, basic literacy was not what was in question. A folk hero like Davy Crockett did not perceive himself as against literacy, or against education. Nor, according to Pessen's account of labor reformers, were workers against literacy. Quite otherwise, says Pessen. "Fairness demanded that the 'children of the poor, as well as the rich, ought to be instructed both in letters and morals.' "[12] Anti-intellectualism, on the other hand, was directed at a particular type of literacy and a particular type of schooling, namely, that which perceived social and political leadership as the exclusive province of the "gentleman." Thus, it is fair to say that insofar as anti-intellectualism *could* have been interpreted as antiliteracy, the accent in both was upon preventing a type of literacy instruction which could be interpreted as antidemocratic. Thus, when literacy was perceived as antiaristocratic, becoming literate and learned was acceptable insofar as it avoided an appeal to traditional social and political distinctions between the gentleman and the commoner.

Promoting Literacy

Among the several sources for the study of an ideology of literacy in early nineteenth-century America, the most readily available and comprehensive are newspapers, school texts, and children's literature. Editors and printers of all three were clearly conscious of their role in promoting literacy, and each had both a moral and an economic interest in promoting his products. The first source—the newspaper—received a good deal of attention from early nineteenth-century advocates of Jeffersonian principles and conservative theologians alike. In the case of theologians, for example, Solomon Southwick indicted newspaper editors as "unprincipled Novelists and Political Pamphleteers" who, as he saw it, propagated a gospel contrary to "sound Christian Education."[13] More representative, however, were those who stressed the social and educational value of newspapers and their importance to a literate and enlightened public. An orator addressing the Phi Beta Kappa Society of Cambridge, Massachusetts, in 1826 declared that the cause of early nineteenth-century Americans' great interest in reading was "to be found in the freedom of the press, or rather in co-operating with the cheapness of the press."[14] A number of citizens of Boston, in a memorial testimony to the Senate and House of Representatives, asserted that

> Without the means of transmitting knowledge with *ease*, and *rapidity*, and *cheapness*, a nation, however free in name, must become the blind followers of the wealthy and the well-informed, or the tools of the designing. Every means, therefore, which renders the access to knowledge more difficult or more expensive, directly *increases the power of the few, and diminishes the influence of the many*, and thus tends to weaken the foundations of our Government.[15]

As a group, newspaper editors had mixed motives for promoting their product. Surely their entrepreneurial concerns were important and profit was a powerful motivating factor; but they also sought to raise public consciousness to the need for literacy by espousing a moral commitment to the latter. Their rhetoric reflected their dual intentions by seeking to blend the enlightenment ideal of a literate citizenry with the commercial interests of promoting newspaper sales. Their commercial interests aside, however, newspaper editors taught their subscribers, and those who listened to their subscribers read aloud, the value of literacy itself. This they did by linking in ideological fashion the concepts of literacy, economic progress, public and private virtue, and nationalism.

Modesty was not one of the salient attributes of newspapermen, and in an age when public schooling had only begun to serve its social welfare function and when teachers were often castigated for being poorly prepared, it did not seem presumptuous for a newspaperman to carry instructional advice in his columns. In 1826, the *Athens Mirror and Literary Register*, Athens, Ohio, featured an article recommending that John Locke's advice on reading be followed so as to reap from a literary work the "treasures of sentiment that are contained therein."[16] In more than one newspaper it was suggested in accordance with a Pestalozzian view of learning (that is, a view which emphasized the importance of sensory perception and the manipulation of objects in learning to read) that a newspaper would be a delightful gift for the young child learning to read "because he reads of names and things which are very familiar, and he will make progress accordingly." In fact, said the paper, "a newspaper one year is worth a quarter's schooling to a child."[17]

The need for newspapers was both broad and deep, according to their editors. In a reprinted article from the *Traveller* (1828), the *Athens Mirror and Literary Register* related the message that the public press "has such an over-powering influence on the morals, the politics, and national character of this country, that it is devoutly wished it may ever be wielded by men of pure hearts, sterling patriotism, and extensively cultivated minds." Approximately twenty years later, its successor, the *Athens Messenger*, credited the newspaper, more than schooling and books, with enlightening the American public "on almost all topics of any real importance."[18] That the promotion of literacy and the promotion of nationalist sentiment were closely linked has been widely recognized by students of literacy. The farmer, indispensable figure that he was in the moral vision of the American republic, received a great deal of attention from editors. One editor, commenting upon the nobility of agricultural employment and generally commending the farmer on his honesty, lawfulness, love of family, and fear of God, juxtaposed his promotional concerns with idealism as follows: "His calling is an honest, honorable one—and the good farmer invariably respects his country and regards the laws, fears God—loves and provides for his wife and family—and takes the Newspaper."[19]

Of the many types of books which explicitly attempted to shape the child's attitudes toward reading, those which probably had the greatest impact in his early years were schoolbooks and formal instructional materials, and a wide variety of stories, poems, and anecdotes which may be classified as children's literature. By the nineteenth century, the value of reading expressed in these books had clearly become multidimensional—its value was part of the value of education and schooling themselves, and proper behaviors *in* and attitudes *toward* school generally related to the acquisition of literacy skills. It has often been noted that propriety and morality taken together were an essential part of the nineteenth-century world view, and it may be remarked that the acquisition of literacy was no exception to this. Even religious thought itself and the accompanying theological concepts (which were linked to the ideology of literacy) were often enfolded within a moral world view so that religious training gave way to training in the "rules for good conduct" through "moral stories calculated to preserve the peace and prosperity of American society by a timely cultivation of the natural virtues."[20]

It was common for both reading and schooling to be used as part of the setting for children's stories or poems, the moral examples contained therein presumably attractive enough to make an impression upon young minds. There was no "neutral ground" in the schoolbooks of the nineteenth century, notes Elson, and the value judgment, which alternately or in concert encompassed the virtues of love of country and

God, duty to parents and family, commitment to thrift, honesty, hard work, temperance, and obedience, and a faith in progress, was considered an essential element in any successful appeal to the juvenile conscience.[21] Moreover, as Macleod has remarked, "the call for order, self-control and discipline, repeated again and again in every story, did echo a dread of disorder, and apprehension that the individual loss of control would end in social disruption at best, in total disintegration at worst."[22]

There is no question that school texts and children's stories urged their juvenile audience to read for the sake of their intellects, their parents, their future success, and their religion, but the most striking change in the expressed value of reading by 1850 was that it had become more than a tool. Its utilitarian garb of colonial times had taken on new colors, allowing the skill of reading to become one among several important virtues to be acquired by the young. While a number of authors and compilers urged selectivity in reading and a few actually forbade reading not sanctioned by teacher or parent, reading had nonetheless become a virtuous activity in itself, and the good child was distinguishable from the bad in part by his ability to read.

The Family and Reading

In the ideology of literacy espoused by editors and printers of nineteenth-century newspapers and authors of children's literature and textbooks, the family remained, as it had been in the past, the moral mainstay of the social order. This, naturally enough, was not a position different from official pronouncements on the importance of the family, particularly when this "institution of institutions" was perceived to be threatened or when the educational duties of parents were thought to be neglected. Of the three "positive institutions"—the family, the Church, and civil government—which the "Almighty has left us," said the governor of Indiana in an address reprinted by the *Zanesville City Times,* Zanesville, Ohio, "the first of these is the Family; and it is in this institution that we must look for the beginning of an education that shall be worthy of the age and the nation in which we live."[23]

It was in the family that an interest in and enthusiasm for reading ought to begin, according to testaments of the period. Printers of catechisms and authors of storybooks, first readers, and primers assumed that children would begin to recite and learn their letters before attending school. The home and school were pictured in a symbiotic relationship, and parents, it seems, though they had less and less time for it, were still obliged to teach the rudiments of spelling and reading to their preschool children. Later eighteenth-century books for children such as Dunlap's *Child's New Play-Thing* and Isaiah Thomas's *Tom Thumb's Playbook* were designed for preschool instruction and clearly express the assumption that parents ought to teach children their letters as soon as they can speak. Webster's *American Spelling Book* made it clear that reading was an activity not to be forgotten at home, and he recommended to children that "when they are at home, [they should] read some good book, that God may bless them."[24]

The very presence of books in the home clearly was perceived as a formative influence on interpersonal relations among family members. Fathers, for instance, if they were not actually given an instructional role, nonetheless reinforced the day's learning. In some cases the rewards for study were direct and tangible: "Young Samuel had been so attentive to his books in the early part of the day, that his father promised to indulge him with a walk, in the evening, to a very fine orchard."[25] Other authors invoked the familiar homey sentiment such as the following found in the *Western Spelling Book:*

1. When my father comes home in the evening from work,
    Then will I get up on his knee,
    And tell him how many fine things I have learned,
    And show him how good I can be.

2. He'll hear what a number I know how to count,
    I'll tell him what words I can spell,
    And I hope, if I learn something every day,
    That ere long I shall read very well.[26]

Newspapers, too, abounded in homespun sentiment and specialized in descriptions of winter evenings spent in the pastime of reading. The book had a conspicuous place in the family circle (particularly on cold winter evenings) and helped moral precepts make their first impressions. The scene was often an idyllic one, such as that painted by the *Athens Mirror and Literary Register* in 1828:

The little family circle is never so closely united and so happy in itself as winter evenings, especially when the storm is beating upon the window; and he ought to be a happy man who listens while one of his children reads, and watches his eyes sparkling when he reads of an act of magnanimity, or his lip curl in scorn at baseness and ingratitude.[27]

Late eighteenth-century and nineteenth-century books alike stressed the importance of the home atmosphere and responsible parentship in learning to read, and it was emphasized, as well, that children, adolescents, and young adults should be encouraged to occupy their leisure time at home with reading. "Think of what you read in your spare hours," counseled Webster's *American Spelling Book,* and Josiah Townsend recommended that after attending church, children "spend the rest of the day

at home, in reading the Bible and other good books.''[28] Mother and child
were often described in a cooperative endeavor to teach the latter the
basic skill of reading. (Occasionally, the role was reversed, as in the
McGuffey story of James Smith, who, through the sacrifices of his hard-
working but poor mother, had learned to read by attending school, and
returned in the evenings to read to her.)[29] A "good" boy such as Master
Edward Goodwill was pictured as experiencing the delights of reading and
"asking his mamma to let him read farther."[30] An early nineteenth-
century *American Reader* addressed itself to the importance of the
mother-child relationship in learning to read in a different way, by describing the plight of poor Hester, who sought to avoid the watchful eye of
a perverse mother who would not let her read. The popular Mrs. Barbauld
pictured the mother-child relationship in a short verse as follows:

Come hither Charles
   come to mamma.
Take haste.
Sit in mamma's lap.
Now read your book.[31]

McGuffey's two-page dialogue conveying his observations of the importance of the mother in the child's performance in reading and spelling
included the following:

7   Well, my child, as you have read your old book through, I have
bought you a new one: here it is. I hope you will keep it neat and
clean, and not tear or lose it.
8   Thank you, dear mamma; I will try and do as you wish me to;
and I hope soon to be able to read all the lessons and spell all the
words in my new book as well as I can those in my old one.[32]

When parents were perceived not to be doing their job, newspaper
editors stepped into the breach in order that they might fulfill their self-
appointed role as protectors of an enlightened and literate society. In
March of 1821 Joseph Buchanan, a democratic-republican and active
educational reformer from Cincinnati, printed in his *Western Spy and Literary Cadet* the first of three essays devoted to the proper modes of instruction. The first essay spoke directly to the proper methods of acquiring
basic literacy and presented in detail the proper sequence of instruction.
After advice on the presentation of the alphabet, syllabification, spelling,
and punctuation, the author said that great "pains should be taken by
teachers, to make correct readers; because by reading all theoretical
knowledge is gained." "Unfortunate for youth," he continued, "but few
parents are competent judges of the matter which their children ought to
learn. . . . But as there is not room in a newspaper for a very lengthy essay,
the writer with all due deference refers his readers to the introduction of

the Columbian Orator, to the preface of the Juvenile Expositor, to Stewart on Education, and particularly to the 189th page of the Columbian Orator, a dialogue between parent and teacher, &c.''[33]

The second essay, ''Education,'' struck at the heart of the ''reading problem,'' namely, that the emphasis upon eloquence ordinarily found in reading instruction often proved an obstacle to reading comprehension itself. Of children attaining a knowledge of elocution, it was remarked that ''not understanding the meaning of words, nor the construction of sentences they cannot comprehend the author's meaning, or express a single idea, even with a tolerable degree of propriety.''[34] Finally, in the third essay, the author concluded that the performing of plays for the purpose of teaching eloquence diverted youth ''from every useful and ornamental part of education.'' He explained that it was not the instruction in oratory itself to which he objected but, rather, the fact that it was not prefaced with a ''due regard to punctuation, to emphasis and to cadence, and to understand the meaning of every sentence which they read.''[35]

The emphasis upon the mother's role in teaching her children to read is one deserving of further comment because it raises the question of whether women, particularly mothers, were expected to be literate or whether the ideology in fact was speaking to, and hence attempting to rectify, the problem of lower literacy rates among females compared with males. Even by the end of the eighteenth century, female literacy was far below that for males, particularly in rural areas. This disparity continued well into the nineteenth century, but the degree of literacy differences between sexes had been reduced dramatically by 1860. Thus, at least by mid-century, mothers in the North could fulfill the expectations of school texts and children's literature insofar as they were able to participate in the teaching of reading to young children. The irony of such a development is that common schools had taken over more and more of the responsibility for the teaching of reading, thus reducing the responsibility of mothers in this respect. A second and closely related question is whether books were, in fact, more prevalent among homemakers than among the unmarried and, if so, whether the ideology of literacy was linked to this basic social fact. Clearly the expectation of newspaper accounts and children's stories was that homes with children would have books present and that interpersonal relations in the family were important to reading achievement.

There is some evidence to support the assertion that, in this respect, the ideology of literacy was based upon an accurate perception of book-owning conditions. In a study of 1,118 estate inventories in two Ohio counties from 1813 to 1859, we have found that marriage, presumed to be a first step in homemaking and, as such, a proxy for family formation, is associated with higher levels of book ownership.[36] Both wealth and marriage have been found to be statistically significant determinants of book ownership. In the case of wealth, the mean personal estate values for decadal intervals between 1790 and 1859 are, without exception, higher for book owners than non–book owners.[37] For our immediate purposes, however, what is important is the fact that the data support the contention that the mother was a key figure in teaching reading (see table 3.1). It is equally important in relating this evidence to an ideology of literacy, however, that book ownership as a function of marriage emerges much more clearly among those above the median wealth line, as shown in table 3.2. Here, the differential effects of marriage on book ownership are apparent, except in Athens County between 1813 and 1829. Differences in book ownership among the married and unmarried are clearly smaller below the median wealth line. Absolute levels of book ownership are considerably less, as well, below the median wealth line. If promoters of an ideology of literacy stressing the role of the mother in teaching reading targeted their efforts in terms of book-owning conditions, then their efforts would be aimed at those below the median wealth line. For this reason, it is likely that the ideology functioned to some extent as a promotional device for the poor (or at least those below the median wealth line), but more as a reinforcement of already existing family conditions for those above the median wealth line. To put it differently, the poor needed encouragement to make the mother's role in the teaching of reading a significant part of family life. For those above the median wealth line, however, the link between motherhood and the teaching of reading was already strong. The ideology of literacy, then, simply reinforced an already existing relationship between mother and child.

Table 3.1   The Differences in Book Ownership Reported in Estate Inventories in Two Ohio Counties, Classified by Marital Status, 1790-1859

County and Date	% Having Books		% Not Having Books		All	
	Married	Unmarried	Married	Unmarried	% Having Books	% Not Having Books
Athens						
1813-29	45	50	55	50	46	54
1830-59	50	32	50	68	44	56
1813-59	49	36	52	64	45	55
Washington						
1790-1829	48	38	52	62	43	57
1830-59	58	35	42	65	50	50
1790-1859	54	36	47	63	47	53

Source: The sample of 1,118 inventories from Washington County, Ohio, Probate Records, 1790-1859, and Athens County, Ohio, Probate Records, 1813-59.

Table 3.2   The Differential Effects of Marriage on Book Ownership above and
below Median Wealth Values in Estate Inventories in Two Ohio
Counties, 1790-1859

County and Date	% below Median Wealth Having Books			% above Median Wealth Having Books		
	Married	Unmarried	All	Married	Unmarried	All
Athens						
1813-29	32	38	34	68	78	71
1830-59	42	30	37	56	34	50
1813-59	39	32	36	56	41	53
Washington						
1790-1829	37	34	35	60	48	56
1830-59	47	38	44	64	32	54
1790-1859	42	36	39	62	38	55

Source: The sample of 1,118 inventories.

Reading and Virtue

Reading was presumed to be important in the development of public and private virtue, and authors competed with each other to convince parents of the moral superiority of their products. Concern for the spiritual welfare of the child was seldom lacking in books for children. The solemnity and ponderousness in children's books of colonial days had begun to disappear, but the evangelical spirit remained strong in late eighteenth- and early nineteenth-century schoolbooks and children's literature. "The Marks of a true Christian" in the early nineteenth century were still, as Fox had instructed in 1743, love for one's neighbor, faith, virtue, knowledge, temperance, and patience. Histories, fables, riddles, and direct moral didactic were standard fare for conveying moral precepts. The exercise of careful scrutiny was often advised in choosing reading material, for its was common knowledge that the minds of youth were easily corrupted. Thus, Asa Lyman noted that "we should be careful what books we put into the hands of children. All publications tending to infidelity, looseness of character, vice, etc. ought to be proscribed."[38] The increasing secularization of traditional culture by the late eighteenth century was evidenced by Benezet's concern that children were being motivated to learn by "covetousness" or a "desire for distinction" rather than by religion.[39] Benezet, a champion of both religious and civil education, would surely have been horrified with those later intrusions into tradition found in some of the new juvenile literature. As Kiefer has remarked, the practice of "enticing children to perform their little duties by bribes," which was condemned in previous decades, was now approved (in the nineteenth century) on the grounds that "whatever stimulated children to a love of virtue or to learning ought always to be applied."[40] By the early nineteenth century, moreover, the range of books available to the young had become of some concern to compilers of school texts. "Do not read any books but those which your parents, or teachers, give you to read," advised Samuel Wood in his *New York Reader*. "It is better not to read at all, than to read bad books."[41]

Juvenile books and school texts were persistent in the theme that good children "mind their books," love their schools, and make every effort to learn. The virtue of reading was often juxtaposed with other virtues, and "a good child," said Webster, "will not lie, swear nor steal," and when at home will "ask to read his book." "Love him that loves his book," he continued, and "if you want to be good, wise and strong, read with care such books as have been made by wise and good men."[42] That this sentiment remained very much alive forty years later is evidenced in Pickett's *New Juvenile Spelling Book and Rudimental Reader*, which gave the following account of the behavior of the "good boy": "He loves his teacher and all who tell him what is good. He likes to read, and to write, and to learn something fresh every day. He hopes that if he lives to be a man, he shall know a great many things, and be very wise and good."[43] "Little Lucy" of McGuffey's *Eclectic First Reader*, when asked, "Would you rather read than play?" responded that she would favor the former "because mamma tells me that play will not be of any use to me, after I grow up; but if I love to read I shall be wise and good."[44] On the other hand, the "BAD BOY hates his book, and takes no pleasure in improving himself in anything."[45]

Books were cherished items, and children who lost, tore, or otherwise abused them were admonished severely. "Only naughty boys tear their books," said Mrs. Barbauld.[46] *The Good Child's Delight*, printed by W. Young of Philadelphia, told the story of a little girl who, having a mother kind enough to teach her to read, abused her books to the extent that "all her friends grew tired of giving her books." "What a sad thing that was," the story continued, "to have no book to read! but to grow up a dunce, and not be able to spell or read pretty stories."[47]

Literacy, the Worthy Use of Leisure Time, and Economic Opportunity

Compilers of school texts, editors of newspapers, and authors of children's literature were not strictly of one mind in the bonds they perceived between literacy, proper socialization, and future material success. Nonetheless, they were in accord with the general theme of common school reformers that the moral object of education would contribute to social amelioration through the prevention of delinquency and crime, and that avoidance of the latter, would, in turn, naturally make it possible for the assiduous youth to apply the basic rudiments of scholarship in an effort to improve himself materially. In the era of intense common school reform during the 1840s when the rhetorical link between schooling and economic success was strong, basic texts continued to stress the moral dimension of education. Thus, at the same time that Sanders's essay "Education" confirmed the notion that "he who wishes to acquire a trade or a profession . . . must expect to work as an apprentice, or to study as a scholar," it explicitly noted that a "good education" would not "always secure wealth."[48]

The theme of proper socialization of the young through literacy was not obscured with the coming of a more explicit concern with the link between literacy and wealth. Men like Webster and McGuffey were persistent in their appeal to the moral mission of education and the moral object of reading. Webster stressed literacy, Church, and school as instruments to ensure proper socialization: "As for those boys and girls that mind not their books, and love not church and school; but play with such as tell tales, tell lies, curse, swear, and steal, they will come to some bad end, and must be whipt till they mend their ways."[49] Later, McGuffey put the case more generally but no less effectively for the moral importance of literacy:

> The boys and girls who can not read must go through the world like the man on his journey. They will never know whether they are on the right road or the wrong one.[50]

The moral purpose of literacy seldom came into open confrontation with the more worldly view that literacy enhanced one's economic opportunity. Neither view really occurred in isolation from the other. A moral world view and the obligation to seek greater economic opportunity through hard work were tenets of nineteenth-century Protestantism whose coexistence made it possible to conceive of literacy and economic opportunity in a mutually supportive arrangement.

In a deliberate attempt to define the important role of the schoolmaster in the conquest of the American West, McGuffey spoke directly to the compatibility of hard work and learning. Thus, Mr. Barlow, the man in charge and the interviewer of prospective settlers, remarks of Oliver, the schoolmaster, that his profession is a "very respectable and useful" one. Of the settlers, he notes, "Though we are hard working men, we do not mean to be ignorant; every one among us must be taught reading and writing."[51] In some texts, hard work and literacy were established parts of a formula for success: "Love your book more than play," said Crandall, "for he who will love his book, and try to learn to read in it, may come to be a rich man; but if you love play most, you will be poor."[52]

The favorite targets for the promotion of literacy and the improvement of reading skills as they related to increased economic opportunity were adolescents and young adults who were apprenticed and farmers who made poor use of their leisure time during the winter months. The favorite theme, like that enunciated later in the *Cardinal Principles* of 1918, was the worthy use of leisure time. The farmer, that moral buttress of American democracy, received his share of attention, although urban youth seem to have been a more favored target. Nonetheless, the *Zanesville Gazette* suggested that the sons of farmers "should employ their winter evenings in the attainment of useful knowledge." The essay noted that farmers' sons were in a better position to do this, since, unlike the apprentice and the clerk, they had long winter evenings to store their "minds with facts, that science has taught and experience confirmed."[53] A decade earlier, in 1828, the *Athens Mirror and Literary Register* had told its readers in an article reprinted from the *New York Farmer* that the farmer's pursuits of the day invite him "to draw near the evening fire—and if he has a taste for useful reading, particularly for that connected with rural pursuits, we scarcely can imagine one to spend his time more rationally and happily." The article then went on to calculate that if the farmer were to spend three hours per day, four days each week for six months "in useful reading," he could consume one thousand volumes, the results of which would be to "prevent him from spending his time and money at improper places" and ultimately to make him a "more valuable citizen, a blessing to his friends and neighbors, and more likely to descend with grey hairs in repose to the grave."[54] The association between reading and social utility was thus made even more appealing by the promise of longevity.

Among newspaper editors, occupational prospects and economic opportunity for urban youth were still of foremost concern. In "A Word to Apprentices," the *Child's Newspaper* of the Cincinnati Sunday School Union advised that "the only way for a young man to prepare himself for usefulness, is to devote himself to study during all his leisure hours." "You can never hope to rise to a respectable standing in the world," the essay continued, "without long, persevering and constant application to study." Specific advice was offered on what type of literature was most suitable for the upwardly mobile youth. Novels and romances were to be avoided, while natural and moral philosophy, geography, history, and the arts were to be engaged.[55]

Commercial papers frequently carried advice to the apprentice and mechanic on the importance of reading to future economic and social advancement. The importance to "young men engaged in either mechanical or mercantile pursuits" of using their leisure time to gain useful knowledge was incalculable, according to the *Newark Daily Advertiser*. However unfavorable their situations might seem, the "paths of knowledge" were open to young men engaged in these pursuits, said the essay, and the result would lead to greater respectability.[56] Other essays simply recommended an hour of reading per day for advancement in life while the more enthusiastic recommended to young men four hours of reading and writing "before retiring to rest." It was calculated that a young man going into business might, if he remained unmarried for five years, accumulate 7,300 hours of "mental application" which would yield future benefits.[57]

The ideology of literacy made it clear that major social institutions were to have a role in the teaching of virtue through literacy. All, in fact, were encouraged to promote the habit of reading for the sake of mind, soul, and success, as well as social utility. In effect, the institutional structure of nineteenth-century America was viewed as a network for the inculcation of virtue and literacy. Family, Church, school, and library were seen as mutually reinforcing as they made their own special contributions to socializing the young through literacy. Consciousness raising itself was seen as a proper function of these institutions as they sought to provide a stable and persistent link between belief and action—a link needed to maintain a moral consensus.

Institutions for an Ideology

It has been noted that the link between belief and action characteristic of ideology at the individual level was also perceived as necessary to the institution building of men taken collectively. In this respect, social institutions were viewed as the carriers of ideology, that is, as vehicles to make the impact of ideology more permanent. Thus, some examination of newspaper circulation, the publishing trade, and the development of libraries must be added to the discussion of an ideology of literacy itself. An Ohio educator commenting upon what he considered to be the national attribute of literacy in 1856 noted, "We are unquestionably a reading people."[58] If he were extending his historical outlook some fifty years previous, it would have been evident that great efforts had been expended, individually and socially, to promote a reading public—to develop those social and commercial enterprises which helped to promote and sustain a literate people. Imprint production, as we have seen, outstripped the increase in population from the late seventeenth century to 1831 (see figure 2.2). In short, the air was filled with the rising expectations which had been generated by the entrepreneurial values inherited from the eighteenth century, by political and educational reform, by the expansion of facilities to bring the printed word to a newly emerging industrial nation, and by an already existing tradition of Bible literacy emanating from Protestant reformism. These enterprises and their accompanying expectations affected a very large proportion of the population. For some, as we shall see in later chapters, the expectation of literacy was unrealistic, however. It will become evident that some groups did not benefit from the promotion of literacy and that the achievement of literacy was a selective process which was determined, in part, by the region of one's birth and the variables of population density, availability of schooling, nativity, ethnicity, and family size.

Newspapers

The importance of the newspaper in promoting an ideology of literacy has already been noted, but it may be added that newspapermen were generally supportive of educational matters including common schools, libraries, lyceums, and other institutions which they viewed as contributing to an enlightened public through expanded literacy. As Louis Wright has noted of the developing Northwest Territory, editors of newspapers were usually advocates of "schools, libraries, lecture programs and other means of bringing literacy and enlightenment to the people."[59] The entrepreneurial spirit of newspapermen made them vigorous spokesmen for their own product, and they sought their customers among adults and youth alike. Preferential postal rates for newspapers also clearly gave them an advantage as instruments for public persuasion, and the frequent congressional debates over postal rates for newspapers generated numerous plaudits for their social value.[60]

The impact of an ideology of literacy was contingent upon giving broad coverage to a codified system of beliefs through an efficient network of communication. While it would be unwise to use the postal system as a model of efficiency, it did play a major role in systematizing communications by 1820. In 1823 there were 4,498 post offices and 82,763 miles of postal roads in the United States—this compared with 195 post offices and 5,642 miles of roads in 1792.[61] The postal system, Brown has noted, constituted a "supra-local" communications system by 1820 in Massachusetts, where 443 post offices "blanket[ed]" the state. The system, which allowed local communities access "to the national communication system," was, along with the growth of printing, a key element in creating a cosmopolitan perspective in rural Massachusetts.[62]

Some idea of the potential effectiveness of this network may be gathered by examining the growth of newspaper circulation in the United States during the first half of the nineteenth century. (The impact of this activity on levels of literacy itself will be examined in chapter 5.) While it is not possible to know directly whether or not a subscriber *read* the paper he bought (any more than it is possible to know if those borrowing books from the library *read* them), we assume that most people who spent their money on subscriptions did so for the purpose of reading the newspapers they bought. In fact, subscriber records probably underestimate the impact of newspapers, since newspapers were shared (a complaint by

editors), thus reducing the profits of the printer and/or editor. One editor
of the *Cleveland Herald* (1841) had apparently exhausted his patience
with a particular form of the pernicious habit of borrowing:

> Cool–Very! We have no doubt many of our country subscribers have
> neighbors who get their newspaper reading by borrowing. One of this
> class of bores has just left our office. He asked for Mr. M———'s
> paper—seated himself deliberately—read it through—folded and
> handed it back, remarking that although he was Mr. M———'s neigh-
> bor he did not know as it would be exactly right to take the paper to
> him without his orders![63]

Weekly papers spread rapidly in small towns and cities throughout the
eastern states between 1783 and 1801, and in the Northwest during the
opening decade of the nineteenth century. By 1790 *daily* newspapers had
appeared in Philadelphia and Charleston, South Carolina. Circulation and
consumption of newspapers varied, depending upon population density,
but the general potential of the newspaper for influencing public opinion in
educational matters may be inferred from examining the paper/person
ratios from 1810 to 1850 (table 3.3). Not every region experienced a high
paper/person ratio, however. Even so, in areas of relatively sparse population, the viability of the newspaper, and particularly the rural, small-
town paper, as a shaper of public opinion and promotor of literacy may be
illustrated. Two examples from small-town, rural Ohio—the *Ashtabula
Sentinel* from northeastern Ohio and the *Mansfield Gazette* from north-
central Ohio—give evidence of this capability. An examination of subscriber records of both papers in the late 1820s and early 1830s shows that
while both served the townspeople where the presses were located, both
actually did the major portion of their business outside the town limits.
Thus, in the case of the *Sentinel,* approximately 29 percent of its business
was in town; 39 percent of the subscribers to the *Gazette* were
townspeople. The remaining papers, that is, the major portion of subscriptions, were distributed (with the exception of a few out-of-state ex-
changes) within a ninety-nine-mile radius, a large geographic region for a

Table 3.3   The Circulation of Newspapers among Whites in the United States,
1810-50

Years	Total White Population	Number of Papers	Annual Circulation	Number per Person
1810	5,862,004	359	22,321,700	3.81
1828	11,500,000	852	68,117,796	5.92
1840	14,195,695	1,631	195,838,673	13.80
1850	19,553,068	2,526	426,409,978	21.81

Source: United States Census, 1860, table 164, p. 158.

local paper. Table 3.4 demonstrates the way in which local papers, taken collectively, could, with the help of canal and mail routes, effectively "cover" a state and help mold public opinion in a crusade for literacy.

Table 3.4   Within-State Newspaper Circulation by Mail and Packet for Two Ohio Newspapers, 1820-33

	Number (and %) of Subscribers Living Given No. of Miles from Home Office				Total Number (and %)
	1-20	11-20	21-99	100 and Up	
Mansfield Gazette (182?-27, 3 years)	62(13.3)	247(52.9)	138(29.5)	20(4.3)	467(100.0)
Ashtabula Sentinel (1832-33)	22(8.9)	109(44.3)	107(43.5)	8(3.3)	246(100.0)

Source: The subscription books of the Mansfield Gazette and the Ashtabula Sentinel. For each newspaper, the sample represents 46.2 percent of the subscribers receiving papers by mail or packet. Mileage for the remaining 53.8 percent could not be calculated from the information available on maps of the period.

The Book Trade and Book Ownership

The importance of the expanding book trade in promoting the "reading habit" was, in degree, comparable to expanded newspaper circulation. Sermons, catechisms, pious biographies, and the Bible had long been a part of a literacy tradition, and this continued into the nineteenth century. By 1750, the almanac (usually serving the several functions of calendar, register, gazetteer, magazine, and diary) had also gained public acceptance. Speaking of his own experience as a printer and compiler of almanacs, Benjamin Franklin observed that the almanac (particularly his own) was "a proper vehicle for conveying instruction among the common people, who bought scarcely any other books."[64] There were other competitors for the tastes of the American reading public. Among the more disdained by literary connoisseurs were the "chapbooks," which offered cheap entertainment in the form of "crime stories, simple fiction and romance, other people's misery, travel, adventure, biography, religious sentiment, songs, jokes, fortune telling, and any kind of excursion into the occult."[65] By the early nineteenth century the cheap secular press, including fiction, magazines, and newspaper serial romances, was a recognized challenge to the traditional motivations for acquiring the reading habit. By mid-century, cheap fiction was a sizable part of the business. Indeed, Uriah P. James, a Cincinnati-based retailer, wholesaler, and auctioneer of books, published a separate catalog in 1840 for his novels, tales, and romances which included *A Voyage to the Moon, Atilla, a Romance, Calavar; or, the Knight of the Conquest, a Romance of*

Mexico, Pic Nics; or, Legends, Tales, and Stories of Ireland, and *The Farmer's Daughter, and other Land and Sea Tales* among its 265 entries. In 1852 a catalog was issued separately for "Cheap Publications" valued between 25 cents and $1.50.[66]

Despite the competition from the morally debilitating secular press (a frequently heard judgment by religious leaders) religious publishing continued to dominate the book trade in the first third of the nineteenth century. The presence of religious titles (and to a lesser extent of works of a more classical and utilitarian nature) on the shelves of country and town merchants in developing frontier regions is ample testimony to the effectiveness of the religious press in distributing its product. The output of the religious presses was prodigious, and the first part of the nineteenth century saw numerous volumes emanating from religious publishing houses, including children's series published by the American Sunday-School Union and the American Tract Society. The former, offering its material at rock-bottom prices, listed fifty-two different series in its 1835 catalog; these were in addition to its popular children's magazines entitled the *Youth's Friend,* the *Infant's Magazine,* the *Child's Companion,* and the *Sunday-School Banner.*

By 1830, 6 million books had been published by the Union.[67] The American Tract Society was no less ambitious under the leadership of Wilder. Of his merchandizing efforts it has been said that "his corps of agents in the field represented 'one of the most ambitious, aggressive, and successful promotion enterprises ever realized by an American publisher.'" Two hundred titles for children alone were available in nicely illustrated and quality printed editions. By 1848, the annual *Report* for the year indicated that an average of "27,000 publications, including nearly 2,400 books, had been printed [by the Society] every day . . . that year."[68] The Methodist Book Concern, publisher of the popular *Christian Advocate,* was particularly effective in penetrating the sparsely populated regions of early Ohio. Through a district system for the distribution of books the Concern was able to increase its sales steadily. Samuel Williams, whose son became editor of the Concern in 1859, took an early interest in making certain that Ohio had its share of books and tracts available for purchase. An invoice of books received from Cincinnati in 1826 indicates that many cheap publications such as the *New American Primer, Watson's Apology,* and the *Family Adviser* were available. A list of books transferred by the Reverend Jones, the presiding elder for the Scioto District in south-central Ohio, to Russell Bigalow and deposited with Williams in Chillicothe in 1825 likewise indicates that 2,816 volumes were available for purchase. The bulk of these were cheap publications ranging from 6.25 cents to 75 cents per item. A few expensive volumes were available between five and fifteen dollars.[69]

The actual consumption of books by individuals is still a little-understood dimension of American cultural history. On the developing Ohio frontier, we do know that wealth was a major factor in book ownership. The study of estate inventories cited earlier shows that the mean estate values of book owners were decidedly higher than those of non–book owners and that this remained true from 1790 to 1859. Wealth differences between book owners and non–book owners were greater above the median wealth line, but the factor of wealth helped to determine book ownership even among those of moderate means. Wealth was also a determinant of the *numbers* of books owned, a fact which can be clearly seen in table 3.5 when we compare the percentage of those above the median wealth line owning three or more books with those below the median wealth line.

Table 3.5   The Distribution of Books among Book Owners above and below the Median Personal Estate Value for Inventories in Two Ohio Counties, 1790-1859

County and Date	% of Book Owners above Median Having			% of Book Owners below Median Having		
	1 Book	2 Books	3 or More Books	1 Book	2 Books	3 or More Books
Athens 1813-59	13	6	81	27	8	65
Washington 1790-1859	12	8	81	32	16	52

Source: A subsample of 478 from the 1,118 inventories.

Some relationships between wealth and *types* of books owned are also evident. As might be anticipated from the fact that the mean estate value of those owning classical works was more than twice the mean for all book owners, wealth and the ownership of classical works showed a strong positive relationship. Other types of books, however, do not show *strong* relationships to levels of wealth. Of the remaining types—school texts, miscellaneous (primarily histories, biographies, travel, collected essays, and poems), religious, and practical aids—the categories of miscellaneous and school texts are significant in their statistical relationship to wealth.[70] The magnitude of the relationship, however, is far less than that of the wealth-classics relationship. The positive relationship between wealth and the ownership of classics held from 1790 to 1859, but was more pronounced before 1830. Of the two counties examined, however, the relationship arose only in the more urbane Washington County. In the poorer interior county of Athens there is little to suggest any such positive relationship. The absence of the wealth-classics relationship in Athens County simply paralleled the general absence of any relationship between wealth and *types* (not ownership) of books. From a statistical standpoint, wealth and reading *tastes* were unrelated in this interior county—an indicator, perhaps, of the greater democratization of culture in an area removed from the wealthier and more urban environment of the city of Marietta and Washington County.

Our analysis of estate inventories also enables us to make some observations on consumer tastes as they are reflected in the *types* of books owned. Two features of the estate data are particularly outstanding. First, it is clear that the ownership of schoolbooks increased approximately 75 percent during the period 1830–59—surely a reflection of numerous legislative actions to build a common school system. The potential impact of an ideology of literacy expressed in these books is certainly evident. Second, as table 3.6 clearly shows, the tradition of Bible-literacy persisted in the early nineteenth century. Undoubtedly, the missionary activity which characterized Ohio during the 1830s and 1840s, in combination with the activities of the American Sunday-School Union and the American Tract Society, contributed to the increase in religious literature among inventories. Ohio was a major target for the 6 million books issued by the Union by 1830 and the 27,000 publications per year of the American Tract Society by 1848. The saving of souls was still an important individual and cultural activity despite some concern expressed by religious spokesmen of the period that Americans were devoting too much of their time to secular activities. Moreover, the marked increase of religious material from 1830 to 1859 and the sizable decrease in ownership of classical literature undoubtedly reflect the ebb of the American Enlightenment period and the reassertion of the evangelical spirit amidst the more general impact of Victorian culture in America. The promotion of religious literature through a vigorous book trade and the broad ownership of religious books through astute merchandizing efforts helped to promote an ideology of literacy consonant with the expression of evangelical Protestantism found in so many dimensions of American culture (and British culture) during this period.

Table 3.6 The Percent of Book Owners Having Selected Types of Books for a Subsample of Estate Inventories in Two Ohio Counties, 1790-1859

Type of Book	1790-1829	1830-59	1790-1859
Religious	63	80	74
Classics	17	8	11
Schoolbooks	31	54	46
Practical	22	15	17

Source: A subsample of 388 from the 1,118.

Libraries and the Worthy Use of Leisure Time

One of the major questions which must be raised with respect to the relationship between the worthy use of leisure time, economic opportunity, and an ideology of literacy is that of the accessibility to books and newspapers of the farmer, apprentice, and mechanic. Whether or not there was, in fact, a relationship between economic opportunity and literacy is a question we treat later. What must be answered first, however, is what, if any, institutional structure existed which could provide the link between belief and action, that is, whether or not a structure existed to provide leisure time reading and whether or not that structure was accessible. Thus, we are speaking here, for the most part, of the potential of the library to affect literacy and the variables which affected that potential.

When the editors of newspapers and compilers of school texts spoke to the worthy use of leisure time through reading, they made certain assumptions regarding the availability of reading matter. We have already remarked that wealth was an important factor in book ownership, as determined by an examination of estate inventories. Wealth was, likewise, a factor in subscribing to newspapers and becoming a member of a social, mechanics', or workingmen's library company. In all of these cases, a very real sacrifice of currency might be expected—currency often needed for the purchase of necessities. A two-dollar subscription for a newspaper was two days' pay for the American laborer in 1840, probably three days' pay for the farm worker, and one to three days' pay for the artisan. Subscriptions to social, apprentices', or mechanics' libraries were at least twice as costly, and this remained true in 1860. If, indeed, a five-dollar subscriber in 1860 were a farm employee, the sacrifice was the equivalent of pay for one and one-half to two weeks' work.[71]

For those who had neither access to nor means for the purchase of books, libraries were of major importance, although it is important to remember that the accessibility of libraries themselves was determined by the critical factors of population density and wealth or income in a community. An ideological appeal to apprentices and mechanics would thus have greater impact in areas of high population density, where capital available for book purchases was greater. To put it differently, because the variable of wealth helped to determine an individual's capability to acquire or use books, it also, in turn, determined the impact of an ideology of literacy itself. From the census of 1850, we know there was a library for every six hundred free adults in the United States and one library book for every two people. From table 3.7 we see that these were not distributed evenly, however, since New York State alone accounted for two-thirds of the libraries and one-third of the volumes. New York and Massachusetts together accounted for one-half of the volumes. The number of libraries increased with the size of the community only to about 25,000 adults, but the number of volumes increased in linear fashion through the whole population range. There is no question about the fact that more densely populated areas had more books; the populated area had twenty times as many as the sparsely populated one, and it would be expected that the availability of books would have an impact on the potential for promoting literacy.

Table 3.7 The Number of Libraries, Classified by Size of Adult White Population (W2OUP) in Each County in the United States in 1850

Size of County (W2OUP, lower class limit)	All		Public		Sunday School & Church	
	Libraries	Volumes	Libraries	Volumes	Libraries	Volumes
100,000-	.23	680	.05	491	.10	66
50,000-	1.81	862	.15	316	.26	130
10,000-	2.86	622	.13	134	.26	69
5,000-	.56	226	.17	83	.16	35
1,000-	.37	142	.10	53	.14	22
500-	.18	42	.02	1	.12	12
100-	.24	36	.02	37	.00	0
10-	.00	0	.00	0	.00	0

Source: The census of 1,565 counties in 1850. Private libraries are generally not included.

Libraries were inherited by nineteenth-century America in a variety of forms of which the most germane to the study of an ideology of literacy were the circulating, social, mechanics', and apprentices' libraries. The apprentices' library was specifically designed to promote upward economic mobility through literacy and the cultivation of proper reading habits. The announced purpose of the Apprentices' Library of Cincinnati, for example, was "to inspire a taste for reading and study, in those youth, who are the most unfavorably situated." It was thought that, this being the case, "the library should therefore consist of books, with which unlettered youth will be most delighted." To accomplish this, it was thought that "witty" and "extravagant" works such as "Gulliver, Munchausen, Robinson Crusoe, and Don Quixote" would be appropriate. After these, providing the youth was not of a "singularly stupid composition," biographies, histories, and books on "practical religion" might be read.[72] Throughout the late winter and spring of 1821, potential supporters of the library were urged to contribute liberally in hopes that the initial goal of seven hundred volumes might be acquired. At this point, the constitution of the library had specified that

> Whenever the library shall contain 700 volumes, it shall be the duty of the board of directors to publish the fact, and authorize the Librarian to deliver books to all young persons who are brought up at any

laborious occupation in the city, upon a parent, guardian, or next friend of the minor becoming responsible, as in the case of apprentices.[73]

On 14 April 1821, the goal had been reached, and the library was opened from three to six o'clock every Saturday to any youth who could "produce a certificate from his master, guardian or parent, promising to be responsible for the safe return of the books."[74] The problems of high fees and restrictive hours of public libraries had clearly resulted in a concerted action to provide for those whose chances to engage in leisure reading would otherwise be minimal.

The so-called circulating library took the most direct promotional approach in its appeal to the reading or would-be reading public. Moreover, along with the social library, it had the most potential for promoting literacy in areas of low population density. Thus, in its appeal to farmers to use their leisure time for reading, for instance, promotors of a reading public founded their appeal in the institutional reality of library formation.

Circulating libraries had appeared in modest numbers by the late eighteenth century, the most notable of which were those operated by ambitious booksellers such as William Rind of Annapolis, George Wood of Charleston, Garrat Noel of New York, and John Mein of Boston. Newspapers in the new western states often carried advertisements for circulating libraries, which, although modest by city standards, nonetheless were able to serve a more rural population. One, which opened in 1833 in Zanesville, Ohio, boasted a rather minimal selection of eight hundred to one thousand volumes for a yearly fee of $4, a six-month fee of $2, a three-month fee of $1.25, and a one-month fee of $.50, payable in advance.[75] Other circulating libraries were city-based, but attempted to promote a reading public in less-settled regions. Adam Waldie, whose home base was at 6 North Eighth Street, Philadelphia, advertised throughout Ohio, offering different types of subscriptions in different areas. In north-central Norwalk, Ohio, Waldie offered a "club" subscription as well as the regular $5-for-fifty-two-numbers subscription which he offered in the southwestern Ohio town of Lebanon. In his promotion of popular reading Waldie put his case before the public in a convincing manner, which no doubt reflected the sober reality that contemporary literary works were sometimes scarce and expensive in rural America:

There is growing up in the United States a numerous population with literary tastes, who are scattered over a large space, and who distant from the localities whence books and literary information emanate, feel themselves at a great loss for that mental food which education has fitted them to enjoy—Books are cheap in our principal cities, but in the interior they cannot be procured as soon as published, nor without considerable expense. To supply this desideratum is the design of the present undertaking, the chief object of which emphatically is, to make good reading cheaper, and to put in a form that will bring it to every man's door.[76]

Lest any of the reading matter be morally suspect, Waldie "confidently answered the heads of families that they need have no dread of introducing the 'Select Circulating Library' into their domestic circle." "The gentleman who has undertaken the Editorial duties," assured Waldie, was aware "of the consequences, detrimental or otherwise, which will follow the dissemination of obnoxious or unwholesome mental aliment."[77] Thus, the major ideological tenet that literacy ought to breed virtue was to be upheld by careful editorial scrutiny.

Social libraries, like circulating libraries sponsored by booksellers, were widespread, and served as a viable institution for the spread of literacy and the nurture of particular reading habits. Unlike the libraries operated by booksellers, however, social libraries were community based and controlled. Selection committees, a common feature of these libraries, were elected by members and were in a position to screen the reading material of their members more closely. This form of library organization was extremely popular in New England between 1790 and 1850. By the mid-1820s it was equally popular in Ohio, where social libraries were scattered through all settled regions.[78] One of the major unanswered questions about these institutions is the critical question of *who* belonged to them. In Great Britain, Kaufman has noted that social libraries played an important role in extending and upgrading literacy to "all but the lowest classes."[79] Some association records are available in the United States but have only begun to be studied from the standpoint of membership characteristics. A preliminary analysis of those who withdrew books from social libraries in Ohio indicates that a wide range of wealth characterized the membership of these institutions. While the average acreage and the value of that acreage are consistently larger for subscribers than for a random sample of the surrounding region, the distributions of wealth for subscribers compared with a random sample show the wealth of the library members to be more evenly distributed than that for the surrounding region. Gini coefficients of inequality were consistently lower for subscribers than for the random sample; moreover, the inequalities diminish as we move chronologically from the second to the fifth decade of the nineteenth century. It is apparent that the very wealthy and the very poor did not belong to such organizations. Yet, despite the exclusion of the extremes in the wealth distribution, there is no doubt that men of very different wealth shared their interests in the literary culture via the social library. Such libraries, then, were not exclusive organizations but, rather, facilitated the mixing of different wealth classes. In the process they helped to extend literate culture to people in a wide range of the wealth distribution.[80]

An examination of the holdings of social libraries shows that they were repositories for a variety of books and functioned as both popularizers of literature and outposts for dissemination of the classics. The Farmer's Library of Wheatland, New York, for example, housed 292 titles and 510 volumes according to its 1827 catalog. The Chillicothe Library Company on the Ohio frontier, organized by John Kerr, held 81 titles and 108 volumes in 1804. The Western Library Association in southeastern Ohio was organized with 51 titles in 1804 and extended its holdings to 144 volumes in 1805. The bulk of material in these associations consisted of religious pieces, history, and politics. Biographies, travels, Greek and Latin classics, and major British authors generally filled out the offerings. Occasionally, works of a scientific nature could be found as could works on education.[81] The holdings of social libraries exhibited greater diversity than did the holdings of most individual book owners. This would be expected in view of the varied individual interests which had a bearing on the purchase of books. Still, religious subjects dominated the holdings of these associations. The literate man who satisfied his bookish habits by membership in a social library remained a man committed to the nurture of his soul. The association to which he belonged provided an institutional structure to satisfy that commitment.

Conclusion

By mid-nineteenth century an emergent nationalism, a tradition of evangelical Protestantism, and traditional virtues associated with proper child rearing and proper behavior had been incorporated into an ideology of literacy. Support for the ideology was widespread and included political and religious leaders as well as those who would reap immediate monetary rewards by promoting literacy: printers and publishers of newspapers, books and magazines. Literacy had become one of several virtues associated with progress while, at the same time, serving the conservative interests of social and political stability. It is evident from school texts that children were taught the value of being literate, that being literate was part of being good, that the unlettered person was clearly considered to be in a state of deprivation. The inference was clear: proper instruction in reading, and to a lesser extent in writing and arithmetic, was needed to help guarantee proper behavior.

The elevation of behavior to an acceptable moral level was clearly a commitment of editors, printers, and textbook authors. In their efforts to increase awareness of the moral value of literacy, these entrepreneurs and self-proclaimed promotors of public enlightenment attempted to define the functions of literacy in American society. They thus helped to interpret for consumers both the reasons for becoming literate and the proper use of literacy, once achieved. They focused their arguments on the morally redeeming value of literacy for the individual and the social utility of reading skills. Neither of these functions was presumed to negate the more secular function of literacy for individual worldly success. In fact, the moral function of literacy and its value for worldly success were mutually reinforcing. In the moral consensus assumed by early nineteenth-century promotors of print, the moral and worldly uses of literacy were compatible.

By the nineteenth century, unlettered youth were *presumed* to be at an economic disadvantage not so much because literacy, per se, was an occupational skill but, rather, because the literate individual was likely to be morally superior and more likely to behave in a manner acceptable to his employer. As we point out in the following chapter, the presumed effects of literacy on moral development became part of the ideology of common schooling itself, the latter serving as a possible convenient method for disciplining the future labor force. To an increasing extent, schoolteachers thus found themselves in the position of administering a simple test of both moral and economic worth: could the individual read? For teachers, as for state superintendents of public instruction, student failure of such a test came to mean that increased efforts at remediation were necessary. For the employer, failure to read became a potentially useful method to select and sort labor. The common school revival and the spread of elementary instruction in reading (discussed in the following chapter) were to lead to even greater simplicity and efficiency in such selection, since the number of years of schooling could be substituted for actual performance in lexical skills. Moreover, years of schooling might be used as a measure of exposure to the socializing process of the school, not the least part of which was accomplished through primers and first readers. Thus, the ideology of literacy developed by promotors of print in general easily became part of the reform rhetoric of schoolmen themselves.

At another level, literacy was envisioned, in the aggregate, as an indicator of social well-being. Thus, it became popular by 1840, and even fashionable by 1860, to collect data on the relationship between literacy, crime, and poverty. As Graff has remarked of literacy and criminality in nineteenth-century Canada, the "stark simplicity of the causal model [assumed by educational reformers] is striking." In unabated linear fashion, ignorance and illiteracy led to idleness, intemperance, and improvidence, which, in turn, led to poverty and criminality.[82] Figures were collected which seemed to speak to causal and self-evident relationships among crime, poverty, and literacy. Prison officials and school reformers who shared a belief in the power of literacy to contribute to the larger social good frequently pointed out the fact that inmates of jails and penitentiaries had higher rates of illiteracy than those which prevailed in the population as a whole. The warden of the Eastern State Penitentiary in Pennsylvania, for example, offered a typical observation in 1838 when he commented on illiteracy among inmates: "These numbers show the gross neglect which most of our personnel have experienced from parents and guardians of their moral and religious training—of their elementary instruction."[83] In Massachusetts, social reformer Frank Sanborn reported in 1854 that 73.7 percent of the prisoners in Massachusetts county jails were illiterate, but by 1864 the figure was only 37.8 percent. The drop in illiteracy, however, was not totally satisfying to Sanford, as Michael Katz has noted: "It was disappointing . . . that in Massachusetts the drop in the percent of illiterate criminals had not been accompanied by a decrease in crime."[84]

Data collected by social reformers and school officials linked an ideology of literacy to social reality in such a way that made educational reform imperative. The social mission of literacy envisioned by the ideology demanded an interventionist policy. The moral well-being of society was not to be left to chance. Control of the environment meant building institutions to spread literacy. These, as we have seen, were founded throughout the first half of the nineteenth century with a remarkable self-consciousness on the part of promotors. Theirs was a self-consciousness born of their belief that, indeed, a moral consensus did exist in the American social order, and the ideology of literacy which they professed and promoted was to function as a link between that consensus and their efforts at institution building.

Yet the possibility for disenchantment was present. The fact was that newspapers and libraries were not available to all who presumably could benefit from them. When a week or two of wages was the price for reading matter, it was a high price to pay for such benefits. Nonetheless, the rapid emergence of a communications network in the first forty years of the nineteenth century made it possible to gain a large audience for ideological persuasion and to ground, at a number of points, an ideology of literacy to the social and economic realities of institution building. This included the establishment of libraries and newspapers, and the consumption of books. Social concentration usually accompanied aggregate wealth increases so that libraries in particular were most accessible in areas of high population density. Social libraries were accessible to a moderately broad economic stratum, but it is unlikely that the very poor benefited from these institutions. Circulating libraries operated by booksellers were also able to penetrate developing frontier regions, but once again it is unlikely that the poor could afford the luxury of a week's wages to nurture the reading habit. The actual consumption of books as a form of investment in culture was related to both wealth and marital status (family formation). As we have seen, mean wealth values for book owners were consistently higher than for those who did not own books. The high culture of the classics was reserved, with few exceptions, for the wealthy book owner, although that culture was available to those of moderate means through social library membership. Ownership of religious works and school texts was found within a broad stratum of the wealth distribution. Marriage itself, as we have noted, increased the probability of book ownership. This basic social fact, in turn, helped to support an ideology of literacy which stressed the family unit as a reading unit.

Like the ubiquitous schoolbook, newspapers were also instrumental in conveying the attitude that the good man was the literate man—that the even better man was the well-read man. The effectiveness of newspapers was not so limited by social concentration as was that of the library, and it is apparent that the newspaper medium had the potential to reach areas of low population density. Moreover, the sharing of newspapers gave both the poor literate and the poor illiterate an opportunity to participate in the popular culture of the newspaper—the latter, of course, by listening to literate men read aloud.

Finally, and perhaps most important in the long run, was the simple but fundamental fact that an ideology of literacy signified the forcefulness of reformers in their intervention in the child-rearing process. The teaching of reading itself was a purposeful intervention into the human developmental process; the ideology of literacy was the orchestration needed to accompany such intervention. Most reformers were still willing, despite the expansion of the common school system, to assign a role to parents in the teaching of reading, yet they were uncertain that parents were able enough to accept such a role. Thus, parents were the target of instructional advice along with frequent reminders of their obligations. Eventually, even these reminders became less concerted as the task of socialization through reading passed from the home to the school. In the mid-nineteenth century, however, few reformers in the United States suggested that the school should replace the home in the matter of literacy. Rather, a cooperative arrangement was sought in which teacher diligence could reinforce parental expectations for the social mobility of their young. As will become evident in the following chapters, parental expectations were hard pressed for realization in the absence of quality teaching. In some communities both proper schooling and parental expectations were lacking. These conditions thus were ready-made for educational reformers whose social conscience and missionary zeal led them, in the name of social and national welfare, to press for universal mass literacy.

Four

The Role of the Common School in Achieving Literacy, 1840-70

Introduction

In this chapter we deal with the context for common school reforms, the level and type of instruction in reading and writing offered in common schools during the period of intense reform activity, and the degree to which reformers achieved their goals in terms of school attendance. A consideration of these factors helps us to judge the efficacy of an ideology of literacy in promoting universal education of the young in the basic skills and knowledge of literacy. Moreover, our examination of reading instruction and the variables which determined school attendance at various ages allows us to speak to the adequacy of reformers' efforts within the context of nineteenth-century American society. Chapter 5, in turn, examines the degree to which the expectations of reformers were met and the social, economic, and demographic variables affecting that achievement.

By the opening of the nineteenth century the political vision of the new republic had linked together an emergent nationalism, basic literacy, and a fundamentally Protestant view of the world. Men of the stature of Jefferson and Rush might differ over the place of Bible instruction in the educational enterprise; others might argue over the merits of financing state-wide systems of education, but a large number agreed with the principle that an enlightened government could not long survive without the aid of an educated people. "In a government founded on the sovereignty of the people the education of youth is an object of the first importance,"

Portions of the latter part of this chapter are based upon Lee Soltow and Edward Stevens, "Economic Aspects of School Participation in Mid-Nineteenth-Century United States," *Journal of Interdisciplinary History* 8 (Autumn 1977): 221–43, and Edward Stevens and Lee Soltow, "Quantitative Factors in the Acculturation of Immigrant Children in Mid-Nineteenth Century United States," paper presented at the American Educational Research Association meeting, Toronto, 27–31 March 1978.

noted James Monroe, and "in such a government knowledge should be diffused throughout the whole society, and for that purpose the means of acquiring it made not only practicable but easy to every citizen."[1] Unfortunately for those of a liberal persuasion, including Governor Monroe, the Virginia legislature preferred an inoperative, county-based statute of 1796 which allowed the liberal demand for popular education to be short-circuited by the discretionary power of each county court.[2] The sentiments expressed by Monroe and shared by Jefferson were not the luxury of a few who possessed political leadership, although the means to fulfilling such high hopes were restricted by wealth. The same sympathies were found in the homespun rhetoric of one William Manning, a Massachusetts farmer who, having assumed that "learning is of the greatest importance to the seport [sic] of a free government," argued that "cheep schools" ought to be made available in every town without tuition. "Purticuler attention," he said, ought to be paid "to teaching the Inglish Langueg & qualifying its scholars to teach & govern Common Schools for little children."[3]

Rhetorically, it was but a short step from the political vision of an educated people to a vision of literary excellence and progressive knowledge. Indeed, the prospects of mass enlightenment were excellent if one were to assume, as did Timothy Dwight, that "a child of fourteen, who cannot read, write and keep the customary accounts, is rarely met with."[4] Judging from our evidence of late eighteenth-century markers, such exuberance fell short of the reality, but remained in line with the expectations of spokesmen for the higher learning. The synthesis of political and literary ideals in a vision of an enlightened people was eloquently expressed by a young Presbyterian clergyman named Samuel Miller in an essay on intellectual history titled *A Sketch of the Revolutions and Improvements in Science, Arts, and Literature in America*. Miller, in a youthful rhapsody to the new federal government—"the last grand epocha in the progress of knowledge in America"—observed that, from 1789 to 1800,

> literary institutions of various kinds were multiplied with astonishing
> rapidity in the United States. Besides Colleges, Academies, and sub-
> ordinate Schools, Scientific Associations were formed; Libraries
> began to be established in the most remote parts of the country;
> Printing Presses and Bookstores appeared in great numbers where
> they were never before known; Newspapers became numerous to a
> degree beyond all precedent; and the rewards of literary labour,
> though still too small, were considerably augmented.[5]

The rhetoric which linked education and public enlightenment in the first years of the nineteenth century easily became part of the message espoused by common school reformers and their supporters. A number of the latter were newspaper editors who, like school reformers, found little argument with the Enlightenment principles which linked liberty and education. The *Cleveland Register,* in a reprinted piece, "Independence of Mind," drew its readers' attention to the Jeffersonian principle that "an ignorant unenlightened people... sunk in the shade and degradation of moral and intellectual debasement, can never be FREE." "A general diffusion of knowledge," it continued, "is the only source from which public spirit draws its essence of vitality—the only foundation of rock on which a nation's liberty can rest."[6] This rhetoric of education, once established in the early years of statehood, became an important element in the crusade for common school reform which followed. Thus, the *Ohio Republican* of Zanesville began a six-part series on public education in 1833 with the question, "What sort of Education is befitting a Republic?" and noted, among other things, that "no system of education which embraces any thing less than the whole people, deserves the name of republican;—and no other system will reform a nation."[7]

By the mid-nineteenth century, a great deal had come to be expected of the public school, including the teaching of behaviors which, it was hoped, would guarantee political and social stability. Yet the major instructional role remained the teaching of the basic skills. Amidst the grandiloquence of schemes for national education, the mass efficiency of the Lancasterian system, and the more restrained efficiency of the graded system, the fundamental instructional objectives of a crusade against ignorance remained the same: "the teaching [to] all children of the State reading, writing, and common arithmetic."[8] "No investment pays so well," said Hiram Orcutt of the common school in 1859, when he echoed the sentiments of teachers and articulate educational leaders such as Mann of Massachusetts, Barnard of Connecticut, Stowe of Ohio, and Pierce of Michigan.[9]

The investment in common school reform of which Orcutt spoke in 1859 had begun some thirty years previous and, in part, was the extension of an ideology of literacy that attempted to synthesize the commitment to modernization with the social conservatism of evangelical Protestantism. The long-range goals of such an investment transcended immediate instructional objectives. No state commissioner's report was complete without its call for an uplifting of moral purpose ("an evangelical exhortative style," as Cremin calls it) and the reassertion of the school's commitment to the eradication of social evils.[10] Recent commentators on American schooling in the nineteenth century agree that the public school had become, by mid-century, a major institutional device for socializing the young.[11] The moral and educational crusade spanning the decades from the thirties to the Civil War (itself a moral crusade of different dimensions) succeeded in large part in transferring the responsibility for social control of the young and the deviant to the formal institutions of the school and the prison. Berthoff has remarked of mid-nineteenth-century America, and particularly of the urban-industrialized sector, that "the capacity of the family to educate its children in either secular or spiritual learning, already considerably shallower than it once had been, now virtually dried up."[12] With publicly financed schooling by 1850 having assumed the primary burden of the formal education of the American young, the claim could no longer be made, as it had been in 1830, for instance, that "the entire state [of Pennsylvania] is destitute of any provisions for public instruction, except those furnished by the enactment of 1809 [which was generally inoperative]."[13]

The raising of the school to the level of a great panacea for society's ills brought with it the imperative that it accept the major responsibility for the attainment of literacy. Reformers were quick to see that the quality and purpose of literacy achieved by the population in general would be important determinants of their long-range successes or failures in social reform. Given the role of the common school in attaining literacy, certain fundamental questions regarding the achievement of literacy in a common school setting and the parameters of attendance at common schools must be posed.

We have seen previously that the meaning and purpose of literacy must be understood within a specific historical context. Part of this context is reading instruction itself, and we would expect instructional practices to have some bearing on the quality of literacy achieved in the common school. The practice of learning to read through the ritual of recitation, for instance, lent itself well to the socializing function of literacy. Questions involving how, when, and at what level children were learning to read are important to our overall considerations. School attendance itself is obviously important, since the effects of population density (rural-urban dichotomy), wealth, occupation, and ethnicity on school attendance probably placed restrictions on an individual's school attendance and the plans of reformers. Finally, it must be interjected that these broader issues should not obscure the importance of individual attitudes in determining school attendance. In his *Personal Memoirs,* for instance, Ulysses S. Grant remarks of his father's "minority" years in Maysville, Kentucky, that "the West afforded but poor facilities for the most opulent of the youth to acquire an education" and that "his time at school was limited to six months, when he was very young...and to a 'quarter's schooling' afterwards." Still, his father "read every book he could borrow in the neighborhood where he lived," despite their scarcity, and acquired "the early habit of studying everything he read" including the newspapers "which he never neglected." Ironically, Grant himself seems to have benefited from his father's lack of formal education, for his father's "greatest desire in maturer years was for the education of his

children." Thus, Ulysses S. Grant "never missed a quarter from school
from the time [he] was old enough to attend till the time of leaving
home."[14]

If we take educational reformers at their word, the problems of irregular
attendance or nonattendance in mid-nineteenth-century America were issues of providing equal educational opportunity. Equal educational opportunity was, in turn, an important aspect of moral discipline through
schooling. It is not, at the moment, our intent to engage in the debate over
the purpose of this discipline: whether the primary purpose was to shape
an emerging industrial work force, to share the responsibilities for child
rearing in an age of emotional stress resulting from rapid social change, or
to cope with an increasing differentiation of institutions (an important
element in modernization) by assigning the school greater "custodial"
responsibilities.[15]

From an instructional standpoint, equal opportunity was a matter of
guaranteeing quality; that is, it was a matter which could be dealt with
through reforms in teacher preparation and certification. From an administrative standpoint, equality of educational opportunity was primarily
a matter of accessibility of schooling and school attendance. It was one
thing, reformers found out, to provide legal sanction for equal opportunity; it was quite another to design a workable plan to carry out the legal
mandate. The state has not fulfilled its whole duty, said the Ohio commissioner of common schools, until the advantages of schooling "bless every
child." He continued, "That child to whom the high duties of citizenship
are soon to be entrusted, has a *right* to be instructed, and the State a vital
interest in that right's not being violated."[16] Private economic interests
also had something at stake. In "The Value of Common School Education
to Common Labor," Edward Jarvis quoted selected employers who had
testified in 1870 to the superiority of literate employees. The commissioner of education posed the following question:

> Do those who can read and write, and who merely possess these
> rudiments of an education, other things being equal, show any greater
> skill and fidelity as laborers, skilled or unskilled, or as artisans, than
> do those who are not able to read and write?

In response to this inquiry, Jarvis cited a Zanesville, Ohio, employer of
five hundred common and skilled laborers working in the iron industry:

> None of our officers doubts the superiority of men who can read and
> write, for common labor, over those who cannot. Men who have some
> education require less supervision. The saving to employers in this
> way alone amounts to fully 10 percent. Employers suffer constantly
> from ignorant employees doing their work poorly and doing less of it
> for the same wages. This amounts to fully 10 percent more.[17]

The obstacles to equal educational opportunity, it appeared, were two. On the one hand, there were those sparsely populated areas of a state where taxable property was insufficient to support levies for school operations. Many such school districts simply could not tax enough to meet the standards of state law, said the Ohio superintendent of common schools in 1867. As Kaestle and Vinovskis have noted, the rural school crisis in Massachusetts (as it was perceived by state school officials) was one of scant resources resulting in poor physical facilities, poor equipment, untrained teachers, and short sessions. The crisis was not one of commitment to education but, rather, one stemming from a decline in the relative productivity of rural areas.[18] School enrollments were high in rural America, but the length of school sessions was short compared with urban areas. Thus, in terms of per capita consumption of schooling, note Kaestle and Vinovskis, rural areas lagged behind urban areas despite higher enrollments in the former.[19]

The second obstacle to equal educational opportunity, and one primarily associated with urban areas, was one of irregular attendance or nonattendance. Put differently, it was one of control—a matter of shaping the attitudes of the poor and the alienated in order to convince them that regular school attendance would be of long-range benefit to them. Morality, school attendance, and social welfare formed a network of concern for nineteenth-century school reformers and officials. The studies of Graff and Katz make it clear that the problem of nonattendance at school was not unique to the United States. The success of popular education, noted the Toronto superintendent of schools in 1854, depended upon "numerous and regular attendance of scholars."[20] By 1863 an Ohio administrator was noting that it was not enough to provide excellence in schooling. "The question of still greater moment," he said, is "how widely and thoroughly are these privileges enjoyed?" Many future citizens of the state, it was maintained, were "growing up 'in open contempt of education'" through the "criminal neglect of their parents," and many were "worse than orphans—born and bred in moral pollution."[21] And as late as 1880, the Pennsylvania superintendent of public instruction was commenting upon the "alarming fact" "that there are many thousands of children in this State who never attend school, and are growing up in ignorance." He continued, "There are many thousands more who attend school so short a time, or so irregularly, that what they learn is of little use to them."[22]

Before 1850, educational reformers had begun to consider the problems of acculturating a rapidly growing immigrant population, and it had become apparent in a rather brief period that the problems of acculturation, school attendance, and the general cultural disorientation affecting families and schools alike were inseparable. The cultural homogeneity of former years, whether illusory or real, had seemed to relinquish its place to a developing American pluralism. Individual families, native and immigrant, struggled to reassess the place of work and schooling in their lives. For example, the long-range economic benefit which, according to the rhetoric of reform, accrued to those attending school depended upon a willingness to delay immediate economic rewards. That it was a better choice to attend school than to work was not readily apparent to children and their parents who lived in abject poverty. The deeper polarization between Protestant and Catholic, foreigner and native, strained reformers' belief in a broad-based consensus of values which underlay the American social order.

The school was only one of several institutions which struggled with the "unfolding religious and ethnic variety of nineteenth-century society."[23] As mid-century reformers began the transformation of the little red schoolhouse into state-wide graded systems, they did not overlook the newly emerging American pluralism. Cultural pluralism was a fact to be reckoned with because it was perceived to threaten the essential homogeneity of the American population. The school, it was thought, could provide the mechanism whereby immigrant children might be assimilated to prevailing behavioral norms. The problem was complicated by the fact that many educators in urban America "persisted in measuring the city schools by a rural standard and the quality of urban life ... by a pastoral ideal."[24] That is, they persisted in their belief that a virtuous America was rural America; that, if urban America were to rid itself of crime, poverty, and immorality, it must attempt to transplant rural America to an urban setting. Fact and ideal competed for the loyalties of schoolmen in their confrontation with the "new" population, in their allegience to, but suspicion of, Hector St. John Crevecoeur's characterization of the American as he "who leaving behind him all his ancient prejudices and manners, receives new ones from the new mode of life he has embraced."[25]

Problems of acculturation were paralleled by problems of class, if not class conflict per se. Large differences in wealth characterized mid-nineteenth-century America, and these differences, as we demonstrate, were translated into inequalities of educational opportunity. At mid-century, only three of every five Americans were property holders. In his *Men and Wealth in the United States, 1850–1870,* Soltow has observed that the accumulation of real estate "depended, in part, on inheritance, knowledge of markets and credit, facility in reading and writing English or at least some foreign language, physical health, desire to accumulate and many other factors, including luck." While the arithmetic mean of real estate held by adult nonslave males in 1850 was a rather high $1,001, extreme deviation from the mean resulted in a large index of inequality

$(G = .857)$. In 1870, total average wealth (real estate plus personal estate) was \$2,399, but inequality was great, as the Gini coefficient of .833 demonstrates.[26]

Despite the great inequality of wealth, however, it was still possible for an individual to accumulate wealth over his entire life cycle even though "the chance of obtaining wealth in any given year was small." Upward economic mobility was a reality in the "jungle of inequality," and individual wealth between ages twenty and sixty-nine increased at about 6 percent per year on the average. The great disparities in wealth, then, were tolerated by the "average" man because, as Soltow remarks, "handsome rates of accumulation of wealth during his lifetime were within the realm of possibility."[27] This was true despite the fact that in 1850 the top 1 percent held 30 percent of all real estate, and in 1870 they held 26 percent.[28] School reformers, while they were probably not aware of the technicalities of wealth inequality, were aware of the inequalities themselves, and this awareness was carried over to their view of education as the balance wheel of the social machinery. The extent to which other reformers shared the view of Horace Mann that education could, in fact, reduce the overall gap between the rich and the poor is uncertain; nonetheless, they usually put forward some argument attesting to the personal economic benefits which might derive from increased schooling. Thus, they were, as Pratte would have it, exponents of the noneducational benefit theory of schooling, the view that the purpose of schooling "is to help allocate the distribution of noneducational benefits in society, such as income, status [and] occupational opportunity."[29] Reformers certainly assumed that proper attitudes and adherence to prescribed norms were important aspects of economic and occupational opportunity, as well as political socialization per se. It required no giant leap, then, for them to link the noneducational benefits of schooling with proper socialization, and thus to envision the school as a great panacea for both individual and social ills. In turn, the broad-based achievement of literacy was seen as a prerequisite to the achievement of this vision.

Pedagogy and the Sequence of Instruction
Reading, Spelling, and Grammar

The period between 1820 and 1860 was an era of great debate about reading instruction. The influence of Pestalozzi and Locke was evident and sometimes explicit in newspapers which addressed themselves to the subject.[30] Still, in the early nineteenth century there is no doubt that tradition weighed more heavily than change. Thus, we find in an 1821 issue of the *Cincinnati Western Spy and Literary Cadet* the following explicit advice on how children should be introduced to reading:

the pupil commencing with the alphabet ought to be taught his letters at sight, until he knows them perfectly, and then the sounds that arise by combining letters; proceeding gradually from one stage to another, until he can read words of one or two syllables, without spelling in the columns, as they are generally placed in our spelling books; but he should not by any means be hurried along through lessons that he does not understand, and cannot comprehend, for the purpose of making his parents think that he improves faster than he really does. . . . Great care should also be taken with the pupil when he first commences reading lessons that are punctuated. . . . If he should not place his emphasis properly, the teacher should immediately direct him in what manner it should be read.[31]

It is unfortunate, continued the article, that "few parents are competent judges of the matter which their children ought to learn, or the course which ought to be pursued by instructors."[32]

Challenges to the traditional ABC approach, however, were soon forthcoming. Within twenty years following Joseph Neef's attempts to popularize Pestalozzian principles through his publication of *Sketch of a Plan and Method of Education* (1808) and *The Method of Instructing Children Rationally in the Arts of Reading and Writing* (1813), John M. Keagy had produced his *Pestalozzian Primer* (1827). This "First Step in Teaching Children the Art of Reading and Thinking" spelled out for future generations the "whole-word" (analytic) approach to the task of reading instruction. At about age four, after having been taught "to *think*" at home through oral expression, Keagy advised that the child "should not be taught his letters at first."[33] Rather, he said, "*whole words* should be presented to his eyes, after the same manner that some teachers of the deaf and dumb commence the reading business with their pupils." Thereafter, he continued, the child should be taught to read his sentences "as if he were *talking*." "This method," he said, "will soon bring him into a natural and musical manner of reading his lessons."[34] In a more traditional mode, modified to take account of Pestalozzian advice on the value of play, Samuel Worcester advised that parents teach their children the alphabet through the use of "letter play" with wooden alphabet blocks.

The pedagogical battle between the ABC'ers and the whole-word advocates continued (and still persists today in more moderate form) throughout the period. By the 1840s a third strategy had made headway in the battle for pedagogical supremacy—the phonetic (synthetic) method. In 1853 Charles Royce stood "ready to prove, that a child can be taught to read and spell the Romanic print much quicker, and at the same time will become a much better reader and speller, by first learning to read the Phonetic print."[35] Thus, in the 1850s the phonetic method, based upon a phonetic alphabet, was a respectable alternative, and it was not long before compromises were being suggested whereby the phonetic and whole-word methods were combined. Suffice it to say, then, that in the last decade of the period under study, these three distinct methods of reading instruction—ABC, whole-word, and phonetic—were in common use, sometimes side by side, sometimes in opposing camps.

As with current experts, opinions differed with respect to the most desirable age at which a child should learn to read and spell, although all agreed that the responsible parent should aid in the teaching of reading. The common school revival brought with it numerous commentators on parental involvement in reading instruction, including Alonzo Potter. Potter was critical of what he called "school reading" (monotonic) and remarked that he had known "several children taught to read by their mothers on the principle of never reading what they did not understand, who always, from the beginning, read naturally and beautifully."[36] In a London publication consumed by numerous Americans, M. Bakewell's *The Mother's Practical Guide in the Early Training of Her Children* warned mothers of the dangerous tendency to make prodigies of their firstborn. She nonetheless offered advice "to facilitate the power of speech" and noted that "a child may with propriety begin to learn to read at three or three and a half years of age." "By the time children are five or six years of age," she said, "they will begin to imitate the forms of printed letters, and to make little words."[37] The question of early schooling and early intellectual training was much debated by the 1830s. As Kaestle and Vinovskis have pointed out, "The early intellectual education of children was generally seen as a positive virtue in the United States before the 1830's, [but] most authorities regarded it as a questionable activity thereafter." Thus, by 1844, Charles Northend's "Obstacles to the Greater Success of Common Schools" included the following objection to early intellectual *discipline* of the type found in schools:

> The disposition on the part of parents to send their children to school at too early an age, I consider detrimental to the schools, and also to the children. Here I must not be understood to affirm, that children begin to *learn*, too soon, but, that they are, very frequently, subjected to the instruction and discipline of the school-room at too early a period of their existence.[38]

Authors of primers, spellers, and readers did not make a point of specifying the level of reading achievement proper for particular ages. Still, their books contained many "hints" with regard to reading progress and age. In 1762, Isaac Watts had recommended that a child begin his catechism at three or four years old, and "Lesson 4" of the 1803 *American Primer* read as follows: "Billy is only five years old, and he can spell all the hard words in his lesson; and he begins to read cleverly. He can say his catechism, and the Lord's prayer, and has learned several fine speeches."[39] This expectation was apparently not unreasonable if we are to accept the testimony of Warren Burton that he had in 1805 at age four "read in class" and by age four and one-half was reading in sentences.[40] Clifton Johnson in his recollections of *The Country School* remarks that children began summer sessions "soon after they passed their third birthday" and there began their learning of the alphabet, "various little poems," and spelling.[41] Later spellers and primers also contained hints on the proper ages for certain educational accomplishments. The 1820 edition of Daniel Crandall's *The Columbian Spelling-Book* told the story of "The Good Boy and Girl" (Orlando and Clarinda, respectively). The former, at age six, "could spell all the words in his book, and could read very prettily; and at the age of eight years, he could read all the stories in his father's library, and had learned the rudiments of English Grammar." Clarinda, his sister, could spell and read at six also. Orlando was undoubtedly precocious and, moreover, obviously had the advantage of his father's library, not a common situation in 1820.[42] In the later McGuffey's, however, we still are told that children of age six could read "quite well."[43]

A more systematic and comprehensive view of the ages at which children could be expected to engage in spelling, reading, and the study of grammar may be gathered from graphic representations based upon a sample population from the state of Ohio between the years 1845 and 1864.[44] From figures 4.1[45] and 4.2[46] it is apparent that most children, if they were in school, were learning spelling by ages three and four. This was true of both sexes during winter and summer terms, and persisted throughout the years from which the sample was taken. The graphs are for 1845–64 inclusive, but the sample itself was subdivided into five-year periods in order that changes during this twenty-year period might be observed. Analysis of the sample, by five-year intervals, however, indicates no significant changes within these chronological subdivisions. It is most interesting that at least 50 percent of the male students between ages fourteen and twenty were engaged in the study of spelling as a separate subject; for girls, spelling instruction persisted until age fifteen in the winter terms. In the summer terms, older girls (ages fifteen through eighteen) all were receiving spelling instruction. An examination of annual reports from urban school systems reveals the same pattern.

Few children, it seems, could receive *too much* spelling, and there is no question that the subject was first in the hearts of American schoolteachers. Pedagogically speaking, spelling instruction was considered a prerequisite to reading instruction, but this is not to say, of course, that reading and spelling involve the same cognitive operations. Reading

Proportion

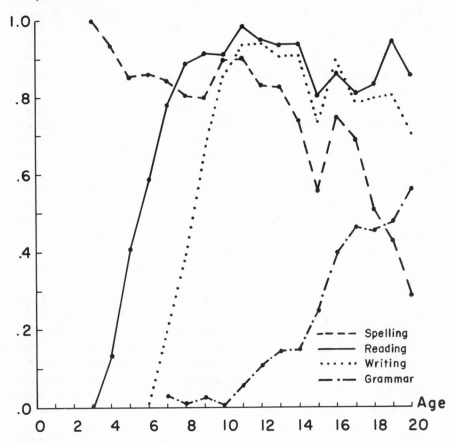

Figure 4.1
The proportion of students receiving spelling, reading, writing, and grammar instruction, winter terms, in selected Ohio school districts, 1845–64. (Source: sample of 1,106 Ohio children.)

began, for a few, at ages three and four. Figures 4.1 and 4.2 illustrate that some 70 percent of children, male and female, were receiving reading instruction by age seven, and by age nine, the proportion was .90–.95. For females, the proportion engaged in reading instruction advanced approximately one year ahead of that for males—quite possibly a developmental phenomenon. During winter terms the proportion of female students age ten and above who were taking reading was slightly above that for males, although for both sexes the proportion was between .75 and 1.0. Summer term patterns did not differ appreciably from those for

Proportion

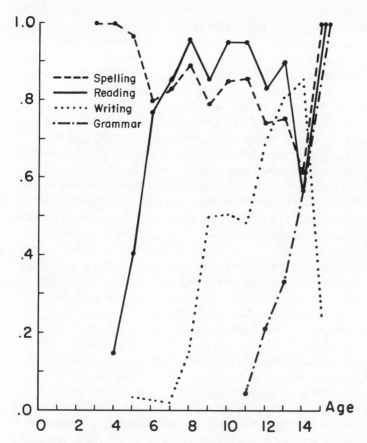

Figure 4.2
The proportion of students receiving spelling, reading, writing, and grammar instruction, summer terms, in selected Ohio school districts, 1845–64. (Source: sample of 333 Ohio children.)

the winter terms, except that males were engaged in learning to read in a greater proportion than females.

Our sample, which does not include high school students, shows that few male students engaged in the study of grammar before age sixteen, and even here the proportion was only .27. Occasionally, a few, probably precocious, youngsters attacked the subject between their sixth and tenth years, but even for ages seventeen through twenty the proportion did not exceed .50. During summer terms, grammar seems to have been offered only on request. Only 20 percent of males attending summer terms were engaged in the study of grammar between ages eleven and fourteen. We may contrast the male participation in the study of grammar with the female participation, where it is evident that the proportion of female students aged twelve through twenty engaged in grammatical studies was considerably higher than that for males. The summer term seems to have been a time during which female students could actively pursue these studies, perhaps in preparation for "keeping school" themselves.

The precise numbers of hours and minutes which children spent reading and learning to read are difficult to determine in any comprehensive or systematic way. It was probably common practice for a school (when in session) to be conducted for six hours per day, summer terms excepted. As early as 1682 in Flatbush, Long Island, school hours encompassed a morning session and an afternoon session, eight to eleven and one to four, respectively.[47] The six-hour school day was still normal in the early nineteenth century, although in the Indiana of Mary Payne Beard (mother of historian Charles Beard) seven hours (8–12, and 1–4) seems to have been the practice.[48] Of this time in school, the overwhelming proportion was devoted to reading, writing, and activities related to learning to read. So much time was devoted to reading instruction in the traditional classroom that it was cause for concern among those who realized that subjects other than reading, writing, spelling, and grammar were continually short-changed in the curriculum. Thus, the editor of the *Ohio Journal of Education* in 1853 lamented that "it seems almost incredible . . . that the mechanical routine of teaching a child the alphabet, reading and spelling, should so long have constituted almost the entire course of instruction in our primary schools."[49] Still, it remained customary in a rural school for young readers at the pre-primer and primer level to recite four times per day for a total of approximately forty minutes.[50] Individual reading practice was continued while other, more advanced reading groups received the teacher's attention. As we demonstrate in our study of attendance and reading achievement, children who attended school regularly in the primary grades achieved a level of reading of approximately that found in *McGuffey's Third Reader*.

Writing

It has been remarked of the handwriting of colonial children that it was "admirably legible and uniform" and that "it was a chief requisite of the old schoolmasters that they should be good teachers of penmanship."[51] Whether such quality persisted into the nineteenth century, however, is not clear. Numerous advertisements for special instruction in writing and penmanship through most of the period under study suggest that a "good hand" was something not to be entrusted to the common school. As it was with most subjects, advice to teachers and parents was abundant. David Page in 1847 advised that "writing may be early commenced with the pencil upon the slate, because it is a very useful exercise to the child in prosecuting many of his other studies."[52] Writing with a pen, however, was to be "deferred till the child is *ten years of age,* when the muscles shall have acquired sufficient strength to grasp and guide it."[53] Jacob Abbot's *Rollo's Correspondence* (part of the well-known Rollo series) portrayed young Rollo, at age seven or eight, writing his first and second letters as follows:

1. Dear Mother,

    I am very much obliged to you for sending me a letter. I am going to write you an answer now. I believe I cannot write any more now.

    Your affectionate son,
Rollo

2. Dear Jonas,

    I am learning to write letters, and am going to write one to you. I have been sick, but now I feel a great deal better. I am almost well enough to go out and work with you to-day in the woods, only it is beginning to snow; and besides, my hachet makes my arm ache, so that I cannot work but a little while.
    Do you think we are going to have much of a storm?

    Yours, truly,
Rollo[54]

Given the opportunity, it is not unlikely that a seven-year-old could compose and write a letter of such quality. Certainly this is evidenced the young hand of seven-year-old Thomas King below, shown as plate 1.[55]

An informative sequence of letters preserved in the William Henry Seward collection at the University of Rochester illustrates the achievement of a young lad in penmanship, and gives us a close look at the developmental process whereby the boy came to his achievements between the ages of six (plate 2), seven (plate 3), and seven and one-half (plate 4), respectively.[56]

These examples, of course, are not typical, yet they do represent the achievements of a youngster who had the advantages of early and continuous schooling. When taken with the data presented in figures 4.1 and 4.2, which show the ages of students engaged in writing instruction during winter and summer terms between 1845 and 1864, they help us to observe the process of children learning to write. Some young boys began their writing instruction at age seven during the winter term, at age eight during the summer term. The proportion of boys taking writing increased rapidly until age eleven (.94) in the winter terms, and then gradually declined to

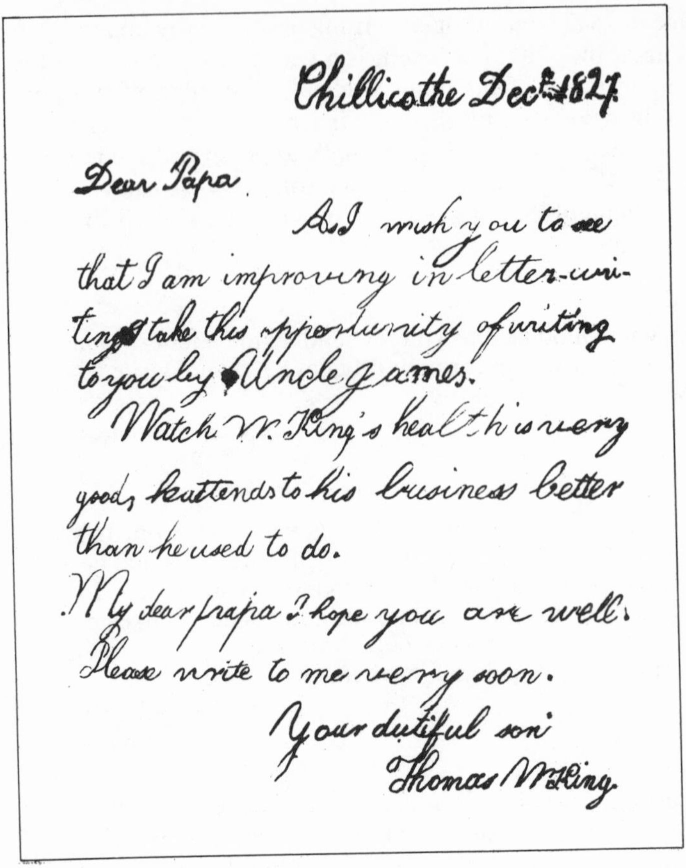

Chillicothe Decr 1827

Dear Papa.

As I wish you to see that I am improving in letter-writing I take this opportunity of writing to you by Uncle James.

Watch Mr. King's health is very good, he attends to his business better than he used to do.

My dear papa I hope you are well. Please write to me very soon.

Your dutiful son
Thomas M. King.

Plate 1
Letter to his father from seven-year-old Thomas King. Reprinted by permission of the Ohio Historical Society.

age twenty. Even with ages twelve through twenty (45 percent of all the males enrolled) the proportion receiving writing instruction did not drop below .70 overall. During the summer terms, the rise in proportion for males was also rapid and reached a high of .88 for those age fourteen.

Girls began learning to write somewhat earlier than boys, although there, too, it was only by age nine that the majority of them were receiving writing instruction. Between ages eleven and fourteen (50 percent of all females enrolled) 94 percent were receiving instruction in writing. Thereafter, a gradual decline to .67 at age twenty is noticeable. During the summer terms, the pattern of writing instruction for females was quite irregular, indicating that following age fourteen the summer terms were probably used by teachers for compensatory purposes.

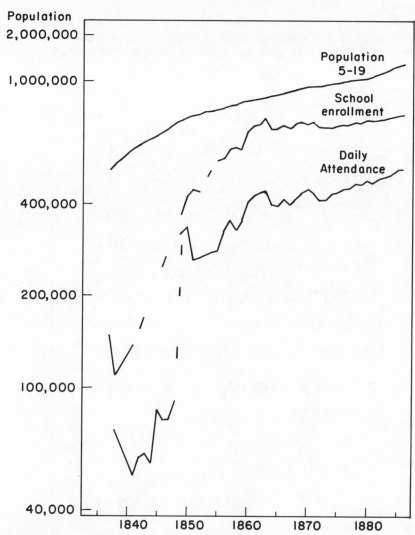

Figure 4.3
The growth in attendance at common schools in Ohio, 1837–86. (Source: *Thirty Third Annual Report of the State Commissioner of Common Schools,* Ohio, 1886 [Columbus, 1887], pp. 204–5.)

School Attendance and Reading Achievement

The years between 1840 and 1865 were ones of rapid growth in school enrollments and daily attendance. Figure 4.3 illustrates this growth for the state of Ohio. The growth testifies dramatically to the implementation of schemes for common school reform, but the aggregate data upon which the growth trend is based unfortunately do not allow us to make the

Plates 2, 3, and 4
Handwriting of William Henry Seward at the ages of six (plate 2),
seven (plate 3), and seven and one-half (plate 4). The original letters
are in the William Henry Seward Papers, University of Rochester
Library.

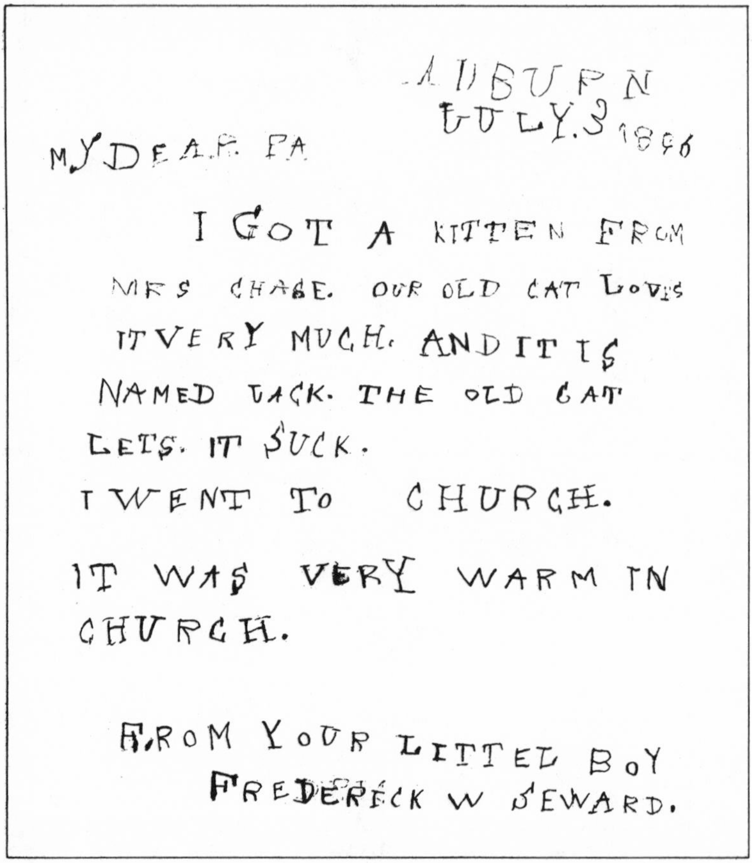

MY DEAR PA

I GOT A KITTEN FROM
MRS CHASE. OUR OLD CAT LOVES
IT VERY MUCH. AND IT IS
NAMED JACK. THE OLD CAT
LETS. IT SUCK.
I WENT TO CHURCH.

IT WAS VERY WARM IN
CHURCH.

FROM YOUR LITTEL BOY
FREDERICK W SEWARD.

AUBURN
JULY.3 1846

2

Auburn Dec 28th 1830.

My. dear Augustus,   I got a man riding
on a turkey in my stocking Christmas.
he looks like a Irish workman.
and a wineglass a candlestick a picture a
book. and some candy. And Cornelia got a
rattlebox. Maria got a picture a book a
little tin basket a pair of gloves and some
candy. Give my love to Pa. We have
made our Newyears cakes. Ma made some
prints. Laura sends her love to you
all. Ma is going to write to you. I had one
motto that said — "Who opens this
            Must have a kiss."

your affectionate   Brother Frederick W. Seward

3

4

Auburn Feb 24 1837

My dear Pa,
            The old cat is dead.
Peter made her a box and her in it.
and buried her in the snow. My cheek
got well Wednesday after you went
away. Augustus has got a new book called
Childs Botany. Augustus' people's magazines
is bound. When Ma and I were down stairs
we heard the cats squeal. Augustus makes
news papers and magazines and Maria and
I take them from his post office.
Maria sends her love too all —
Uncle Jennings is here he gave me a book
to day.   Your affectionate son
            Frederick W. Seward.

attendance/age or attendance/age/subject breakdowns necessary to approximate the time which children were exposed to formal instruction in reading.[57] The separate sample of attendance data from local school records, together with descriptive statements, however, does allow us to make an approximation of hours devoted to reading instruction. There are, inevitably, ecological problems associated with comparing cross-sectional analyses of this type of data. Local issues (not recorded and long-since forgotten) relating to year-to-year difficulties in financing, changes in school board personnel, and teacher-parent conflicts may have influenced attendance. Yet for the limited purpose of determining the number of hours of reading instruction received by children in rural areas who *attended* school, the usefulness of local attendance records outweighs possible difficulties in statistical analysis.

Attendance data for this section were analyzed with step-down and multiple regression techniques from two samples: one of children in the state of Ohio for the years 1840 to 1869, the second of children from the city of Rochester, New York, for the years 1861 to 1874. For both samples there were wide *ranges* in attendance figures within age groups, and coefficients of inequality calculated for each age group are relatively high. (Most fall within the range of .23 to .33.)[58] For both samples attendance was regressed on the factors of age and sex.[59] In the case of Ohio, we are dealing with rural school districts, although one large district was a Union Free School District and was organized, as were city systems, according to a graded plan of instruction. Of course, in the case of Rochester, New York, we are dealing with an urban graded school system, albeit not a major metropolitan area.

The most obvious fact emerging from figures 4.4 and 4.5 is that overall days attended rose dramatically, by 70 to 76 percent, following 1860 in the winter terms of Ohio. It would not be unlikely that this rise in the decade of the sixties could be attributed to the increased pressure for attendance following the reorganization of the state commissioner's office according to a constitutional provision of 1853. A similar rise in attendance figures may be noted in figure 4.6 for the Rochester sample from 1870 to 1874, and this coincides with the move toward universal compulsory attendance in that state. Levels for attendance in Rochester were still seemingly above those for Ohio between 1860 and 1869, although this is probably misleading, since in Rochester we are dealing with a September to June school period and for Ohio an October to March period. It is more than likely (since many student names are carried from winter to summer terms on the attendance rolls) that summer term attendance in rural Ohio made up for the shorter winter terms as compared with the urban three-term, nine-month schedules.

Second, while some variations according to sex do appear in the data

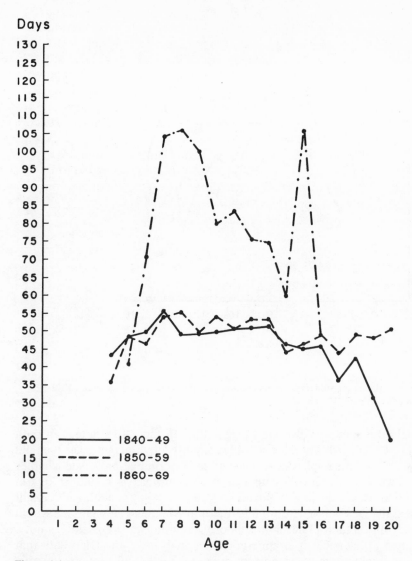

Figure 4.4
Mean attendance for students, winter terms, selected Ohio school districts, 1840–69.
(Source: sample of 1,569 Ohio children.)

used in compiling figures 4.4, 4.5, and 4.6, an overall evaluation of the
data by multiple regression indicates that sex, by itself, was not a
significant factor in determining attendance. The same finding was evident
in the Kaestle and Vinovskis study of school attendance in Massachusetts
as they comment: "The sex of the subject has surprisingly little impact on

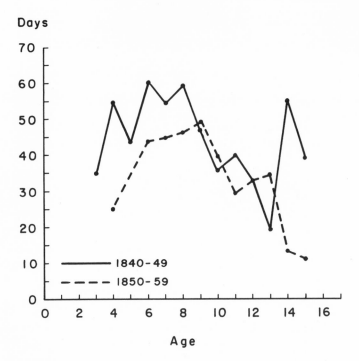

Figure 4.5
Mean attendance for students, summer terms, selected Ohio school districts, 1840–59.
(Source: sample of 719 Ohio children.)

school attendance [in the age range 4–8]." In fact, they note, "in both 1860 and 1880, girls attended school in slightly larger percentages than did boys."[60] In our sample the absence of sex discrimination is true whether or not we are dealing with winter or summer terms. (It should be kept in mind that we are dealing only with children attending school, and it might well be that sex was a determining factor in whether or not parents would initially enroll their children in school.) Even though sex itself was not a factor in attendance, it is apparent from analysis of the Ohio data that sex-age interactions are significant in both summer and winter terms. No significant sex-age interactions were observable in the Rochester data. The absence of sex-age interactions in the Rochester data and their conspicuous presence in the rural Ohio data might well be a reflection of rural-urban differences attributable to differing work patterns of children on farms compared with those in urban areas. In rural areas even young male children were a necessary part of the work life of the *family* and could be productive members in doing light farm chores. "Picking" coke or rags could also make young children in urban areas productive family

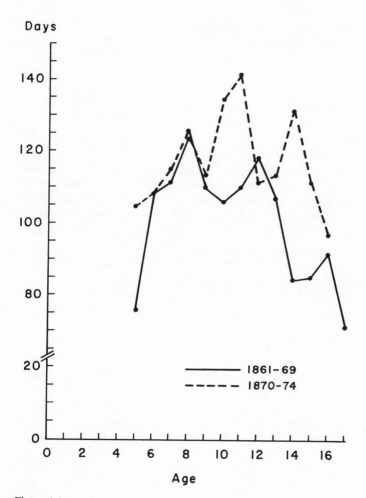

Figure 4.6
Mean attendance for students, September–June terms, Rochester, New York, 1861–74.
(Source: sample of 1,334 children, Rochester, New York.)

members, but it is likely that performance of this type of work was confined to children of poor parents. For farm children, on the other hand,
light labor at young ages was not confined to poor families but was, rather,
a part of growing up. In other words, the economic value of *young* children was greater in farm families because the division of labor among
family members easily accommodated different age-groups. Thus, in the
language of microeconomics, the young farm child was more easily conceived of as a "producer durable" contributing to the income of the
family.[61]

Age was a significant factor in determining the number of days of school attendance, but once again it is only those who *did* attend that we are considering at this point.[62] (Later, we shall look at enrollment patterns to identify which, if any, socioeconomic factors were helping to determine enrollment.) It is noted, first, that during winter terms for male children between ages four and eight school attendance rose rapidly. This was true in all three decades sampled for Ohio. The same was true for the Rochester sample of male children between ages five and eight. For female children, the same pattern is observable to age seven. Thereafter, for both sexes, the number of days attended declines, although there are wide variations in mean attendance for males seven to eight years old and for females six to nine years old. One exception occurs in the 1840 to 1849 data for fourteen-year-olds. After ages nine to ten years, attendance figures are marked by large fluctuations in both directions, although the overall trend is downward. Probably at about ten years of age, work-related activities (though not full-time) became increasingly important in the lives of children and surely competed for their school time.

Numerous complaints by teachers and state commissioners of education lead us to believe that regularity of attendance was crucial to achievement. This was particularly true for students who went only to three-month winter terms. Geal Grover Norris, a district school teacher, recalled of his early school days in the 1830s that even at age fourteen he "had forgotton nearly all [he] had learned [in the prior three-month term]," and that it "would take at least 2 out of the 3 months to get back to the place where he left off."[63] In urban districts the longer winter terms probably rectified this problem to some extent, although contemporary parents are well aware of the lapse in achievement over the three-month summer vacation period.

In order to better understand the relationship between school attendance and reading achievement, a separate sample of 117 students was selected from the attendance and achievement records of the Rochester, New York, schools for the year 1870. Analysis of this sample (with children having an attendance range of 25 to 195 days, a median of 171.5, and a mean of 151) indicates that attendance was an important factor in achievement, but only among ages five, six, and probably seven years old.[64] Thereafter, to age fourteen, attendance was statistically insignificant for achievement. In combining attendance and achievement data from this sample with census data for each of the 117 students, it was found, also, that the nativity and wealth of the parent were insignificant determinants of achievement in reading. This was true for all age-groups, and it must be assumed that with regular attendance the child of an ethnic minority would achieve basic literacy quite as well as those of "established" stock.

Estimates of the hours of formal reading instruction to which school children were exposed are difficult to make, and rest upon certain assumptions about the quality of literacy expected by common school instructors and the time devoted to reading instruction per day. Until age eight the typical curriculum consisted of only spelling, reading, and writing. Arithmetic, if undertaken at all, did not receive much time until age nine. We conservatively assume, then, that two hours per day were devoted to reading instruction (group recitation and individual preparation) from ages five to eight.[65] With more demands made upon the curriculum after age nine, we assume one hour per day devoted to reading instruction. Sex differences were very small, and it makes little sense to weight sex as a factor in our calculations. Second, while there are major sex differences in the proportion of students receiving instruction in grammar, it is assumed that children had achieved basic literacy before the taking of such instruction. A child entering school at age five, for instance, was reading McGuffey's fourth or fifth reader by age eleven or twelve, provided he had attended regularly. At age eleven we could also expect the child to begin the study of grammar. Reading in McGuffey's fourth reader was probably no mean task, and even the mastery of the third reader was probably sufficient to classify the student as having achieved basic literacy. In fact, as Nietz has observed, the application of the Yoakam Readability Formula to McGuffey's second reader indicates "that its vocabulary was at the eighth grade reading level."[66] That literacy was achieved at this level of a graded series of instruction is further supported by a set of unique data collected by the newly formed state superintendent's office of Ohio in 1853. In that year, teachers were requested to complete reports to township clerks which included enrollment, average daily attendance, length of summer and winter sessions, tuition, textbooks, enrollment in the various branches of study, and, most important, the number of scholars able to read and write. We thus have at our disposal judgments made by teachers with respect to literacy. These data were then combined with various financial data from the several counties and reported in aggregate form in the commissioner's annual report. Analysis of the data does not show any statistically significant relationship between per capita wealth in each county and scholars able to read and write; the same is true for total dollars used to support schooling in each county. What is significant is the relationship between enrollment in grammar study and scholars able to read and write. Other subjects do not correlate significantly with literacy. The implication is that teachers were willing to classify their students as literate by the time they enrolled in grammar, and this tells us that students were generally classified as literate by the time they were twelve to fourteen years of age. This undoubtedly reflected higher expectations on the part of teachers, but it nonetheless sets an upper limit on the amount of instruction needed to classify a student as literate. The minimal literacy revealed in census figures would not require this level of instruction.[67]

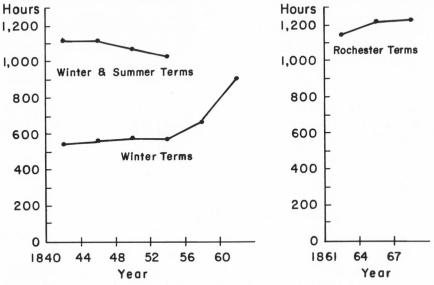

Figure 4.7
Estimated mean number of hours of reading instruction in selected Ohio districts and Rochester, New York. (Source: samples of 2,288 Ohio children and 1,334 Rochester children.)

The hours of formal reading instruction to which children were exposed is conservatively estimated in figure 4.7. For Ohio, a rise in mean hours of reading instruction in winter terms begins in the 1850s and continues through the 1860s. An increase of approximately 60 percent was achieved in this period. When winter and summer terms are combined, the approximation is very close to that level shown for the Rochester data. In the 1840s, a combining of summer and winter terms led to almost twice the hours of formal instruction which a child would experience had he or she attended only the winter terms. The magnitude of the differences decreases somewhat by the 1850s, although here, too, summer-term attendance increases the mean hours of reading instruction by some 75 percent. The age distribution for summer terms as shown in table 4.1 indicates that it was quite common for children between ages five and eleven to be attending in the summer. It would be realistic to assume that five- to eleven-year-olds attended both terms. If we calculate the number of hours of reading instruction received by children as they progressed through schooling between the ages of five to eleven, we estimate that each student, had he or she attended regularly, would have received 1,050 to 1,100 hours of formal reading instruction.[68] This certainly would have been sufficient to classify a youngster as literate. For rural children, the summer term was certainly an important adjunct to the winter term, and, if the child were to attend regularly, the summer term would enable him or her to receive nearly the hours of reading instruction given to the urban child. Certainly the child who attended school regularly became literate early in his or her life. Reading literacy was undoubtedly achieved by age eleven, but writing literacy followed soon after and was likely to be accomplished by age twelve. Many children were probably literate in both by age nine.

Table 4.1 Ages of Students Attending Summer Terms in Ohio, 1840-69

	Ages (%)						
	5	6	7	8	9	10	11
1840-49	8.2	13.4	17.7	12.9	7.3	9.1	5.6
1850-59	10.6	9.8	9.5	11.7	10.2	12.1	10.6

Source: Subsample from the 2,146 Ohio children, 1840-69.

Note: Ages 3 to 4 and 12 to 18 are omitted because of small cell size.

For the child unable to attend school regularly, on the other hand, the attainment of literacy must have been difficult. Comparative and cross-sectional analyses of 1840 and 1870 census data (see table 5.8) demonstrate the positive, linear relationship between illiteracy and low school enrollment rates. Certainly those children whose parents did not have the leisure time to teach them would have reached adulthood as illiterates; more than likely, the availability of leisure time itself was restricted by family wealth. For the poor, it was only with the greatest difficulty that literacy might be transmitted without the aid of formal schooling. Those without schooling undoubtedly made up the greatest proportion among illiterates recorded by the federal censuses and army enlistee records. It remains, now, to consider what factors were likely to influence the accessibility to the school for different subpopulations and, hence, the extent to which it could be said that the school afforded equal educational opportunity in the sense of an equal chance to become literate. It is these two related questions to which much of our attention will be devoted in the remaining sections.

Illiteracy and Patterns of School Attendance

While the quality of instruction undoubtedly varied greatly from district to district in both rural and urban areas, the greatest obstacle to equality of educational opportunity defined in terms of achieving literacy lay in nonattendance. In this section we look briefly at the general level of school attendance in mid-nineteenth-century America and, in greater detail, at the regional disparities and the social, economic, and demographic variables which affected that attendance. In a unique set of data for northern soldiers in the Civil War provided by the United States Sanitary Commission, we may observe the large inequality in the years of education of adult whites in 1862–64. It should be remembered that the data in table 4.2 reflect the educational experience of these men in the 1850s and, in some cases, before.

Those with no education or possibly slight education may be taken to be almost totally illiterate, and indeed, the overall rate of 5.8 percent to 7.2 percent is consistent with our census statistics for 1860 and 1870. We find that up to 20 percent of those born in Kentucky, Tennessee, and Canada had never been to school. These are followed by Irish born at 15 percent and French born at 5 to 12 percent. The illiteracy rate among Scandinavians and Germans was very low, while the Scottish had the fewest of any group who had never been exposed to education. Among native born in northern states we find very low illiteracy, with the rate in New England being the lowest of all.

Table 4.2 shows that almost half of the soldiers were classified as having limited common school education. A small minority of these men may not have been able to sign their own names. The proportion in this category climbs from .34 for New England born to .44 for those born in New York, New Jersey, and Pennsylvania to .52 for those born in Ohio and Indiana to .66 for those from Michigan, Wisconsin, and Illinois; thus, there is a clear gradation in the number of years of education as we move further west. The regional variations in these data will be explored more fully in the succeeding pages on school enrollments, but it is readily apparent that inequality in the years of education of young adult males was very large. As displayed in table 4.2, the Gini coefficient of inequality in this case was .26. The counterpart coefficient for adult white males twenty to twenty-nine years of age in 1970 was .12. This age-group for the years 1862–64 and 1970 is compared in table 4.3.

The evidence from the United States census displayed in tables 4.4 and 4.5 clearly indicates that *fewer* white children per adult male were in school in 1870 than in 1860. This was the result of lower absolute numbers in 1870 and slippage in the probability of individual attendance. It is possible that some of the decrease during this decade was attributable to fewer enrollments of five-year-olds. By 1860, towns and cities had become increasingly reluctant to admit children under six years of age to school. Kaestle and Vinovskis have noted that "school officials discouraged parents from sending their very young children to school and often tried to raise the school entrance age." In their study *Education and*

Table 4.2 Education and Nativity of Soldiers in the Northern Army, 1862-64

Nativity	Number Sampled	Number per 1,000[1]							Years Education Mean	Gini Coefficient of Inequality
		None	Slight	Limited Common School	Good Common School	High School	Collegiate	Professional		
Total	10,472	58	14	473	408	39	5	3	4.4	.26
New England	1,174	25	1	343	548	73	7	3	5.2	.22
N.Y., N.J., Pa.	3,699	36	10	440	459	45	6	4	4.7	.24
Ohio, Indiana	1,637	39	26	524	375	28	4	4	4.3	.25
Mich., Wis., Ill.	1,001	24	8	655	286	23	4	...	4.0	.21
Coast slave state	338	171	21	411	358	27	6	6	3.9	.36
Ky., Tenn.	266	199	19	481	293	4	...	4	3.3	.36
States west of Miss. Riv.	41	24	24	366	513	73	...	...	4.9	.23
Brit. Prov. ex. Can.	38	27	...	263	605	105	...	...	5.5	.19
Canada	508	181	20	466	299	26	6	2	3.6	.36
England	287	56	10	516	397	14	7	...	4.2	.24
Scotland	81	12	25	482	370	86	25	...	4.9	.27
Ireland	720	147	14	526	292	17	4	...	3.6	.32
France, etc.	42	48	71	524	262	47	24	14	4.3	.33
Germany	494	30	26	458	425	49	4	8	4.6	.33
Scandinavia	31	32	...	517	451	...	...	...	4.3	.25
Other countries	115	104	9	417	383	52	26	9	4.6	.33

Source: Benjamin Gould, Investigations in the Military and Anthropological Statistics of American Soldiers (New York: United States Sanitary Commission, 1869), pp. 570-71.

[1] The years of education have been assumed to be 0, 1, 3, 6, 10, 14, and 16 for the seven classes.

Table 4.3 The Proportion of Total Years of Education of Young Men in the Northern Army in 1862-64 and of Males Twenty to Twenty-Nine in the United States in 1970

Proportion of Men Cumulated from the Top (N_E)	Proportion of Total Years of Education of the N_E Group	
	1862-64	1970
.10	.19	.14
.20	.33	.26
.30	.46	.38
.40	.60	.48
.50	.70	.58
.60	.77	.68
.70	.84	.77
.80	.91	.87
.90	.98	.95
1.00	1.00	1.00
Mean	4.4	12.3
Gini coefficient	.262	.122

Source: Same as table 4.1 and United States Census, 1970, vol. 1, p. 627.

Table 4.4 The Average Number of Children in School (SCHN), the Average Proportion of Children in School (SCHNP), and the Proportion of Men with at Least One Child in School (SCHCHI) for All Free Adult Males in 1860 and Adult White Males in 1870 in the United States

Age Class of Adult Male	1860	1870
	SCHN	
20-29	.04	.03
30-39	.85	.66
40-99	1.37	1.03
	SCHNP	
20-29	.01	.01
30-39	.24	.19
40-99	.32	.27
	SCHCHI	
20-29	.12	.10
30-39	.39	.33
40-99	.49	.42

Source: Samples of size 4,833 in 1860 and 9,125 in 1870. See note 72.

Social Change in Nineteenth-Century Massachusetts they point to the sharply declining attendance of children of ages four to eight: "from 69.3 percent in 1860 to 54.6 percent in 1880." Most five-year-olds attended school in 1860, but only 38.3 percent were enrolled by 1880.[69] The greatest decline in enrollment rates was in urban communities, where, it should be added, graded systems of education were predominant and where educators probably found the presence of youth under six disruptive to their efforts at greater efficiency through a formal graded structure. The figures may also have the implication that there was some deterioration in the school system, that the handiwork of the 1840s and 1850s had begun to deteriorate in the throes of a warring country. The proportion of children attending school had dropped even in the North, where 65.7 percent of children between ages five and nine had attended in 1860 compared with only 55.7 percent in 1870.[70] If the 1870 data were for 1865 or 1866, we could understand the decrease. However, the 1870 information comes five years after the war. It is assumed that the census school enrollment statistics had less measurement error than did those for illiteracy and that decade comparisons are valid. It may have been that there was some lessening in the effectiveness of school systems occurring in the aftermath of the Civil War.

It is not likely that reversal in school enrollment figures can be attributed to an increasing percentage of foreign born, because we observe the same phenomenon for native born classifications. Moreover, the decrease certainly cannot be attributed to an urban movement, since rates were generally lower in urban areas in both years and the population was more urban in 1870 than in 1860. Retrogression in the South was to be expected, since the educational upheaval was great because of property destroyed during the war. Levels of school enrollment in the South had been lower for some decades before the war, but it is interesting in percentage terms that retrogression in the South was from 3 to 4 percent less than in the North.[71]

Table 4.5   The Proportion of Free Children Enrolled in School (SCH) in the North and South Living in Families, 1860-70

Age	1860		1870	
	North	South	North	South
5-9	.66	.34	.56	.22
10-14	.78	.57	.78	.51
15-19	.50	.42	.43	.32
5-19	.656	.436	.605	.353

Source: The sample is of 6,790 children living in 3,085 families, each having a father.   There was no mother in 165 of the families.   Corresponding counts in 1870 are 10,112 children in 8,556 families and 569 with no mothers.

Regional Disparities

The discussion of regional disparities which follows and the later discussion of wealth and school enrollments are based upon a random sample of 4,833 males twenty years of age and older from the 1860 federal census manuscripts for the free population of the entire country and a sample of 10,235 adult males twenty and older in 1870. All information pertaining to the families of the adult males was recorded. In the enumeration returns, each member of the family was asked whether or not he or she had attended school at any time during the year.[72]

The strongest statistical differences in schooling are found between North and South as demonstrated in table 4.5. Differences are pronounced at all age levels, but particularly so in age groupings five to nine and ten to fourteen, where enrollments in the North were twice as great among very young students and 30 to 35 percent greater for young adolescents. Judging from enrollment figures in 1860 and 1870, the average southern child was more likely not to attend a school in any given year than to attend one. Part of the regional disparity might be explained if southern children were taught at home. The above figures do not cover children outside families, and it is possible that there was a greater proportion of southern scholars living away from home. A separate sampling of boys ten through nineteen in the United States, however, indicates that this was not a large group. It is considerably more likely that school systems in the South did not provide the same level of access as in the North. This does not imply that the South was without its common school advocates. As Church and Sedlak have noted in *Education in the United States*, "The South, far from being restrained by its aristocratic tradition from establishing schools, made a major educational effort relative to its resources before the Civil War."[73] The rub, of course, was in the lack of *available* educational resources. With so much invested in a system of private schools and academies, available resources for public schooling were minimal. The Civil War itself, as we remark in chapter 5, brought with it a violent redistribution of wealth in the South, and for public education, the beginning of a new era. We cannot say, of course, that the development of public education in the South would have stagnated without the war, but it is evident that the South, under the prodding of self-righteous Yankees, began a new move toward publicly financed education after the war.

It would be expected that the enrollment rate would be lower for young people living in the Northwest (Ohio and west) than in the Northeast, where the common school system had developed earlier. The school enrollment figures do not yield this result, however, as shown in table 4.6. Despite the efforts of reformers to raise the age of school entrance, there was a greater tendency for children in the East to enroll in school at an

Table 4.6   Enrollment Rates (SCH) in the Northeast and Northwest in 1860 and
1870 for Children Living in Families

Age	1860		1870	
	Northeast	Northwest	Northeast	Northwest
5-9	.70	.61	.60	.52
10-14	.81	.75	.77	.80
15-19	.42	.59	.36	.51
5-19	.661	.652	.600	.612

Source: Same as table 4.5.   The sample includes 4,517 children in the North.

earlier age; the rate of enrollment was somewhat less for older children,
the result being that average participation was about the same in each
region. The typical enrollee was a little older in the West, the average age
being 11.2 in the West and 10.7 in the East. (The two age-specific curves
have maximum values at age 11—88 percent in the East and 8 percent in
the West—but they cross each other between ages 13 and 14.) On the
basis of these observations, two suggestions might be made. First, unlike
the situation in the South, county formation, wealth, and population density in the West were rising. As we see in chapter 5, county formation and
the consequent increase in population density were strategic in the development of educational institutions. School enrollments in the West thus
did not suffer as they did in the South. Second, it is certainly possible in
the Northeast that a mature system of manufacturing enhanced child labor
and earlier departure from school. This would level aggregate rates despite the greater systematization of public schooling in the Northeast.

Since agriculture was so much more dominant in the West, one might
expect school participation in the North to be more an occupational than a
regional problem. We turn now to classifications based on whether the
fathers of enrollees had a farm occupation (such as farmer, farm laborer,
gardener, planter) or were nonfarmers. The results are shown in table 4.7.

Participation among farm children matched that of nonfarm children in
the younger and middle years and was substantially larger among those in
the fifteen to nineteen age-group. This was the case in both the Northeast

Table 4.7   Enrollment Rates (SCH) in the North in 1860 for Children Five to
Nineteen in Families, Classified by Occupation and Residence for
the Father and Age of the Child

Age of Child	North		Northeast		Northwest	
	Farmer	Nonfarmer	Farmer	Nonfarmer	Farmer	Nonfarmer
5-9	.65	.66	.72	.69	.61	.61
10-14	.78	.78	.81	.81	.76	.72
15-19	.58	.38	.51	.35	.64	.46
5-19	.676	.636	.689	.642	.666	.620

Source: Same as table 4.6.

and Northwest, and also in attenuated form in both the Southwest and Southeast. This occurred in spite of the fact that transportation costs to and from school were greater for rural children, and that wages foregone while attending school (opportunity costs) for an older boy would be larger than those for a younger boy. Seasonal labor demands undoubtedly were stronger in rural areas. Some schools included planned vacations for harvesting. In the spring, it was noted by an 1835 observer, the "large scholars" were absent for their "spring work and sugar-making," thus reducing class sizes considerably.[74] A young farm lad could obviate opportunity costs to the extent that he could adapt attendance to slack periods in the growing and harvesting of crops. One-half the farm boys ages fifteen through nineteen with listed or stated vocations attended school. An examination of local school district records indicates that older boys, after having helped with the fall harvesting, returned to school for the winter months. The decision to leave school at times when seasonal labor opportunities were promising and to return during slack times was a reasonable one for the older farm lad. Periodic absence from school of this type was, during a year's time, not an either-or choice in the sense that it sacrificed schooling to work.[75] From the point of view of school officials and pedagogues, the practice had deleterious effects on learning; from the point of view of the farm family, an older boy could have the benefits of both work and school simply by adjusting his schedule.

The Alternative of Work

For children, obvious alternatives to attending school were employment either on the family farm, in a business owned by another, or in some small private enterprise.[76] In all three cases the motivation very likely was to enhance the immediate income and wealth of the family rather than that of the individual. We will discuss in chapter 5 the tendency of lower-order-of-birth children (the older children) within the family to have lower school enrollment rates. Modell's study of ten northeastern states for 1889 tends to support our findings. He observes in the case of the Irish that "in a majority of age-ethnic-income classes, larger families clearly *did* tend to send their oldest child into the labor force." The same pattern (but less pronounced) was common to native born, working-class families.[77] The finding for 1870 of lower school enrollment rates for lower-order-of-birth children we interpret as evidence that older children in the family helped younger siblings attend school for a greater number of years by earning part of the wages necessary to support the family.

It has been pointed out by Stephan Thernstrom in his *Poverty and Progress* that "the relentless pressure of poverty—stemming from the depressed wage level for common labor and from the sharp seasonal fluctuations in employment opportunities—forced the children of Newburyport's laborers into the job market at an early age."[78] Similar conditions existed elsewhere in rural regions. In the mining country of Ohio in 1878, a Trumbull County miner noted that "the schools are first class. I have nine children, but none of them go to school. Three of them are at work, and earned nearly $200 in the year, while I earned $103.70. Poverty prevents their going to school."[79] Another, in Athens County, attested to a similar situation. He noted that "school facilities first rate, but my children cannot go, because I cannot clothe them, work has been so poor."[80] Records of the Ohio Bureau of Labor Statistics show that five of eleven families had expenses greater than their net wages during 1878.[81] That the family budget could be balanced by sending children to work instead of school seems evident.

Second, we must consider, in addition to the immediate stimulus of supplementing the family income, that if children could easily have found jobs at some meaningful fraction of the adult wage rate, there would have been a counterbalance to the desire for further education and greater expected, although postponed, income. Information on child labor is not readily available, but it is certain that significant numbers of children were employed. Children accounted for about 6 percent of manufacturing employment in 1870, while their numbers in the population as a whole may have been not more than 16 percent.[82] As would be expected, urban counties tended to have a greater proportion of children in manufacturing than did rural counties. In both the 1870 and 1880 censuses of industries, employers were asked questions regarding the number of employees, sex thereof, and months of operation during the year. Though small in numbers, the examples in table 4.8 illustrate some of the findings.

There is an extensive literature relating income differentials of various professional and education classes to the income foregone while obtaining an education. The yearly differential during the working life of a person can be discounted (using an annuity table and assuming a prevailing interest rate of 6 percent) back to the year of graduation or completion of schooling. This sum, in turn, may be related to the cost of education.

Table 4.8 Examples of Child Labor in Manufacturing for a Few Selected Employers in Manufacturing in Ohio and Wisconsin, 1870

| Type of Industry | Number of Employees | | | Months of Operation in Year |
	Males over 16 Years	Females over 15 Years	Children and Youth	
Woolen mills	18	9	5	12
Cooper	2	...	6	3
Nursery	4	...	12	6
Hand press	2	...	1	12
Cheese factory	1	2	1	6

Source: Manuscripts of the Census of Industry, Ohio, Wisconsin, 1870, selected employers.

Table 4.9 Earnings of Boys in Wage-Earner Families in Massachusetts in 1874-75 and Their Annuity Equivalent at Age Twenty, Assuming 6 Percent Interest and Payments from Age Twenty to Sixty-Five

Age of Boy (A)	Number of Boys	Average Annual Earnings (Y)	Earnings Equivalent at Age 20, $Z = Y(1.06)^{20-A}$	Annual Equivalent as an Annuity Payment from 20 to 65, $E = Z/15.45$	Equivalent as Proportion of Father's Earnings $E/\$574$	Cumulated Differential
9	1	$ 76	$144	$ 9	.016	.016
10	4	152	256	17	.029	.045
11	6	129	205	13	.023	.068
12	33	145	218	14	.024	.092
13	48	157	222	14	.025	.12
14	69	200	267	17	.030	.15
15	41	245	309	20	.035	.18
16	26	299	356	23	.040	.22
17	10	388	379	25	.043	.27
18	1	416	440	29	.050	.32
19	1	520	520	34	.058	.37
	240	207	3,316	215	.374	

Source: Massachusetts Bureau of Statistics of Labor, Sixth Annual Report, March 1875, Public Document no. 31, pp. 359, 364, 220-355. See also United States Bureau of the Census, Historical Statistics of the United States, Colonial Times to 1790, p. 309. Data were collected in fifteen cities and twenty-one towns.

Note: The average annual earnings of fathers was $574; an annuity of $15.45 is the equivalent of an annual payment of $2 for forty-five years at 6 percent interest.

A more detailed view of this relationship may be had by examining a set of age-specific income data reported by the Massachusetts Department of Labor in 1875. This gives us a rough guide in understanding the decisions made by boys and their fathers concerning the trade-offs between work and schooling. The earnings of boys reported in table 4.9 increased in linear fashion from the rate at age nine to the adult rate of $574 after age twenty for those who were employed. An individual working from age nine to twenty might have the equivalent of $3,316 at age twenty if he invested all of his earnings at 6 percent per annum. This sum would purchase an annuity paying $215 for forty-five years, or about 37 percent of the average earnings of adult workers as reported. This means that a differential in wages of perhaps 3 percent a year would cover the opportunity cost of remaining in school an extra year.

A more exact calculation given in the last column of table 4.9 indicates the break-even level at various ages. A 15 percent differential in earnings between those with education to age nine and those remaining in school to age fourteen might be the signal to others to remain in school until age fourteen if they could in some way borrow money at 6 percent or finance the investment from accumulated assets. For example, from table 4.9 we see that the average annual earnings (Y) of a boy of fourteen was $200. If this were placed in a bank at 6 percent interest, it would accumulate to $267 when the boy was twenty years old. If he then purchased a forty-five-year annuity with the $267, it would pay him $17 each year for forty-five years. The $17 is slightly more than 3 percent of an average father's salary and can be considered the differential necessary to cover the opportunity cost for the education at age fourteen. Finally, the cumulative differential for age fourteen and also for ages nine to thirteen is 15 percent. If we compare these findings with the differential suggested in table 4.10 for Pennsylvania, we see that it would be more than ample to cover the school investment, if one could obtain funds and were capable of pursuing education.

The employment opportunities and prospective earnings of children who stopped schooling before achieving literacy were not good, and tended to support the claims of school officials and common school advocates that literacy was an important element in upward economic mobility. The following study done in 1867 by the Commonwealth of Pennsylvania indicates that salary was a function of the degree of literacy and that illiterate employees could not expect to be rewarded at a level commensurate with semiliterates. The results are shown in table 4.10, where it is clear that level of reading achievement and wages per month were positively related. Thus, in linear fashion, wages rose with level of education.

Urban and rural differences in work-school patterns for the age-group fifteen through nineteen can be explained in part by examining the limited

Table 4.10 Differentials in Salary according to Levels of Literacy and Education
in Pennsylvania in 1867

Level of Literacy and/or Education	Number of Employees in Sample	Number of Counties in Sample	Range of Mean Wages/County in Dollars/Month	Mean Wages in Dollars/Month
Those who cannot read	4.860	18	16-78	36
Those who can read a little	4,886	19	19-80	42
Those who can read well, but are otherwise poorly educated	4,937	21	25-100	52
Those who are well educated in all aspects	4,767	20	45-173	90

Source: Calculated from county averages as in Superintendent of Common Schools, Report, 1867, Harrisburg, Pa., pp. 274-75.

data available from the census of manufacturing in 1870 and the censuses of occupations for 1860 and 1870. The statistics indicate that children under seventeen were employed extensively in urban (nonfarm) areas, perhaps from age fourteen, and that the industries least related to agricultural production tended to operate with less seasonal movement. It is possible, then, that urban young in the age class fifteen through nineteen might be expected to have low school enrollment rates since employment was an alternative to schooling. Farm children provide a contrast since their farm and farm-related employment tended to be more seasonal and probably had its impact among those of twelve and thirteen years of age. Seasonal employment dictated school attendance patterns in rural districts where farm children had higher school enrollment rates for the age-group fifteen through nineteen because they could attend in seasonally slack periods, though they had not attended in busy seasonal periods when they were younger.

Statistics presented on school enrollments are for both boys and girls. The school enrollment proportions for boys are somewhat larger than those for girls for any particular classification. Thus, while sex was not a statistically significant determinant of days attended, it did have some bearing on enrollment in school itself. One exception to the sex pattern for school enrollment occurs in the northern farm sector, as shown below for the ten to fourteen age-group (described in table 4.7):

	5–9	10–14	15–19
SCH for boys	.68	.77	.63
SCH for girls	.62	.80	.52

The proportion for boys is more stable than that for girls and is actually less than that for girls in the middle age-group—again an indication that seasonal employment, at least for males, was a factor in the pattern of school attendance in the rural sector, but much less so in the urban sector.

Table 4.11 Earnings in Dollars per Week for Selected Manufacturers, 1879, Ohio

	Skilled	Unskilled	Boys (youth)
Cooperage	12.00	6.60	3.00
Planing mills	10.52	6.14	2.92
Furniture	10.85	6.00	2.71
Woolen mills	11.08	7.17	3.41

Source: Ohio Bureau of Labor Statistics, Second Annual Report, 1878 (Columbus, 1879), pp. 139, 143, 144, 163.

The relationship between literacy and employability is confounded by the uncertainty pertaining to levels of worker skills required in the middle stages of industrialization. Alexander Field has taken the position that it is of dubious truth to contend "that the common school revival resulted from an increase in the derived demand for skills brought about by the shift to factory production."[83] From this viewpoint, then, the level of job skills possessed by potential adolescent factory workers was not crucial in determining their employment; thus, it is likely that the low-skill, low-paying jobs were those most open to adolescents leaving school. We should not infer, then, that boys and girls were paid well enough to make early work an attractive economic prospect. Of course, to many, work was not an option but a necessary condition for keeping the family solvent. Table 4.11, while not age-specific, gives an indication of how little (less than half that of unskilled adult workers) a boy could expect to earn, compared with an adult. Where age-specific data are available, in returns for manufacturers of boots and shoes, for instance, 1878 figures indicate that male and female youth under fifteen earned only an average of $5.40 per week compared with $14.70 for males over fifteen and $8.60 for females over fifteen; in paper mills, boys under sixteen earned $3.62 per week compared with $6.69 for unskilled men and $10.01 for skilled men. Similar differences existed for "men" and "boys" engaged in mining, where per-week wages for boys were 50 percent below those for men.[84] Lower pay for younger workers does not necessarily mean that employers did not value "schooled" youth. Three years of common schooling, for instance, did offer some degree of assurance that a youth at least knew his letters. Five years of common schooling was probably enough to classify the youth as literate. To be literate, as we have seen, did not simply mean to be competent at a specified level of reading mastery. It meant, perhaps more importantly for the employer, exposure to a set of values compatible with a disciplined work force. In short, literacy through schooling was a step toward the moral discipline so prized by mid-nineteenth-century school officials and employers alike.

Wealth and School Enrollment

We turn now to a discussion of those relationships between wealth and schooling which seem to have characterized mid-nineteenth-century America. It may be assumed that if parents had substantial wealth, they were in a superior position to provide education for their children. The expenditure may have been considered to be not only an investment of broad cultural or moral value, but also one of a narrower vocational value. The aims of common school reformers spanned both these dimensions. The following questions remain: Was America in 1860 a country offering opportunities for literacy through schooling to all classes, or were these opportunities stratified by wealth? What were the enrollment proportions for different wealth classes? In dealing with these questions we consider only common schooling, since it is at this level that literacy was usually attained, providing the child had attended regularly. Thus, we do not consider the great inequalities of opportunity which existed through private schooling; nor do we consider inequalities at the high school level despite the best efforts of reformers and school superintendents to publish materials which indicated that children of all socioeconomic classes participated in high school education.[85]

Table 4.12 Enrollment Rates (SCH) of Northern Children Living in Families in 1860 Related to the Wealth of Their Parents

| Wealth Class of Parents ($) | SCH by Age of Child | | |
	5-9	10-14	15-19
0-99	.66	.65	.25
100-999	.62	.77	.43
1,000-9,999	.70	.81	.56
10,000 and up	.69	.88	.58

Source: A sample of 4,517 children in 2,357 families.

We begin our discussion by considering northern families where wealth did not include the value of slaves. Table 4.12 for 1860 shows that participation among the young of ages five through nine was not a function of the wealth of the parent. Approximately two of every three children were in school for our four economic classes, which, though broad, capture both the very poor and the affluent. Enrollment for the ten through fourteen age class is a function of the wealth of parents since there is a clear gradation for the four total-estate classes in the table. The effect of wealth is even more demonstrative for children of ages fifteen through nineteen. For the latter age classification, almost two and one-half times as many children of the affluent were likely to be in school as were children of the poor. We know that in 1860 and 1870 (see chapter 5) literacy and wealth were positively correlated, that in 1860, for instance, the top 20 percent of wealthholders included only 7.8 percent of the illiterates. In relationship to our school enrollment figures, then, it seems likely that if the wealthy perpetuated an intellectual elite in the United States, they did it partly by making it possible for their teenage children to attend school at least part of the year.[86] Then, too, perhaps there was less necessity for the children of the wealthy to work on the family farm or business. The opportunity costs or immediate earnings foregone by youth would not have been as important to affluent parents. They could hire servants or laborers for their farms and businesses with relative ease.

Table 4.13 Enrollment Rates (SCH) in the North in 1860 by Occupation of Father and Wealth of Parents

Wealth Class of Parents ($)	Age of Farm Children			Age of Nonfarm Children		
	5-9	10-14	15-19	5-9	11-14	15-19
0-99	.57	.64	.35	.61	.66	.23
100-999	.53	.74	.48	.67	.79	.40
1,000-9,999	.70	.80	.60	.70	.84	.43
10,000 and up	.73	.86	.64	.64	.92	.47

Source: Same as table 4.12.

We obtain some hints of the impact of wealth in the rural and urban sectors from table 4.13. The pattern previously described persists within each sector, with the affluent children, ages fifteen through nineteen, being twice as likely to be enrolled as the poor children. The relationship demonstrating that children in cities were more likely to attend from ages ten through fourteen and less likely to attend from ages fifteen through nineteen is still apparent in the figures of table 4.13. The older son of a wealthy man living in a city was no more likely to attend than the older son of a farmer with modest wealth.

Studies of specific cities have shown that the children of foreign born did not attain the occupational levels of the children of native born.[87] They were less likely to be skilled or to have nonmanual jobs. If this is the fact throughout the country, we should expect that school attendance of children with foreign born parents should be less than that of children with native born parents for our data. The comparisons in table 4.14 indicate that foreign born parents had fewer children enrolled, not only in each age-group, but also at each wealth level. This was the case in both the Northeast and Northwest and was not confined to urban areas. Stephan Thernstrom has properly documented the importance of ethnicity in upward occupational mobility.[88] It is noted here, however, that the level of wealth within the foreign born group was very important in the

Table 4.14 Enrollment Rates (SCH) in the North in 1860 by Nativity of Parents

Wealth Class of Parents ($)	SCH by Age of Child and Nativity of Parents					
	5-9		10-14		15-19	
	Native	Foreign	Native	Foreign	Native	Foreign
0-99	.64	.55	.71	.59	.37	.10
100-999	.66	.57	.83	.68	.51	.28
1,000 and up	.72	.65	.84	.76	.61	.41

Source: Same as table 4.12. Foreign born encompasses classes where one parent is native born.

determination of schooling and probably in the ultimate occupational attainment of children.[89] The problem is exceedingly complex since ethnicity and education are entwined at the parental level and illiteracy rates for poor foreign born parents were three times those of wealthy foreign born parents. Because of the complexity of this topic, we treat it separately in the next section.

School Attendance, Ethnicity, and Wealth

Many immigrant children were members of different cultures at different times. For a number of Catholic children, for example, one culture was represented by the traditional Catholicism of the parent and, perhaps, the grandparent. Another culture was represented by the unrelinquishing Americanism of the public school, the curriculum of which, notes Wilkie, stressed nationalism, Protestant morality, and economic individualism.[90] The problem of identity—of cultural demands and individual psyche alike—was a most serious one for the child. In order to better gain an intergenerational perspective on the problem of acculturation through schooling and the relationships among school attendance, ethnicity, and wealth, we first analyze grandparental characteristics as they relate to characteristics of children in nuclear families for northern (nonslave) states in 1870. (This distinction is made because the preponderance of foreign born lived in the North, and it is desired to compare foreign born and native born living in areas with similar economic and institutional backgrounds.) We then proceed with an analysis of parental characteristics and their relationships to the activities of children.[91]

Our data for this aspect of the study were drawn primarily from the federal census manuscripts of 1870, the first to ask information about the nativity and place of birth of an individual's parents. Some data from our 1860 federal census sample are also used. For the 1870 enumeration, each individual was asked if his or her father was foreign born and if his or her mother was foreign born. For the parents of children in nuclear families, the place of birth is also available. This means we can obtain some knowledge of ethnicity in three generations in the case of census families with children. Moreover, we can determine the proportion of children whose grandparents were foreign born and the number of grandparents of native birth. In short, for those children enrolled in school, information may be obtained about four branches of a family tree instead of two, and we are in a position to relate the nativity and/or ethnicity of the four branches to socioeconomic characteristics of the family and children.

The sample from 1870 consists of 11,360 children living in families with both father and mother. Excluded are children living outside the family (nonnuclear) and those families in which either parent has died or is not otherwise recorded. The siblings of each child are also part of the sample, so we are dealing with only 3,866 families with children. Large families will have greater weights in the results, but this is exactly what is desired, since the emphasis is on the activities of children, not those of their parents. The children are most often under twenty and usually under fifteen years of age, the average being nine years.[92]

Intergenerational Nativity and Children's
Activities

An important aspect of the subject of acculturation was its quantitative dimensions in terms of the proportion of children in 1870 who had both sets of grandparents born in other countries. It is commonly believed that there were very few such children at the time, that perhaps less than one in four were not purely Americans of two generations. The analysis of census data indicates that the proportion was actually 34 percent and, as table 4.15 shows, approximately one-third of children had all four of their grandparents born abroad. Some children probably were in families which immigrated after the Civil War, and others were likely among those arriving in the 1850s. Unfortunately, there are no data available from the federal manuscripts enumerating the years of residence in the United States. We can capture at least some of the change over time, however, by classifying the children by age-group.[93] Classifying in this manner indicates that older children in the United States were more likely to have

Table 4.15 The Proportion of Nuclear Children in Northern States in 1870 Who Had One, Two, Three, or Four Foreign Born Grandparents

Number of Grandparents of Foreign Birth	Number of Children by Age				
	All Ages	0-4	5-9	10-14	15-19
0	.56	.53	.52	.55	.62
1	.01	.01	.01	.01	.01
2	.08	.09	.08	.07	.07
3	.01	.01	.01	.01	...
4	.34	.36	.36	.36	.30
	1.00	1.00	1.00	1.00	1.00

Source: The sample of 11,360 children in 3,866 families.

native born grandparents, a reflection of an earlier period in American history when intergenerational ties were closer, that is, less affected by immigration. Among younger children, the somewhat larger proportion having grandparents of foreign birth reflected the emerging ethnic diversity which began to characterize American society.

The great majority of children with foreign born grandparents also had parents who were born abroad; 41 percent of all children had at least one parent who was foreign born. This means that there were very few foreign grandparents whose children (the parents of the children of our sample living in nuclear families) were born in the United States. In terms of our sample this meant that a little over one in three American children intimately faced problems of acculturation, and we might expect that two in five were cognizant of their foreign heritage at the grandparental level. A cognizance of one's heritage, however, ought not to be equated with a continuous, direct, and intimate experience involving one's grandparents. In fact, such continuous, intimate experience was more likely to be lacking in the homes of the urban Irish and German foreign born than in the families of the native born in general. In an important study, "Ethnicity and Family Structure in Nineteenth Century America," Glasco has demonstrated for the city of Buffalo, New York, that "extended and augmented households were a distinct minority, particularly for the immigrants." "Taken together," he notes, "extended and augmented families made up only fifteen percent of the German households and 26 percent of the Irish." On the other hand, the number of "extended households" among the native born was "quite substantial, comprising forty-two percent of all native born households in the city."[94] We would expect, then, that grandparental influences (in any continuous, direct manner) on grandchildren among the foreign born would be lacking compared with grandparental influences among native born children. In an experiential sense, the child in the immigrant family was likely to be one more step removed from his family heritage than the child in the native family. It may be inferred, then, that the tendency of the grandparents to be absent from immigrant families actually *removed* one obstacle to the rapid acculturation of the child.

When we turn to the relationship between grandparental characteristics and the activities of children, the most salient finding is that children were more likely to attend school if all their grandparents were native born than if they were all foreign born. This was true particularly at the later stages of childhood. Children whose grandparents were a mixture of native and foreign born held an intermediate position with respect to school attendance. This mixed group is of interest for several reasons. We know that at least one of the grandparents immigrated to the United States and that there was intermarriage of nativity groups. These grandparents had at least some exposure to the role of education in American culture. Their children (the parents of our sample children) would presumably be further along the path to acculturation if such exposure had not resulted in hostility and alienation, that is, if they could adjust to the ideology of nationalism, economic individualism, and Protestant morality taught by most public schools. On the other hand, it might be expected that Catholic parents or grandparents who had been intimidated and/or alienated by the public schools would encourage their children to remain within the fold of the many parochial and ethnic organizations which helped the Catholic immigrant contend with a hostile environment.[95] Even in the case of the Catholic child attending public school it should be remembered that public school attendance would not be evidence of assimilation, although attendance at a public school might be a good training ground for behavioral conformity.[96]

Table 4.16 Enrollment Rates (SCH) of Nuclear Children in the North in 1870 by Age of Child and Nativity of Grandparents

| Age of Child | Nativity of Grandparents | | |
	All Native Born	Mixed	All Foreign Born
5-9	.56	.56	.55
10-14	.82	.77	.74
15-19	.54	.43	.24

Source: The sample of 11,360.

We now examine the relationship between the school enrollment of nuclear children and the nativity of grandparents. Table 4.16 indicates there is little difference in school enrollment for the young of ages five to nine. Some differences begin to appear for ages ten to fourteen, with children of the native born more likely to be enrolled. The differences in enrollment become accentuated for children fifteen to nineteen years of age, with the probability of enrollment being twice as great for the native born as distinguished from the foreign born category. These patterns also held generally within the rural and urban sectors of the northern economy, particularly the distinction between *all* native and *all* foreign born. It should be stressed, then, that the role of the school in the acculturation of the immigrant child was confined within the ages of five to fourteen for the most part and that the differential impact of the acculturating experiences were particularly important for the ten to fourteen age-group. This fact takes on added significance when one realizes that within this age-group, the child's peers become increasingly formative in shaping his or her behavior. For the immigrant child whose training within the family was an inadequate guide to coping with American social institutions, peer experiences with children of the native born in the pubescent stage of development might well have outweighed the earlier, more restrictive environment of the family.[97] Even if one assumes that the early childhood experiences in one's life are the most formative, it still must be recognized that the experiences of early adolescence are re-formative and often determine the patterns of social behavior with which a person enters the economic life of society.

Table 4.17   The Proportion of Nuclear Children with Stated Occupations (OCC) in the North in 1870 by Age and Nativity of Grandparents

| Age of Child | Nativity of Grandparents (number per thousand) | | |
	All Native Born	Mixed	All Foreign Born
10-14	24	14	57
15-19	174	203	254

Source: The sample of 11,360.

The complement to schooling activities of children may be considered by looking at information in the occupational column of the manuscripts, which listed activities such as farm laborer, farm helper, day laborer, worker in the specific trades, and hundreds of other titles. It is very likely that children working for their parents did not state such activity as an occupation, so that figures giving the proportion of children with occupations will be an understatement. The figures are interesting, nonetheless, as indicators of activity. As seen in table 4.17 children with stated occupations were less likely to be attending school. Among children with foreign born grandparents the proportion engaged in occupations was considerably higher than among those of native born grandparentage. For those children with both grandparents foreign born, it was probably those in impoverished circumstances that accounted for the greater share engaged in occupations.

The Economic Environment of Children

The analysis of children's economic environments may be related to the nativity of their grandparents, as in table 4.18. It is noted, first, that families with children of foreign born grandparents had only one-half of or less than the average (mean or median) wealth of the native born. Children of mixed grandparentage were in families whose wealth ranked between that of the other groups. In both farm and nonfarm sectors of the country, the economic environment of the child was better among those families having both sets of grandparents native born than among those in which both grandparents were foreign born.

Knowing these wealth positions may lead one to hypothesize that school attendance proportions should differ much more among nativity groups in urban areas than elsewhere and that such proportions should

Table 4.18   The Average Wealth of Father (W) of Children in the North in 1870 by the Age of the Children and the Nativity of the Grandparents

Age of Child and Occupation of Father	Nativity of Grandparents		
	All Native Born	Mixed	Foreign Born
All			
0-4	$3,130	$2,460	$1,740
5-9	4,725	3,494	2,129
10-14	5,810	3,716	2,329
15-19	6,087	5,653	2,922
Farmers			
0-4	3,130	2,925	2,982
5-9	4,803	4,535	3,222
10-14	5,685	3,681	3,921
15-19	6,274	5,493	4,086
Nonfarmers			
0-4	3,129	2,099	1,222
5-9	4,624	2,591	1,564
10-14	6,002	3,743	1,496
15-19	5,772	5,782	2,342

Source: The sample of 11,360.   Wealth equals real estate plus personal estate.

differ more by economic class among the foreign born. This proves to be the situation especially in the sensitive fifteen- to nineteen-year-old group. Overall, the foreign born enrollment proportion for this group is less but substantially over half the native born proportion in the farm section; it is appreciably under one-half in the urban sector as shown below:

School Enrollment by Grandparent Nativity

Occupation of Father	All Native Born	Mixed	All Foreign Born
Farmer	.60	.58	.36
Nonfarmer	.43	.31	.18

Consider also that the school enrollment proportion for children with farm parents is twice that for those with nonfarm parents among the foreign born, but urban-rural distinctions are much less than this among native born. An investigation of proportions of children with occupations conveys the same general relative magnitudes and reinforces our findings for school enrollment data. Surely economic conditions of parents were a most fundamental determinant of activities of children as those activities related to school and work. These economic conditions in turn were related to the nativity of grandparents.

More direct information on the economic environment of children may be gathered by examining the wealth of their parents. This wealth, as recorded by the federal census, was the declared value of real and personal estate no matter where it was owned. As a child grew older and his

Table 4.19 The Average Age and Wealth of Parents in the North in
1870 by Age of Child

Age of Child	Average Age of Father	Average Age of Mother	Average Wealth of Parents
0-4	35.3	30.4	$3,377
5-9	40.6	35.6	4,686
10-14	45.4	40.0	5,598
15-19	50.0	44.9	6,380

Source: The sample of 11,360.

parents proceeded through their life cycle, the average parental wealth increased. As table 4.19 illustrates, children had fathers averaging thirty-three years older and mothers twenty-eight years older than themselves, and it is quite possible that children born into the family later benefited from the economic accumulation of the family. Among those families which experienced poverty in their early child-rearing days but experienced some upward economic mobility in their middle years, it is quite plausible that the frustrations of the firstborn to achieve success led to a greater support of those born later. Moreover, as we have observed earlier, the earnings of the eldest child could probably ease the financial difficulties of the poor, thus allowing for increased school attendance by those following the firstborn (see table 4.20). The assertion that younger children were likely recipients of greater educational opportunity must be qualified to some degree, however. First, it is evident that the differential is greatest among children aged five to nine, and this is true regardless of whether fathers of the children were literate or illiterate. It is equally as clear, however, that children of illiterate fathers had much less chance of attending school than children of literate fathers. Among children with illiterate fathers there is a clear gradation from the first child to the fourth. Beyond the fourth child, however, the linear relationship does not hold. Among children aged fifteen to nineteen, the higher order child certainly had greater access to schooling; however, in this age range the differences, while persistent, are not as dramatic.

Table 4.20 The Proportion of Children Attending School during the Year
(SCH) in 1870 in the North by Order of Birth

Order of Birth in the Family	SCH of All Children		SCH of Children of Illit. Fathers	
	Age 5-9	Age 15-19	Age 5-9	Age 15-19
Oldest child	.46	.42	.34	.35
Second oldest	.59	.43	.41	
Third oldest	.60	.45	.54	
Fourth oldest	.61	.55	.61	.40
Fifth or higher order	.55	.57	.36	

Source: The sample of 11,360.

Note: The sample of 903 children of illiterates includes only 119 of age fifteen to nineteen.

Parental Country of Birth and Children's
Activities

Between 1815 and 1875, some 9 million immigrants—6 million from Ireland and Germany alone—made their way to the new American republic. Our sample of nuclear children reflects this massive shift in population, as it shows that about one-quarter of the nuclear children in the North in 1870 had fathers who were born in Ireland or Germany. Unfortunately, we do not know from the data where in the respective countries an individual was born or his or her religious affiliation. It might be anticipated, however, that parental experiences before emigration would combine with those expectations for the new land to affect children's activities. We may assume, for example, that many of the Irish Catholics had experienced the tensions of attempting to establish a national system of schools in Ireland after 1812, and that some had turned to the famous "hedge schools" of early- and mid-nineteenth-century Ireland for their instruction in the basic skills.[98] Despite the fact that the Irish came from a land where 40 percent of the Catholics five years and older were illiterate, it would be unwise to postulate any general antipathy to education among them. In fact, in the state of Wisconsin in 1844–45, when a free public school system was being established in Kenosha County, Father Kundig and the Irish Catholics of the county gave their support because, in view of their relatively low economic status, "a free school system was to their advantage."[99] It is evident that they believed, as did many native and immigrant families, what the ideology of literacy had taught: that improved economic status was a reward for becoming literate through schooling.

The many Prussian emigrants (if they were schooled) were probably products of the well-known and efficient Prussian state system of education. Among Catholics in Prussia aged ten and over, the illiteracy rate in 1871 was approximately 18 percent compared with an overall illiteracy rate of 12 percent.[100] In 1850, adult (ten years of age and up) illiteracy was 20 percent. The image of the "bookish German" in American textbooks was undoubtedly an exaggeration, but it indicates, nonetheless, the perspective that Americans held and continued to hold toward the American-German population in the nineteenth century. Unlike the Irish, the Germans were viewed as people who took their education seriously because they were one of the few nations "outside of the United States, who believe[d] in common school education for all."[101] Ironically, in the matter of school enrollment Irish children outperformed German children in all age-groups, as is evidenced in table 4.21.

Irish paternal illiteracy was high in 1870 as compared with rates for those born in other countries and in various sections of the United States. Table 4.22 shows that only among the Canadian born and those living in the southern United States do we find higher rates.[102] It is almost certain that rates differed between Catholic Irish and Protestant Irish with the

Table 4.21   School Enrollment (SCH) of Children in the North by Age of Child
and Country of Birth and Occupation of Father, 1870

Country of Father's Birth	SCH by Age of Child			Age Standardized SCH, 5-19		
	5-9	10-14	15-19	All	Farmer	Nonfarmer
Ireland	.60	.78	.28	.59	.62	.58
Germany	.53	.77	.21	.54	.53	.55
England & Wales	.52	.64	.27	.51	.48	.52
Scotland	.70	.87	.28	.66	.73	.60
Canada	.56	.67	.30	.54	.71	.45
United States						
Northeast	.60	.84	.50	.66	.70	.62
Northwest	.49	.78	.64	.63	.63	.61
South	.43	.76	.54	.57	.56	.61

Source: The sample of 11,360.   The northern populations of children for
the age-groups within each occupation have been used in the standardization.

former having considerably higher rates of illiteracy than the latter.[103] But
what effects, for instance, did parental educational experiences, a low-
level of literacy, and the depressed conditions of many Irish laborers have
upon the occupational and school activities of Irish children?[104] We may
gain some insight into the question by noting, first, that foreign born
children of foreign born fathers were much more likely to have stated
occupations, even between the ages of ten and fourteen, than native born
children, regardless of whether the latter had native born or foreign born
fathers. Although the numbers are rather small in some categories, attention should be given to the fact that in the ten to fourteen age-group for
children with Irish-born or German-born fathers the actual proportion of
children with occupations is quite low, .07 and .03, respectively.[105] William V. Shannon has remarked in his work *The American Irish* that the
premature deaths of so many heads-of-families led younger members of a
family "at the age of five or six to peddle papers, pick coke, run errands
and rummage through junkyards for useful and salable items."[106] "At
twelve or thirteen," he continues, "boys took on full-time jobs wrestling
freight or carrying a hod."[107] While it is not at all unlikely that many of
the young supplemented the family income, our data indicate that if the
young of impoverished immigrants were expected to help in a substantial
way to balance the family budget, they did not, as a rule, engage themselves in occupations until age fifteen or older.

   The findings for occupational activities of children are in accord with
the school enrollment pattern among the same. The relationship between
paternal ethnicity and child participation in school must be interpreted
with care, however. First, it may be supposed that parents of particular
ethnic backgrounds would have held different values regarding education
and that those values would be internalized by their children. The tie
between religious and educational values is a case in point, and without
belaboring the question we need only point to the fact that within thirty

Table 4.22 The Proportion of Nuclear Children in the North in 1870 with
Illiterate Fathers (ILF) by Age of Child and Country of Birth
of Father

Country of Father's Birth	ILF by Age of Child		Number of Children per 100
	0-9	10-19	
Ireland	.18	.18	13
Germany	.05	.06	13
England and Wales	.06	.06	5
Scotland	.00	.00	1
Other European	.08	.11	2
Unknown	.17	.14	2
Canada	.24	.26	3
United States			
Northeast	.04	.03	40
Northwest	.06	.08	15
South	.21	.23	6
All in North	.08	.08	100

Source: The sample of 11,360. The smallest sample size is that for
Scottish children (N = 139).

years following the New York school crisis of 1840–42 and the Philadelphia Bible riots of 1844, parish budgets were sufficient to allow Catholic
churchmen to accommodate numerous Catholic children in parochial
school systems in every major city (see table 4.23).[108] Still, in larger cities
exposure to public schooling was still the rule. Even in a city like New
York, where the parochial system of schooling expanded rapidly following the Civil War, most children were still enrolled in public schools. The
basic fact was, as Dolan has remarked, that "despite thirty years of vigorous campaigning, Catholic education could not keep up with the increase
in population."[109] In small-city America, and most likely in small-town
and rural America, where Catholics made up a far smaller percentage of
the population, children were, of course, exposed to public schooling
rather than private or parochial schooling.[110] Thus, for our purposes, it is

Table 4.23 Estimated Number of Private and Parochial Students as a Percent of
All Children Enrolled in Schools for the United States, 1875, 1880

Total Population of City	East	Midwest	West	South	Total
1875					
7,500-49,999	16.5	24.1	19.4	22.2	19.8
50,000-99,999	27.6	32.8	...	45.3	30.7
100,000-1,000,000	31.9	31.3	17.7	35.5	31.5
Total	25.1	28.2	18.0	32.1	25.7
1880					
7,500-49,999	16.6	21.8	27.0	24.0	18.5
50,000-99,999	15.7	23.0	...	37.5	19.7
100,000-1,000,000	27.4	29.7	14.8	27.0	27.1
Total	21.7	25.5	19.3	26.6	28.0

Source: United States Commissioner of Education, Report, 1875, pp. 555-60;
1880, pp. 414-21.

important to note that the bulk of children enrolled in school were enrolled in public schools.

Second, we must be aware of more general confounding effects due to urbanity (farm and nonfarm) and to residence (Northeast and Northwest). For separate studies of the Northeast (Pennsylvania, New Jersey, and north) and the Northwest (Ohio and west) some differences of importance are found among age-groups, but overall school enrollment rates were approximately the same in each region. Standardization for age, occupation, and region made little difference in the final results.[111] Over half the Irish children were in the urban Northeast, and it might be thought that the endeavors of schoolmen in this area to increase attendance might have increased school enrollment rates. Yet the Irish did sufficiently well elsewhere in farming areas and the Northwest that alternative weightings give approximately the same results. Irish school enrollments, it turns out, were higher than those for both German and British children. At one extreme were the Scottish, greater in school enrollment than any other ethnic group for ages five to fourteen, the native born not excepted. At the other extreme were those of Canadian born fathers. One very firm distinction appears, however: twice as many United States born children of ages fifteen to nineteen in nuclear families were in schools as those associated with other countries.

Finally, we must attempt to ascertain the relative effects of wealth and nativity on school enrollment within a particular region of the country for particular ethnic groups. Previously, we have noted that children not enrolled in school had the opportunity to enhance the immediate family income by working but that opportunities for children to be employed at a meaningful fraction of adult earnings were not good. Nonetheless, the family budget could be balanced by sending children to work instead of school. It will be recalled that we examined school enrollments as a function of parental wealth in table 4.12. For children of ages five to nine, school enrollment was not a function of parental wealth, and two-thirds of children were enrolled for all economic classes. Similar findings are reported by Wilkie for children in the city of Boston in 1850.[112] School enrollment for the ten to fourteen age bracket, however, began to differentiate according to parental wealth, and for the age class of fifteen to nineteen, parental wealth was decisive.

These previous findings from the 1860 federal census, however, do not enable us to determine the *relative* effects of wealth and nativity on school enrollment, and we turn now to the northeast sector of the United States in order to examine the interaction of wealth and nativity on school enrollment, and hence the degree to which wealth in association with a particular ethnic identity influenced the process of acculturation via the school. While the relationship between ethnicity and wealth is complex to say the least, we assume, as did Kaestle and Vinovskis in their recent study of school attendance in Massachusetts, that ethnicity did operate as a significant factor in school enrollment. However, as we show below, such an assumption must be severely qualified. We pursue this line of investigation by noting that a cross-classification by wealth and father's birthplace for children aged fifteen to nineteen enables us to observe important distinctions in the school enrollments for the two major immigrant groups in the urban Northeast. Table 4.24 presents this cross-classification, and it may be observed that within these groups the factor of wealth operated differentially: among German children aged fifteen to nineteen school enrollments decreased above the median wealth of $1,250; among Irish children there is a sizable increase in school enrollments above the median wealth line. The differences in children's activities, as measured by school enrollments, reinforce the validity of the traditional distinction between the "shanty" and the "lace" Irish. Similar differences for the German born, however, are not reflected in enrollments of children with German born fathers. When we compare both the Irish and the Germans for the urban Northeast and the entire northern United States, the differential impact of wealth is dramatic for those belonging to families with an income less than the median. Among families from the two major immigrant groups whose economic fortunes left them below the median wealth line, school enrollments were cut by more than half in the Northeast relative to enrollments for all children in the same region; on a national scale, school enrollments were cut by slightly less than half compared with children in the entire northern sector. Thus, wealth and father's place of birth combined to reduce school enrollments for children of ages fifteen to nineteen of the two major immigrant groups relative to the mean in the Northeast and the northern United States.

Table 4.24   School Enrollment (SCH) for Nuclear Children Fifteen to Nineteen Living in the Urban Northeast in 1870 by Birth of Father and Family Wealth

Country or Region of Father's Birth	SCH by Median Wealth ($1,250)	
	Below $1,250	Above $1,250
German	.10 (N = 31)	.04 (N = 26)
Irish	.17 (N = 86)	.37 (N = 30)
Northeast	.35 (N = 118)	.38 (N = 135)
All	.22 (N = 291)	.33 (N = 219)

Source: Samples of 5,539 for median wealth below $1,250 and 5,821 for median wealth above $1,250.

Conclusion

By 1840 it had become clear that the common school was to shoulder the major responsibility for the achievement of mass literacy in the United States. Educators had not, at least in their rhetoric, dismissed the home as an important environmental influence in achieving basic literacy, nor had they overlooked the importance of the Sunday school and religious tract societies in bringing the proper moral vision to the young. Nonetheless, they had engaged themselves in the process of modernization which brought with it a greater differentiation of labor among social institutions. Increasingly, the concerns of school reformers turned to eradicating inequalities of schooling prior to the age of adolescence, since it was critical before this age to stress the teaching of literacy skills and the importance of schooling to moral economy. Common school reformers had committed themselves to the idea that universal public education at the primary level was a necessity in the face of demographic, social, and economic change and that the skills of literacy offered the most efficient way to deal with such changes. These changes were uneven to be sure, and the problems of educational reform differed according to geography and population density. Still, the settling of the frontier, a persistent inequality of wealth amidst a growing industrial economy, a religious confrontation which brought a new source of violence to major urban areas, and the emergence of a new pluralism were basic conditions which affected most Americans at some point in their life cycles. To contend with these conditions and at the same time fulfill the expectations of those who looked to the common school both as a means to the acquisition of basic literacy and as a panacea for social ills was a formidable problem for the reformer. The ideology of literacy which had emerged prior to 1840, and which continued throughout the period of common school reform, asserted that literacy was a virtue in its own right as well as an instrument to achieve social amelioration and to extend to the dispossessed the prospect for upward economic mobility. By mid-nineteenth century, the school was to be the major institution for effecting that ideology. It is no wonder, then, that the teaching of reading became a topic for national debate in mid-nineteenth-century America, and that school administrators and teachers were expected to offer some assurances that their efforts to achieve mass literacy were productive. In short, they were asked to demonstrate that the common school could, in fact, function as the institutional guarantor for the promises of an ideology of literacy. This they attempted to do in their annual reports and professional journals.

The quality, sequence, and regularity of instruction were key issues among all who saw fit to speak on the topic of reading instruction. While accurate comparisons with the period prior to 1840 are difficult to make, the common school did well following 1840 in providing instruction for basic literacy and in socializing the young in matters moral and civic.

As we have seen, the great majority of children in the age category five to nine attended school in the North, and this fact helped to guarantee the efficacy of the school in terms of socialization; moreover, from an experiential standpoint, the meaning of literacy and the meaning of schooling were much the same in these early years. The approximately eleven hundred hours of reading instruction given by the common school to children who attended regularly between the ages of five and eleven was sufficient for the attainment of literacy. As we have noted, the ability even to read in McGuffey's second reader was a substantial achievement. To meet the expectations of teachers who equated the study of grammar with the achievement of literacy was to move beyond basic literacy itself. Achievement of reading skills at either level undoubtedly met the literacy requirements of all but the most technical occupations. The substance of reading matter itself over this period of instruction surely was sufficient, also, to properly socialize all but the incorrigible.

Both sexes in both rural and urban areas were able to participate extensively in schooling in their early years as students, although some advantage may have belonged to the urban youngster because of the longer, and hence more regular, winter term. Rural children who attended both summer and winter terms might receive nearly the hours of reading instruction given to the urban child. The child who attended school regularly undoubtedly became literate early in his or her life. Reading literacy was probably achieved by age eleven, and writing literacy soon followed. Many children, as we have already remarked, were probably literate in both by age nine. This situation itself, however, was all the more frustrating for the child unable to attend school regularly. Indeed, the simple fact that parents had become dependent upon the common school made this great panacea a source of disillusionment. In all likelihood, those children who were unable to attend school regularly and whose parents did not have the leisure time to teach them would have reached adulthood as illiterates. For the poor, it was only with the greatest difficulty that literacy might be transmitted without the aid of formal schooling.

By 1880, it was with some misgiving that reformers looked beyond the individual in their moral vision of social amelioration and the eradication of crime and poverty through schooling. With obvious disillusionment they began to observe by 1880 that prisons were "filled with men and women the great majority of whom can read and write." While their short-range objectives were achieved in terms of school attendance for younger children, their expectations for the social utility of education were unfulfilled: "It is easy to see that something more than these acquirements is necessary to prevent crime, to reform criminals. The school therefore should have a broader outlook [which encompasses industrial training]."[113] A similar disillusionment was apparent in the reports of school commissioners and superintendents when they addressed their commentaries to problems of absenteeism and irregularity of attendance, both of which were related to the work-school patterns of youth. The relationship of schooling and work in the lives of children had already become one of the major concerns for educational reformers by 1870 and later was to become a major topic for theory building among progressives concerned with the place of leisure time in a work-school–oriented economy. Already by 1850 the problematic relationship between work and school had become one of several elements in the issue of nonattendance and irregular attendance. These problems were, in turn, part of the broader concern with properly socializing the young through schooling and the attainment of literacy. Thus, not only was school attendance itself critical in the technical achievement of literacy skills, but the continuity of experiences provided by regular attendance was considered important to internalizing the social values for which the school was responsible.

By mid-century, educational reformers had good reason to believe that literacy and economic status were related variables and that a higher level of literacy would lead to greater wealth. Wage differentials for literates and illiterates certainly reinforced this element of the ideology of literacy. Schooling itself had become the major institution through which literacy was achieved, and, by inference, it was then to serve as a gateway to economic success. The link between school attendance and economic success, then, was intimate in the eyes of reformers. Inequalities of schooling would be transformed into inequalities of literacy. In a very real sense, the success of the mission of the school seemed to rest on the capability of reformers to induce children to attend school regularly and to persist in their efforts at attendance. If most youth could attend up to their early adolescent years, there was a good chance that writing as well as reading skills could be mastered at a level to permit entry to most occupations.

As we have noted in this chapter, inequalities of educational opportunity unquestionably persisted in the mid-nineteenth century and were linked to factors of age, region, urbanity, ethnicity, order of birth, and wealth. The disparities in school enrollments between North and South persisted, and as we see in chapter 5, the same regional differences were present in literacy rates. The factor of urbanity in the South had abated in importance, however. In one sense, the redistribution of wealth in the South following the Civil War helped diminish the strong link between wealth and illiteracy. Yet the destruction of wealth which accompanied the war left the South, temporarily at least, in a disadvantageous position with respect to the expansion of public schooling. Eventually, as the

South experienced economic recovery, it is likely that the political commitment to cultural intervention through education became a major determinant of declining illiteracy rates.

We have seen that school enrollments differed between farm and nonfarm groups of children, and it is likely that this was true because of differing work patterns among rural and urban youth. More important, however, was the relationship of age to school enrollment. Here it was evident that up to age nine, wealth was not an important determinant in school enrollments. For ages ten to fourteen, however, it was; and, as we noted previously, it was between ages nine and eleven that one could expect children to be classified as literate. Thus, removal from school prior to this age (unless attendance had been continuous) was a major decision facing parents, but especially those whose wealth classification was low. Children leaving school before achieving literacy probably received lower wages than those who left after having achieved literacy, and we must observe that leaving school for early work was not a viable alternative unless it would keep the family from poverty.

The interaction of wealth and ethnicity is one of the most important themes developed in this chapter. In our examination of the quantitative dimensions of acculturation it has been pointed out that the problem of acculturation as it related to the public school extended beyond the child to the parents and grandparents alike. It was noted that differences in school enrollments related to the nativity of grandparents began to appear modestly in the ten to fourteen age-group and were accentuated in the fifteen to nineteen age-group. In the case of the latter, the probability of enrollment for children of native born grandparents was twice as great as for children with foreign born grandparents. Concordantly, the proportion of children engaged in occupations is considerably higher among those of foreign born grandparents than among those whose grandparents were native born. We would expect that both school enrollment and work would contribute to the acculturation of the immigrant child—the former through the deliberate proselytizing efforts of the teacher and the textbook, the latter in the more circuitous but nonetheless effective way of employer demands in the way of behavior conformity.

Between the ages of five and fourteen, and particularly between the ages of ten and fourteen, the children of the foreign born participated in school at a level commensurate with those of native born parentage. The school played a lesser role in the acculturation of children who themselves were foreign born, although it is certainly possible that their occupational experience outside the school at an early age offered a different route to Americanization. It is quite evident that the school, if it were to affect the process of acculturation among immigrant children, would have done so between the ages of five and fourteen, where enrollments were highest among the different ethnic groups—as high or higher, in fact, than among the children of the native born.

It was during these ages that children, if they attended regularly, mastered the basic learning skills, and one would expect that former disadvantages attributable to the higher illiteracy rates among adult immigrant parents would be overturned by teacher diligence. Moreover, the importance of peer group relations in early adolescence in conjunction with the high rates of school enrollment among major ethnic groups in this age range suggests that among children of ages twelve to fourteen there was ample opportunity for the school to inculcate behavioral norms which would lead to upward economic mobility. We do not know, however, whether such inculcation actually took place. We know that school texts promoted these norms; we do not know whether children learned them, nor what teacher values intervened between text and child.

The native versus foreign born differences in school enrollments for the age group fifteen to nineteen were likely to affect the future chances of these youngsters as they entered the meritocratic structure of American society. In chapter 5 the nature of this structure is explored more fully, but it should be emphasized at this point that with the achievement of mass literacy at the basic level, differences in the level of literacy skills would become increasingly important for occupational selection. The level of literacy achieved by youngsters fifteen to nineteen who had attended school regularly no doubt far exceeded most occupational demands for literacy. Critical in this respect was that employers had some efficient means to select personnel and, as we have observed previously, that literacy was a convenient and easily applied measurement of achievement. Thus, despite having attained basic literacy, children of the foreign born were likely to be at some disadvantage in economic advancement from having left school in early adolescence. This was not because basic literacy had not been achieved, but because so many had achieved it that the usefulness of literacy as a tool for job selection was diminished. For those youngsters who had not attended school even to age ten, the prospects for economic advancement were severely diminished, although, as we observe in chapter 5, not completely denied. Among these latter youngsters, the sons of illiterate fathers were conspicuous. As we observe later, the intergenerational perpetuation of illiteracy was an important dimension in explaining literacy rates.

Finally, the impact of wealth was certainly a significant (although a differential) factor in the activities of children between the ages of fifteen and nineteen, and its impact may be measured both within and between ethnic groups—the Germans and the Irish, for example. Among those families whose income was below the median, the effects of both wealth and country of origin combined to influence the activities of children in the later stages of adolescence. The Irish children provide the most dramatic example of the decisive impact of wealth on school enrollment between the ages of fifteen and nineteen. A comparison of the German school enrollment proportions with other groups, however, suggests that the German family valued the educational experience of the public school less than did other groups for their children in later adolescence, but that this particular attitude of the German family was accentuated by those in the upper half of the wealth distribution. We must conclude, then, that family wealth was a significant but differential variable in the process of acculturating the children of immigrants within the public school. Among older adolescents the process of acculturation probably did not include the achievement of basic literacy; such achievement would only have occurred if these older children had attended school very irregularly or entered school at a later age. For the most part, fifteen- to nineteen-year-olds attending school had probably achieved basic literacy in the early grades. What they had to gain from longer attendance was a higher level of literacy. In this respect, it is clear that children of the native born had a distinct advantage over those of Irish born or German born parents, that greater school attendance by children of the native born in the fifteen- to nineteen-year age-group could lay the foundation for an intellectual elite in the United States.

Five

The Extent of Illiteracy and Its Socioeconomic Consequences, 1840–70

Introduction

Between 1800 and 1840, the efforts of editors, publishers, printers, school officials, and advocates of expanded common schooling had resulted in an ideology of literacy which linked the traditional values of home and religion to an emerging nationalism. Accolades to the enlightened conditions of the new republic were common and, undoubtedly, inspirational. They did, however, miss the mark of reality in many instances, although, as we have seen, reformers were highly successful in their efforts to enroll children of ages five to nine in school. Some of the instances alluded to above have been documented in court actions involving illiterate individuals. In looking at the judgments handed down by courts in these matters, we are able to take note of the various ways in which illiterate individuals were dependent upon the reading and writing skills of others and to observe the extent to which the law protected illiterates.

Decisions and statutes pertaining to affadavits, bills and notes, contracts, deeds, elections, evidence, executors and administrators of estates, juries, mortgages, perjury, and wills all have aspects relating to our subject matter. It is unfortunate that the records of decisions are often confined to higher courts and frequently cannot be found even there. Decisions of lower courts may have described numerous situations involving unlettered individuals; yet these are unavailable, and the vast majority of possible adverse decisions would not likely be appealed since the illiterate was likely to lack economic resources. Probably the most salient instance of illiterate dependency is found in the making of wills. It is of the utmost significance in decisions concerning wills that a testator unable to read or write is often treated the same as one who is blind. This reasoning seems valid because, when the unlettered testator is deceased,

148

he is not there to describe the visible or audible circumstances of the making and signing of the will.[1] There is a strong implication that a will with a signature had been read and understood by the testator if evidence to the contrary is not presented. For illiterates, however, the entire question of the circumstances existing at the time of the making of the will has been the subject of many suits. An appreciable number of these have been appealed, and the extenuating circumstances for the specific cases, as ascertained in courts of law, have been published.

The general principles governing the conditions or circumstances under which the will of an illiterate testator was valid or invalid were those established for the signing of deeds. These principles had been set forth early in English law (Thoroughgood v. Cole, 1582) and were compiled by Blackstone for later use.[2] Thoroughgood's case was an action in trespass which had resulted from the signing of a deed by the unlettered Thoroughgood. The case is often cited because of its great importance in the history of contract law, but its discussion of illiteracy also made it a frequent precedent for later cases involving illiterate or blind testators. In Thoroughgood it was held

> 1st, that a deed executed by an illiterate person does not bind him, if read falsely either by the grantee or a stranger; 2ndly, that an illiterate man need not execute a deed before it be read to him in a language which he understands; but if the party executes without desiring it to be read, the deed is binding; 3rdly, that if an illiterate man execute a deed which if falsely read, or the sense declared differently from the truth, it does not bind him; and that though it be a friend of his, unless there be covin.[3]

It has been considered indispensible that an illiterate or blind testator understand the contents of his will. In the case of Thomas Hemphill et al. v. James Hemphill et al. (1830) in North Carolina, however, it was declared that the valid execution of a will of a blind or illiterate man did not depend upon the will having been read to him in the presence of witnesses. The decision, which reflected what could be termed a laissez-faire principle of contractual relations, noted that it was undeniable that "illiterate and blind men are liable to be imposed upon." It concluded, however, that "at all events, they are allowed to make contracts and wills without the law laying down any inflexible rule that the validity of their acts depends upon its being proved that they were read to them."[4] Thus, the illiterate person, like others, was to have freedom of contract, although it is obvious that he was at a greater disadvantage in exercising his intent.

The reading of a last will and testament in the presence of a testator was not considered sufficient evidence to establish the fact that an illiterate or blind testator understood the contents of the document. The opinion in an

1849 case (Clifton v. Murray) stated that the perpetrator of fraud may act as easily by falsely reading the will as by falsely writing it. As the court recognized, the problem is further complicated by the right of the testator to make his will in secrecy, since he is subject to pressures from interested parties. This might be increasingly true in the case of an illiterate, since secrecy is more difficult, if not impossible, to maintain in the presence of witnesses in the instance of an oral reading.[5] In the eighteenth and nineteenth centuries, school arithmetic books contained sections on commercial arithmetic and legal documents, and a literate individual could copy the form for a will, make appropriate additions, and have it witnessed by a disinterested party. Thus, secrecy was maintained. This was a relatively simple process and quite understandable. To one unable to read and write, however, this simple procedure was unavailable without the aid of a literate friend.

With other types of personal and business documents, such as bills, notes, and mortgages, there are numerous examples illustrating the handicaps of unlettered individuals when engaging in the "signing" of such agreements. The opinion of Chief Justice Shaw in Nathaniel Atwood v. James Cobb (1834), a case to "recover damages for the nonperformance of an agreement to convey...real estate," described the difficulties of illiterates when they were confronted with a written document:

> considering how often agreements are necessarily drawn up by illiterate persons, incapable of expressing their intentions with clearness and certainty, and the injurious consequences which would follow if effect should not be given to such agreements, it must be a rule of construction governing courts of justice, not wholly to reject such instruments, as uncertain, if it is possible, with the helps allowed to be brought to the aid of such construction, to ascertain the meaning of the parties.... And in construing all instruments, and especially those which are informal, illiterate, hastily and unskillfuly drawn, the intent of the parties, if possible, is to be ascertained, without regard to technical rules.[6]

A reading of other cases gives the impression that courts have been surprisingly lenient in assuming that illiterates did not understand the written nature of the agreements. This has tended to mean that the literate parties to these agreements must make great efforts to ascertain that the illiterate parties have understood the stipulations attached to the contract. Ironically, the burden of illiteracy would fall, in some cases, on the literate party, particularly if the illiterate, knowing the leniency of the courts, were lax in his commitment. On the other hand, there was probably a certain reluctance of the illiterate individual to enter into such engagements at all.

Two additional cases will illustrate the handicap of illiteracy in the economic world and document the problems of the illiterate in business transactions. The first (1870) involved the defense in a fraud case, the plaintiff being Mr. Atchison, a man who was unable to read and write and who had signed a note for $140. In 1868 two men had gone to the home of Atchison proposing that he become an agent to sell reapers, screw-forks, and mowers. At first he declined to do this on the ground that he would not become bound for anything. The strangers assured him he would incur no obligation, and he then assented. The implements were to be sent to him and sold on commission, the terms being agreed upon. The two men then proposed to give him an instrument for Atchison's protection in making sales since the articles had been patented. The document was presented to Atchison for his signature, and, since he was unable to read it without difficulty, he requested that it be read to him. One of the men then purposefully "misread" the document. They then produced another paper, which they assured Atchison was a duplicate of the one read to him, and he signed both papers. The papers were much larger in size than an ordinary note, and Atchison was unaware that he had signed a note. The papers, as it turned out, were merely a ruse to obtain Atchison's signature on a $140 note. Fortunately for Atchison, his credibility was greater than that of the opportunists, and the litigation was settled in his favor.[7]

The second case, that of Walker v. Ebert (1870), involved Mr. Ebert, a German by birth and education who was unable to read and write the English language. Ebert alleged that the holders of a note bearing his signature had cheated him by falsely claiming that he would become the sole agent for his town of a certain patented machine for a period of ten years. One of the machines was to be delivered to him free of cost, excluding freight, and Mr. Ebert was to receive 50 percent of all profits from his sales. The holders then presented to him to sign, in duplicate, an instrument partly written and partly printed which he was unable to read and which was stated to be simply a contract covering the oral agreement. The original decision in favor of Walker was reversed and a new trial ordered.[8]

The cases reflect the dependent position into which the illiterate individual was cast when dealing with contractual agreements. It would be inaccurate to describe the illiterates in these instances as "marginal" people, that is, people who had been separated from the mainstream of American society by their illiteracy. Rather, they may more properly be described as dependent and, in these particular cases, exploited. A similar description, it will be remembered, was also used to portray illiterate parties entering into contractual agreements during the colonial period. The dependency of the illiterate person in 1870, however, was more acute than in 1670, for contractual instruments (particularly executory ones) had become more sophisticated by mid-nineteenth century. Consequently, they were also more liable to abuse. The foregoing cases illustrate the principle of dependency, as formulated in an earlier 1821 Pennsylvania case involving a misunderstanding because three individuals were "unlettered men not understanding the English language."[9] The described particulars of that case made it clear that in business dealings, an illiterate "marksman" must have the agreement correctly read to him and that this places him in a special position of dependency. The observation made in Hemphill v. Hemphill (1830) that "illiterate and blind men are liable to be imposed, and that they are sometimes imposed on" was of even greater moment as written documents became increasingly sophisticated in the later nineteenth century.[10]

We do not know the extent to which social theorists, political observers, and critics of mid-nineteenth-century schooling were aware of the difficulties of illiterates in dealing with contractual matters, although it is certain that these difficulties existed. We know, however, that criticisms of the existing state of education and literacy emanated from a variety of sources, and among the most poignant of these were social theorists such as Davies, Simpson, Sedgwick and Wright, the workingmen's political unions, and, in the case of Massachusetts, the state legislature. In part, the problem was one of differing estimates of educational opportunity and the quality of literacy among youth in the working force. A number of reformers no doubt realized what Charles Davies had axiomatically declared: that "the diffusion of knowledge becomes . . . the distribution of power."[11] This surely was the principle assumed by Frances Wright when she asserted that the common school, while rightly conceived in the "noble example of New England," could not possibly operate in a way to reach the children of the poor. The acquiring of reading and writing skills—the chief instructional (not socializing) objective of the common schools—could not be achieved in manufacturing districts where children worked twelve hours a day. The appropriate corrective action, said Wright, was a system of graded schools within each district to be financed by a "moderate tax per head for every child" and a graduated property tax.[12]

Poverty and child labor were frequent objects of criticism for those committed to social amelioration through education and the achievement of basic literacy. The twelve- to thirteen-hour day of the child laborer, reported the Senate Committee on Education in Massachusetts, left "little opportunity for daily instruction."[13] The same was found in the Philadelphia factories, and of the children employed in Pawtucket manufacturies in 1830, it was estimated that "not more than one-sixth [of them] are capable of reading and writing their own name[s]."[14] William Shaw, in sworn testimony before a Senate investigating committee in

Pennsylvania, thought that "no attention is paid to education during the time [children] are employed in factories, except what they receive from Sabbath schools, and some few at night schools, when they are in an unfit condition to learn." He added, "the children attend Sabbath school with great reluctance [and] many will not attend in consequence of the confinement of the week."[15] In New York City in 1830, an urban center with a "much more efficient system of education" than Philadelphia, 24,000 children between five and fifteen years of age were said to "attend no schools whatever."[16]

The reasons for differing estimates of the equality of educational opportunity and the extent of illiteracy are not too obscure. First, the United States had entered into the nineteenth century with an illiteracy rate of approximately 25 percent in the North, and a figure from 40 to 50 percent in the South. Within this rather sizable rate, however, were wide variations at both state and county levels. Second, the idea of a common school for every locality had achieved immense general popularity by the late 1820s and early 1830s, but was inoperative for a number of particular communities. For critics and optimists alike, however, the fundamental problem was the fact that there were still too many illiterates to guarantee that the moral mainstays of American culture would not waver. The price for illiteracy was a social and moral price, and commentators on the social and economic costs of illiteracy were fond of putting their case in terms of the link between crime, poverty, and illiteracy. The warden of the Eastern State Penitentiary in Pennsylvania offered a typical observation in 1840 when commenting on illiteracy among the inmates:

> [The] smaller offences [larceny and horse-stealing] are generally committed by the most ignorant and debased; ignorant of both the common rudiments of school learning, and also in moral culture; for it appears that 593 could read and write; 312 could only read; and 377 could neither read nor write. In fact, of those who are thus indicated as being able to read and write, and read only, there are but a small portion who can read with *facility,* and still fewer who can write a sentence correctly. While it appears that only 233 were bound and regularly served an apprenticeship, 269 were bound and left their masters, and 785 were never bound. Of their debaseness, 914 admit they were intemperate, and 104 used spirituous liquors occasionally.[17]

Social order and moral stewardship continued to be favorite themes for the reform-minded through the Civil War, and officials at all levels of government translated their concerns into statistical reports. Thus, we find at the local level, for instance, the February 1851 Report of the Cuyahoga County Jail (Cleveland, Ohio) listing sixty-five inmates, 72 percent of whom were illiterates, a finding remarkably consistent with that of 73.7 percent illiteracy among inmates in Massachusetts county jails in

1854.[18] Twenty-one percent and 65 percent of Cuyahoga County Jail inmates were between the ages of eleven and nineteen, and twenty and thirty, respectively. These boys and men were convicted usually for the crimes of larceny and assault and were 92.4 percent Catholic, 49 percent Irish, and 38 percent American.[19] Lengthier and more comprehensive reports were also published at the state level as may be seen in table 5.1 for the case of Pennsylvania.

Table 5.1   Reading Proficiency of County Jail and Poor House Inmates in Pennsylvania, 1867

	Number	Proportion
Jail inmates		
Read well	64	.15
Read a little	200	.48
Cannot read	156	.37
Poorhouse inmates		
Read well	174	.20
Read a little	225	.27
Cannot read	443	.53

Source: Report of the Superintendent of Common Schools of Pennsylvania, 1867 (Harrisburg, 1868), pp. 374-75.

By the time of the Civil War, the rhetoric of moral consensus, nationalism, and enlightenment through public education had been linked ideologically to a moral crusade against slavery. "Our present national difficulties," said the Cleveland Leader in 1863, "show the value of our free schools and the danger and cost of neglecting to educate the masses of the people. Without free schools, a free government cannot long survive."[20] A year later the same paper took note that "two thirds of the Rebel hordes now in arms against their country are unschooled." "How is the government to protect itself against the people?" it was asked. "Not by standing armies as in the old world," was the answer, "but by a school system that shall reach every child." Two weeks later, the Leader continued its argument by contrasting the famous Massachusetts statute of 1647 which required each township having fifty householders to appoint a person to teach all children to read and write, with Virginia Governor Berkley's now infamous statement in 1671 thanking God "there are no free schools." The message was clear, according to the Cleveland Leader: "These characteristic documents show that in this instance 'coming events cast their shadows' sometimes 'before.' They are remarkably correct condensations of the antagonistic civilizations that have come to maturity upon the continent since they were written."[21]

Once the war had ended, the educational message was apparent to northern reformers: bring civilization to the South. In some cases, reformers acted with a vengeance, supposing—incorrectly, of course—that the South was unfamiliar with the concept of the free common school. Some were more judicious in their efforts and acted in the spirit of benevolent paternalism. The latter was undoubtedly the guiding spirit behind the following advice offered in 1868 to those who would remake the South in the educational image of the North: "All the encouragement and assistance given them by the people of the North will be judiciously bestowed, as we may hope for more good results from the education of the poorer classes in the South than from the most comprehensive reconstruction legislation."[22]

Within the context of military confrontation, moral suasion, and a political commitment to social homogeneity, efforts to move the United States toward universal literacy persisted. In the remainder of this chapter we examine the social, economic, and demographic variables which intervened between the rhetoric of reform and the success, or lack thereof, of achieving mass literacy. These variables, as it were, reflect the basic social realities which confronted reformers and which, in the long run, determined whether their efforts were well spent.

Variations in Illiteracy Rates
The National Perspective

The national picture of illiteracy as given by the 1840 census was one of 550,000 illiterate white adults twenty-one and over in an entire population of 6.4 million aged twenty-one years and over. If we make allowance for illiterates exactly twenty years of age, and for counties not reporting, this yields an illiteracy rate of .093, or approximately 9 percent.[23] This illiteracy rate is considerably less than the .35 rate of markers among army enlistees in the same period. In the case of army enlistees, a comparable rate of .07 is not reached until about 1880. Regionally, the variation in rates was what we might expect from our assessment of literacy in the late eighteenth century; that is, the Northeast and Northwest had illiteracy rates of .03 and .09, respectively, while the rates were .19 and .17 for the Southeast and Southwest. These rates for all regions are minimal since they measure only those who were avowedly illiterate. No test was given the individual, nor was he asked to sign or make his mark on the census return. Some recent findings might help illustrate the problems associated with census enumerations of illiteracy. For 1969, the Census Bureau had determined that the proportion illiterate was .077 for whites.[24] This figure is substantially less than the 16 percent of white adults whose 1975 performance level in reading was minimal from the standpoint of functioning in the economic world.[25] By 1860, the illiteracy rate had decreased somewhat to about 7 percent; in 1870, the illiteracy rate rose slightly to approximately 9 percent. The reasons the rate in 1860 was lower than in 1870 are difficult to assess with certainty. It is possible that differences for the two years may be only a matter of measurement error. More detail was gathered on literacy in the latter year, and the inquiry by census takers was expanded to include those ten to nineteen. Two questions were asked: Can you read, and can you write? It was found that 25 percent more could not write than could not read, and this fact alone could account for the difference. The 1870 definition of illiteracy was made more explicit for the enumerators by inclusion of the statement, "Very many persons who will claim to be able to read, though they really do so in the most defective manner, will frankly admit that they can not write." This warning was not included in the instructions of 1860 and 1850. We do know that there was a long-run trend toward increased school learning, but we also know that the Civil War brought about great disruption in the schooling process. We are not prepared, however, to assert any real changes, or cause for these changes, in the figures for one decade. Thus, it is not the changes in this one decade which are of interest but, rather, the differences in illiteracy rates *within* the 1860 and 1870 data. These differences will allow us to examine more thoroughly the demographic, social, and economic variables affecting illiteracy rates.

Sex and Age and Illiteracy

Differences in illiteracy rates, because they may be associated with labor patterns and commercial activity, raise certain questions regarding the possibility of sex differences in illiteracy due to different work patterns of males and females and the greater importance of the family in the transmission of literacy in sparsely populated areas. Our sample of 3,493 married couples in 1860 and 6,607 in 1870, not standardized for age,[26] indicates a definite sex differential in illiteracy. The magnitude of the difference varied from an illiteracy rate of .09 for women in 1860 compared with .07 for men. In 1870 the rates for women and men, respectively, were .10 and .09. Differences were accentuated in the South, where the illiteracy rate in 1860 was .15 for women compared with .11 for men. In the North the comparable rates were .06 for women and .04 for men.

One explanation for the sex differential is that the women did not have the occupational experiences which would demand the use of letters. Our sample of married women for 1860 and 1870 has only 2 percent of women with a stated occupation, although nearly 100 percent of the males listed an occupation. The property of these married women averaged but $35 in 1860 and $145 in 1870, and, indeed, only 1 percent were recorded as owning property above $100 in 1860 and 6 percent in 1870. The census results reflected the dominant view that the place for the woman was in the home. Occupational listings for women in the urban sector alone were also low, with only 3 percent having stated occupations.

Illiteracy rates of married women, classified by age, give some indication of an upward trend in literacy. Women of younger age had lower rates, and the tendency was toward a methodical increase with age. This was true for 1870, where our sample was much larger, and specifically for women in the North; in this case the rate by five-year intervals from age twenty to fifty-nine was thus:

Age Class	IL
20–24	.06
25–29	.06
30–34	.09
35–39	.08
40–44	.08
45–49	.09
50–54	.09
55–59	.11

This positive relationship could be attributed to natural selectivity, whereby women who married early were more likely to be literate. It also could be attributed to the fact that women were more likely to forget how to read and write because of disuse; this could occur because their occupations of housecare did not demand reading and writing. More likely, however, the positive relationship between illiteracy and age arose because of a general improvement from decade to decade, from 1830 to 1860, in the schooling of women. By 1840, common schools did not discriminate in terms of the number of hours of instruction they provided females and males in reading and writing. If school attendance itself increased among females, then literacy rates would likely increase according to an age differential, as we have just observed.

Some hints concerning the use women had for reading and writing can be obtained from the occupation and nativity figures of table 5.2. The lowest illiteracy rate is found among native born women in northern cities, who were probably exposed more frequently to newspapers, libraries, schools, manuals of child rearing stressing the importance of reading, and churches, even though the great majority of them did not work away from their homes. It is significant that the illiteracy rates for native rural women in the North were roughly half-again as large as those of their counterparts living an urban life, and this appears to have been the case in the South, at least after the war. The ordinary work patterns, and greater isolation from institutions promoting and serving literacy, would seem to have mitigated against equality of literacy, despite formal schooling, in rural areas. Ratios of female illiteracy to male illiteracy indicate that native born women in cities did not suffer from sex discrimination in basic education after the Civil War:

Female-Male IL Ratios in
the North in 1870

Native born, farm	1.14
Native born, nonfarm	1.03
Foreign born, farm	1.18
Foreign born, nonfarm	1.26

For the remainder of the nineteenth century the long-run downward trend in sex differences might be anticipated from the 1870 data, since we know that women at young ages had no higher illiteracy rates than did men. The published statistics for 1890 allow us to observe this trend. We may note, for example, that the ratio of female to male illiterates in the United States in 1890 for the age classifications ten to fourteen, fifteen to nineteen, and twenty to twenty-four were .81, .76, and .96, respectively; for age classifications twenty-five to thirty-four, thirty-five to forty-four, forty-five to fifty-four, and fifty-five to sixty-four, the ratios were 1.07, 1.15, 1.37, and 1.64. The ratio for those sixty-five and older was 1.78.[27]

Rates for foreign born women in the North were two to four times as large as for native born women, and with respect to the former, the rural-urban distinction was not important. Like the wives of farmers, the options open to foreign born wives in cities to participate in schooling and the cultural or lettered life of the city seem to have been limited either by traditional familial patterns mitigating against female participation or unfamiliarity with available opportunities. Unlike the native born married women in northern cities, among whom equality of literacy with men had become an established fact by the late nineteenth century, the wives of farmers and those who were foreign born retained, at least temporarily, their traditional lexical inferiority.

Table 5.2 Illiteracy Rates (IL) of White Married Women by Nativity and Residence of the Woman and Occupation of Her Husband, 1860 and 1870 in the United States

	IL North		IL South	
	1860	1870	1860	1870
All	.06	.08	.15	.18
Native born	.04	.05	.16	.19
Foreign born	.12	.14	...	.14
Farmer	.06	.07	.16	.20
Native born	.05	.06	.16	.20
Foreign born	.11	.12	...	...
Nonfarmer	.06	.08	.14	.14
Native born	.03	.04	.16	.14
Foreign born	.12	.15	...	...

Source: Sample of 3,493 married couples in 1860 and 6,607 in 1870.

State and Regional Variations in 1840

The presence of large state and regional variations in illiteracy rates merits considerable attention, and we turn for this to a detailed analysis of the 1840 federal census. Census enumerators in 1840 were directed to ask the head of each family, "How many white persons in your family over twenty years of age cannot read or write?" The definition of illiteracy, then, was given as one who cannot read and write, as determined by inquiry. One who could read and write in a foreign language or in English was considered to be literate. Unlike the 1840 census, the federal census of 1850 gathered data for individuals rather than for each family. Thus, it becomes possible, using 1850 data, to learn about illiteracy for individuals within the nuclear family. For instance, if a twenty-one-year-old son were illiterate, was this also true of his father and mother? If a father were illiterate, was he more or less likely to have his children enrolled in school? What were the illiteracy rates for different age-groups of males and females?

The data in the following list show the disparity in illiteracy levels that existed among different states. While the figures for the unlettered of Connecticut were really no larger than the number who might be placed in institutions, illiteracy rates five hundred miles farther south, in North Carolina, were dramatically larger. As we may observe below, the rate for adult whites rises steadily in 1840 as we travel from .003 in Connecticut to .04, .04, and .05 in New York, New Jersey, and Pennsylvania, to .08 in Maryland, .19 in Virginia, and .28 in North Carolina.

North Carolina	.28	Maryland	.08
Tennessee	.24	Louisiana	.06
Arkansas	.22	Iowa	.06
Georgia	.20	Ohio	.06
South Carolina	.19	Pennsylvania	.05
Virginia	.19	New York	.04
Delaware	.18	New Jersey	.04
Alabama	.18	Rhode Island	.03
Kentucky	.17	Michigan	.02
Missouri	.15	Vermont	.02
Indiana	.15	Maine	.01
Illinois	.14	Massachusetts	.01
Mississippi	.12	New Hampshire	.006
Florida	.10	Connecticut	.003

(source: *United States Census*, 1840). The same North-South vector may be observed in 1850 census data also. The pattern of increasing illiteracy from North to South is the most important of our initial observations and certainly is the one which first needs explanation.

Table 5.3 State Illiteracy Rates (IL) of Army Enlistees
       in the United States, 1799-1829

	IL
North Carolina	.58
Virginia	.47
Maryland	.50
Pennsylvania	.46
New Jersey	.41
Connecticut	.25
Massachusetts	.21
New Hampshire, Vermont, and Maine	.26

Source: Sample of army enlistees, National Archives,
Record Group 9, various boxes.

A most obvious explanation for the variation among states along a North-South axis is that states with high illiteracy rates at the beginning of the century continued to have high rates as they approached mid-century. Some support for such a contention may be found by observing illiteracy rates among our army enlistees, classified by place of enlistment, for the period 1799–1829. These are noted in table 5.3. Thus, while the absolute levels of illiteracy vary substantially between the two sets of data, the same regional differences are found. A second explanation of the North-South vector focuses on climate and terrain and suggests that the fertility of the land determined, at least in part, the vocational activities of men and that these, in turn, affected the demand for skills in reading and writing. The proportion of men engaged in commerce, manufacturing, and the professions rose from .07 in North Carolina to .17 in Virginia, .27 in Maryland, .31–.37 in New York, New Jersey, and Pennsylvania, to .35–.46 in Connecticut and Massachusetts. The complements of these proportions essentially represented those engaged in agriculture. The assumption could then be made that nonagricultural pursuits would be more likely to demand the use of reading and writing, at least on a sustained day-to-day basis. This hypothesis of positive correlation of the degree of commercial activity and literacy, or conversely, the magnitude of subsistence farming and illiteracy, can certainly be tested statistically. While we cannot undertake such an analysis here, the relationships would undoubtedly be quite complex, varying with the size of operation. Thus, an area of many small retail, wholesale, and manufacturing concerns could have a literacy rate higher than an area dominated by one or a few manufacuring concerns. Agricultural communities with many farms of moderate size might very well have had higher literacy than those dominated by a few plantations.

A third explanation of the trend would focus on illiteracy–school attendance configurations. Regional variations are very evident as observed in figure 5.1 and show the high correlation between school attendance for white children and illiteracy among adults aged twenty and over in

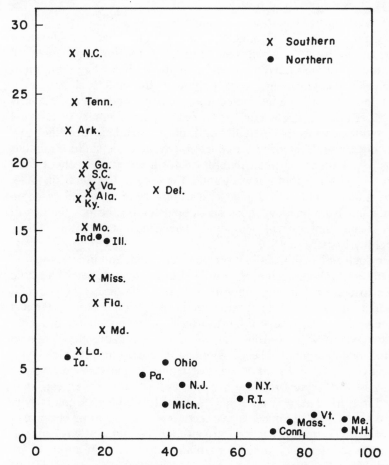

Figure 5.1
Relation between illiteracy and school enrollment for twenty-eight states in 1840. (Source: *United States Census*, 1840.)

twenty-eight states. The hyperbolic shape of the relationship is dictated largely because there is little variation in southern attendance. There is a strong negative pattern for northern states, however, with the more recently settled states tending to have less-developed school systems. The inverse pattern is far from perfect, but the rank ordering relates perfectly with our direction vector as we move from Connecticut to New York, New Jersey, and Pennsylvania and on to Maryland, Virginia, and North Carolina.

There were large variations particularly before 1850 in available schooling for the young. Connecticut, for instance, had a tradition of schooling dating to 1650 which had been given the force of law: "All parents and those who have the care of children, shall bring them up in some honest and lawful calling, or employment, and shall teach or instruct them, or cause them to be instructed to read, write, and cypher, as far as the four first rules of arithmetic."[28] Of course, enforcement of this and similar statutes was exceedingly difficult, but it nonetheless testifies to a general concern with the need for education in the basic skills. From our previous list of states and their illiteracy rates according to census data, we may also observe that illiteracy rates for 1840 in Connecticut, Massachusetts, and New England in general were very low, and bordered on levels not much larger than those accounted for by the populations of blind, deaf and dumb, insane, and idiots. The same states continued their low illiteracy rates as of 1850.

A state such as North Carolina, on the other hand, had little in the way of a tradition of schooling and, in 1840, had fewer schools per white child aged five to eleven than any other state except Arkansas. Moreover, it had the highest illiteracy rate of any state in the Union. In understanding the depressed literacy levels of North Carolina, the comments of a concerned citizen of North Carolina are instructive because they point to attitudinal, demographic, and economic factors contributing to high levels of illiteracy. His remarks, in a series of letters to the Raleigh *Register* beginning in 1829, categorize the problem according to seven causative factors. First, he said, was poor and uninspired teaching. Second, there was an aversion to taxation because of economic hardship and because of the belief that taxation was contrary to a republican form of government. Third, he noted intergenerational perpetuation of ignorance, during which the uneducated "become avowed partizans of mental darkness against light, and are sometimes seen glorying in ignorance as their privilege and boast." Sparse population and a lack of commercial opportunities which would bring a flow of funds from abroad and from other areas and thus raise income sufficiently to allow greater expenditure on education were cited as factors four and five. There was a further need, he noted, to illustrate for the unlettered that benefits derived from the cotton gin, steamboat, and locomotive engine were related to education; the utility of education must be demonstrated. Finally, an unwillingness to surrender individual liberty by having society run schools with the concomitant regulation and compulsory measures was cited as an obstacle to general enlightenment.[29]

The fact that less than 20 percent of southern children from five to fifteen years of age were attending schools in 1840 may mean that only about half really had even the most minimal schooling. This is a distinct possibility if the relative distribution of attendance in the South was at all similar to that in northern states with known distributions. Given such a possibility, why, then, was illiteracy for southern adults not higher than it was? Surely it might have been that many children and young adults learned to read from their parents, friends, employers, and fellow workers, in which case the availability of handwritten or printed materials in the form of letters, broadsides, newspapers, pamphlets, and books must have had a major impact on literacy rates. Thus, we are able, in accord with our previous discussion of ideology and institution building, to suggest a fourth explanation of differing illiteracy rates which postulates a relationship between literacy and the availability of printed materials.

By 1840 there was good reason to believe that the enthusiasm for printed materials of an earlier period had been translated into economic activity; that, in turn, such activity had borne fruit in terms of reducing illiteracy; and that an ideology of literacy had made its impact as had the institution building which accompanied it. Newspapermen of the early nineteenth century were beset by difficulties in the manufacture of rag-pulp paper, and advertisements for clean linen and cotton rags in exchange for cash or books were common. The following, for example, appeared in the *Western Spy* of Cincinnati in 1821:

RAGS WANTED

American Preceptors
School Bibles, on fine paper
Picket's Juvenile Spelling Book
Webster's American Spelling Book
Writing and Letter Paper,
Will be given for clean LINEN or COTTON RAGS, at
four cents per pound....[30]

Guaranteeing a regular supply of paper in frontier areas was complicated by the difficulty in financing local paper mills. As the nation expanded westward, however, enterprising founders of paper mills in the early Northwest made their appeals to the area's residents by arguing that the regional production of paper would reduce the cost of books and newspapers. To support their appeals, they spoke of the virtue of frugality and the good of the community when they asked "the industrious and good people of the neighboring towns and settlements" to preserve their linen and cotton rags. "Certainly it is respectable to save, but shameful to waste," said the proprietors of a newly founded paper mill in Steubenville, Ohio, while adding a final patriotic note in their attempt to establish a local paper mill: "The reflection of doing good things for our country, surely must be a gratification to every generous mind."[31]

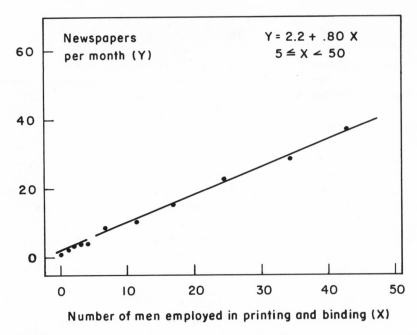

Figure 5.2
The average number of newspapers per employee in printing and binding for 1,163 counties in the United States in 1840. (Source: *United States Census*, 1840.)

The causal relationship between level of literacy and level of imprint production or men employed in print production is a difficult one to establish. Our findings, however, suggest an alternative to the causal model implicit in Schofield's warning that "changes in the volume of production [of publications] may be influenced by many factors other than changes in the level of literacy." Schofield's point is well taken as is his observation that "there is no necessary relationship between the volume of production and the size of readership."[32] Yet it is a point which assumes that the direction of causation is from literacy to imprint production. The model may have severe restrictions, however. When illiteracy is very high, that is, when no general commitment to mass literacy is in evidence, it makes good sense to assume that printers produce in limited quantities for a select and stable literate group. Once an ideological commitment to mass literacy is made, however, the possibility of expanding markets for print becomes a vital consideration. Expanded markets lead to greater profits if the widespread availability (and potential attractiveness) of print materials can serve as an inducement for illiterates to learn to read. In short, one can promote the reading habit by making print materials easily accessible. Nowhere is this promotion more evident than among newspapermen themselves, and it is here that one must con-

Percentage
Illiterate

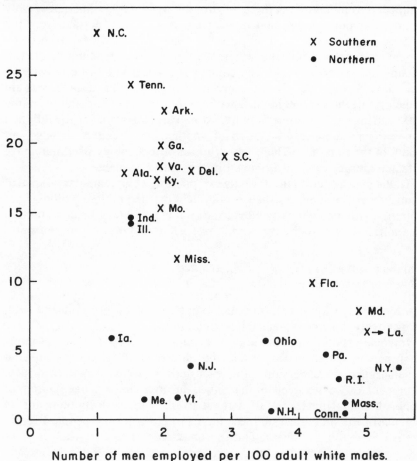

Figure 5.3
Relation between illiteracy and number of men employed in newspaper production in 1840.
(Source: *United States Census*, 1840.)

sider the possibility that the direction of causality in the literacy-print linkage is reciprocal.

By the mid-nineteenth century, advances in printing and paper-making technology had helped to create the conditions necessary for mass consumption of printed materials. Newspaper production increased rapidly in the first half of the nineteenth century; printing and binding rose accordingly. For 1840 this relationship is expressed in figure 5.2, which expresses the linear relationship between increased employment in printing and binding and the number of newspapers produced per month. Moreover, labor force participation in printing showed an inverse relationship to illiteracy, as the configuration in figure 5.3 illustrates. Only Maine, Vermont, Iowa, and most likely New Jersey detract from the general scheme. We might expect this finding for Iowa because of its recent settlement, and the others by their close proximity to Massachusetts and New York. The capital invested in the printing industry was about 5 percent of that invested in manufacturing, and the figures are indicative of the general importance of written or printed materials in the total scheme of economic activity. Moreover, a state with roughly five times the newspaper production of another could expect to have but one-fifth the illiteracy. Thus, the diffusion of technology itself may have affected literacy rates as it made printed matter available.

Having suggested four alternative or possibly complementary explanations, we now attempt to shed further light on the problem by looking at counties with high illiteracy rates to see if it is possible to be more precise in explaining why such large variations in illiteracy rates were present.

Illiteracy at the County Level: Urbanity and Indices of Development

Each of the 1,161 and 1,565 counties reporting illiteracy in 1840 and 1850, respectively, may be classified by its illiteracy rate (IL). The data of table 5.4 indicate the exceptional area dispersion in the 1840 data. Assuming each person within a county had the illiteracy rate of that county (an assumption of no dispersion within each county), we can say that, in 1840, 5 percent of adults lived or had lived in areas having one-quarter of America's total illiteracy, 10 percent lived in areas accounting for 44 percent of the illiterates, and less than 15 percent of the people lived in areas accounting for one-half of the unlettered. The Gini coefficient of concentration, a measure of relative dispersion, is .63 (table 5.4) in the 1840 case, although it had abated somewhat to .52 by 1850.[33] For 1870 there was even further abatement. The published data for 1870 allow us to compute the illiteracy rates for all males and separately for white males twenty-one and over.[34] The main thrust of the figures is that there was much less dispersion in area inequality than existed in 1840. Examination of table 5.5 illustrates the fact that the Gini coefficient was significantly smaller than it had been previously. This means that counties in southern Ohio, Indiana, and Illinois had had marked improvement and that the new counties added west of the Mississippi had little population weight. Figure 5.4 illustrates the fact that southern portions of middle-west states and southwest Pennsylvania still had higher rates than farther north.

Our list of the counties with the highest illiteracy rates for northern states and those which had essentially no slavery prior to the Civil War

Table 5.4   Counties in the United States in 1840 and
            1850, Classified by Illiteracy (IL) of
            Adult Whites

IL (lower class limit)	Number of Counties	
	1840	1850
.001	343	279
.05	162	268
.10	242	343
.20	190	264
.30	115	148
.40	68	105
.50	41	58
Average IL	.089	.104
Gini coefficient of concentration	.63	.52

Source: United States Census, 1840 and 1850.

Note: Counties reporting no cases of illiteracy have
        been iliminated. The concentration coefficient
        is computed assuming each individual in a
        county had the county IL rate. The class
        limits of the table are .001-.0499; .05-.099,
        . . . , .40-.499, and .50-1.00.

includes four counties in Kansas, two in Minnesota, and four in Texas.
The Minnesota counties were in the very northwestern part of the state
and are contiguous to Canada. At least three of the Texas counties were
near or contiguous to the Gulf of Mexico. All ten reported illiteracy rates
of over 71 percent, but they represented only .1 percent of the population.
At the same time that these new frontier areas of low literacy were
created, we find that former areas of low literacy had substantial
improvement. Thus, as increased settlement resulted in greater population density, our list of the ten counties with the highest illiteracy rates in
1840 exhibited marked improvement in thirty years; the average dropped
from .47 for whites in 1840 to .19 for males in 1870.[35]

The rapidly expanding Northwest more than held its own relative to the
Northeast in terms of basic literacy. Counties were forming rapidly but
not so rapidly as to keep pace with the population, since it is evident that
the average number of people increased more than 10 percent in the
decade. The population density was increasing in counties, and this was
likely to be strategic in the formation of educational institutions such as
libraries, schools, and churches. The thesis that population density is
closely related to illiteracy—a thesis for which a mathematical model was
suggested in chapter 2—may be further investigated by observing figure
5.5, which plots size of county by IL for 1850. There is tremendous
variation in population size from county to county. The Gini coefficient of
.60 in this case is as much as that arising from wealth distribution among

Figure 5.4
Illiteracy in the United States in 1870. (Source: *The Statistics of the Population of the United States*, Ninth Census, vol. 1 [Washington: GPO, 1872], p. 392.)

individuals in farm communities, and it was much larger than it is today. (Adjustment to the number per square mile in each county would only accentuate the difference, since sparsely populated counties tended to have larger land areas.) Thus, any learning characteristics related to size of population might be expected to have, in turn, a substantial effect on literacy.

Table 5.5 Northern County Illiteracy Rates (IL) for Males Twenty-One and Older, Weighted by Size of Adult Male Population, 1870 and 1840

Average County IL for Adult Males (lower class limit)	Adult Males, 1870 White and Colored	White	Adults, 1840, White
.001-	.013	.016	.306
.01-	.032	.039	.146
.02-	.181	.204	.132
.04-	.235	.288	.076
.06-	.235	.193	.137
.08-	.096	.102	.054
.10-	.159	.131	.024
.20-	.027	.021	.073
.30-	.010	.004	.036
.40	.012	.002	.016
	1.000	1.000	1.000
Average	.079	.068	.049
Gini coefficient	.373	.339	.625

Source: United States Census, 1840 and 1870.

Note: The number of counties in the North was 458 in 1840 and 1,158 in 1870. The Gini coefficient has been computed assuming each adult had the illiteracy rate of his or her county.

Illiteracy rates shown in figure 5.5 are not perfectly correlated with population size, but they do show definite inverse relationships for population ranges from the very smallest to those with 20,000 to 30,000; illiteracy tended to rise a little beyond this level. Thus, the importance of population density in our analysis of literacy rates in colonial America is reaffirmed for the nineteenth century, although, as we will see, certain qualifications are in order. The Gini coefficient of illiteracy, sorted by population size, is .184 for the North and .156 for the South.[36] Certain aspects of the mathematical formulation stated in chapter 2 have been explored in greater detail with regression techniques. It was necessary, however, to limit our analysis to differences among counties in 1850 and to rule out change over time because of the limited availability of statistics. It was found that county wealth per capita was a more sensitive factor than county density in its negative association with illiteracy.

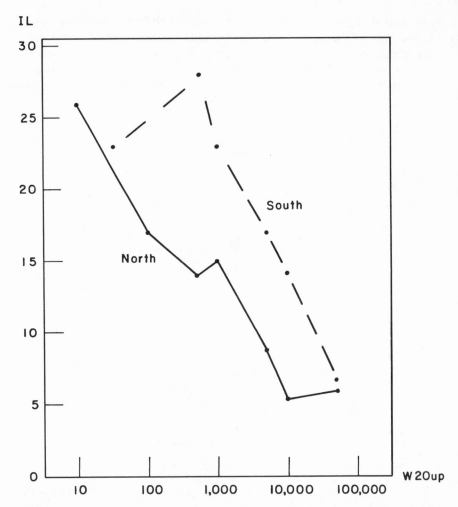

Figure 5.5
Relation between the illiteracy rate (IL) and the adult white population twenty and older
(W20up) in each county in the United States in 1850. (Source: *United States Census*, 1850,
for 1,565 counties.)

Other factors lessening illiteracy were the number of books per
capita and the larger proportion of persons native to the county (a function of settlement history). The most significant factor of all in terms of
sensitivity or in terms of elasticity was the number of schools. The county
with 10 percent more schools per person had an illiteracy rate over 20
percent less than an otherwise comparable county, as determined by
holding other variables constant. A multiple regression analysis of county
data for 1850 demonstrates that the number of schools is paramount in

lessening illiteracy rates. The wealth of the county has a greater statistical importance in curtailing illiteracy than does population density; the number of books is highly related to lower illiteracy, but an anomaly occurs in the case of church accommodations. One possible formulation stems from the data for northern counties: $ILL = -2.10 - .17P - .28W - 2.28S - .51V + .43C - .87B + .47R$, where ILL is the logarithm of the proportion of adult whites who were illiterate, P is the log of the white population twenty and older, W is the log of the wealth (aggregate cash value of farms plus capital invested in manufacturing) per white adult, S is the log of the number of schools per white adult, V is the log of the number of book volumes per white adult, C is the number of church accommodations per white adult, B is the proportion of the population born in the state, and R is the proportion of accommodations which were Roman Catholic. (Values of W, S, and V which were zero are entered as 1 or .1; counties with more than 50,000 adult whites have been excluded and $N = 657$ and $R^2 = .17$. The equation for southern counties has coefficients for P, W, S, and V, respectively, of $-.04$, $-.50$, $+1.63$, and $-.14$ with $N = 865$ and $R^2 = .26$.) It should be understood that this is an analysis in only one year, capturing only differences reflected by variation among counties. Our mathematical formulation of chapter 2 conveys more importantly the impact of change over time. The 1850 data reflect time only insofar as some counties had had longer settlement histories than others.

The theme that sparseness of population is associated with a general low level of literacy may be further investigated by observing the general quantitative relationships which held between illiteracy and commonly accepted measures of economic and cultural development. It is apparent from table 5.6 that a general inverse correlation exists between county IL and the variables of (1) commercial and manufacturing activity, (2) the number of schools, and (3) the number of students. If we compare illiteracy rates for the lower-class limits of .01 through .60 and up with the proportion of the labor force engaged in commerce, manufacturing, and the professions, the inverse correlation continues unabated in linear fashion. For example, the proportion of the labor force engaged in commerce, manufacturing, and the professions is .35, .12, and .05 for the illiteracy classifications .01–.049, .20–.29, and .60 and up, respectively.

For 1870, as in 1840, it is noted that illiteracy classes for counties are obviously associated with indices of development, as pictured in table 5:7. The relationship, as before, is an inverse one and dramatizes the fact that illiteracy patterns, urbanity, and wealth were meaningfully related. The last two, in turn, helped determine the manner and extent of publicly financed schooling. The proportion of improved acreage, the cash value per acre, and the capital employed in manufacturing per adult male decline, with one exception, as male illiteracy increases. Thus, for example,

Table 5.6 Indices of Development for Counties in the United States in 1840, Classified by Illiteracy

Illiteracy Rate (lower class limit)	Number of Counties	Number of White Males 20 and Older (average)	Proportion of Labor force in Commerce, Manufacturing, or Professions	Number of Schools per 100 White Children 5-15	Number of Students per White Child 5-15
.01-	343	10,633	.35	1.22	.54
.05-	162	4,893	.22	.92	.37
.10-	242	2,991	.15	.72	.24
.20-	190	2,535	.12	.61	.17
.30-	115	2,408	.09	.54	.15
.40-	68	2,468	.09	.44	.11
.50-	28	2,116	.07	.41	.10
.60 and up	13	1,992	.05	.17	.06
	1,161				

Source: United States Census, 1840.

Note: Not shown are the ninety-two counties reporting no illiterates since they were in areas of appreciable illiteracy and obviously constituted cases of noncompliance. Weighted averages have
been employed using county adult white populations. An exception is the column of adult
white numbers, in which weights of one per county were used.

Table 5.7   The Proportion of Improved Acreage to Total Farm Acreage (IMP),
the Average Cash Value per Farm Acre (CV), and the Capital
Employed in Manufacturing per Adult Male (CAP) Related to
Illiteracy Rates (IL) for Adult Males in Northern Counties of the
United States, 1870

IL (lower class limits)	IMP	CV	CAP
.0001-	.66	$ 9.60	$210
.05-	.70	14.60*	365
.10-	.58	9.50	265
.20-	.46	6.20	159
.30-	.34	2.70	84
.40-	.22	1.80	24
.50-	.18	2.30	17

Source: The census data for 1,185 county averages, weighted by the adult
population.   Not included are 32 counties reporting no illiteracy.

*New York County and Philadelphia County were eliminated.

the proportion of improved acreage declines from .70 to .18 as county
illiteracy rises from .05 to .50; the cash value per acre drops from $14.20
to $2.30 for the same county illiteracy rates. Capital employed in man-
ufacturing per adult male drops from $365 to $159 to $17 as county illiter-
acy rates rise from .05 to .20 to .50.

For 1840, the linear relationship between indices of economic development and literacy is also observable when illiteracy values are plotted
against number of schools per 100 white children five to fifteen years of
age and number of students per white child five to fifteen. For an illiteracy
rate classification of .01–.049, the number of schools per 100 white children five to fifteen is 1.22 and the number of students per white child five
to fifteen is .54. At the other end of the spectrum for an illiteracy rate
classification of .60 and up, the number of schools is .17 and number of
students is .06. These values taken from table 5.6 imply not only that urbanity is associated with a drop in the number of uneducated and illiterate, but that it causes this drop by making educational facilities available.
We find, for instance, that those counties with illiteracy rates ten times as
large as other counties had one-fifth the number of libraries and three-
tenths the number of books:

	Adult Illiteracy Rates	
	.0001–.049	.20–.29
Number of Counties	379	264
Number of libraries per 1,000 adults	2.5	.5
Number of volumes per 1,000 adults	620	180

Table 5.8   The Number of White and Black Males Attending School as a
            Proportion of the Male Population Five to Eighteen (SCH) for
            Counties in the United States in 1870, Classified by the
            Proportion of Males Twenty-One and Older Who Were Illiterate
            (IL)

	SCH, 1870		1840 School Enrollment Rate, White Males and Females, Adjusted to Age 5-18	
IL	North	South	North	South
.0001-	.75	.40	.47	.14
.05-	.72	.62	.37	.15
.10-	.70	.53	.27	.14
.20-	.53	.40	.17	.12
.30-	.34	.29	.14	.11
.40	.18	.24	.13	.08
.50 and up	.17	.16	.15	.07

Source: 1870 and 1840 census data. A factor of .8 has been used in
adjusting 1840 age data from five to twenty-one to five to eighteen.
Tables 5.4 and 5.6 describe the 1840 counties.

Note: County rates are weighted by the male population twenty-one and
      older in computing class averages. There were 1,158 counties in
      the North and 1,027 in the South.

Table 5.9   Publication Indices and Illiteracy Rates for Counties in the
            United States in 1840

Illiteracy Rate (lower class limit)	Number of Newspapers per 20,000 White Males 20 and Older	Number of Binderies per 10,000 White Males 20 and Older	Number of Men Employed in Newspaper Production per 100 Adult White Males	Capital in Printing and Binding per 100 Adult White Males
.001-	3.8	1.0	4.9	$25
.005-	2.7	.4	2.5	12
.10-	1.9	.3	4.7	13
.20-	1.7	.1	1.2	6
.30-	.7	.04	.6	3
.40-	.8	.0	.5	2
.50-	.2	.0	.2	1
.60-	.0	.0	.0	0

Source: United States Census, 1840.

In table 5.8 it will be noted that the inverse relationship between school attendance and illiteracy is even stronger in 1870 than it was in 1840, probably indicating that with the surge in public school development, areas of low population density and little wealth were falling behind in a relative sense, although over a period of twenty years they had gained in an absolute sense. Further evidence of the positive relationship between the availability of print and lower illiteracy is apparent in table 5.9, which compares publication indices and illiteracy for counties in 1840. It may be observed that some counties indicated no newspapers, but did report men engaged in printing and binding. This meant that there were at least some broadsides, notices, and documents that were in circulation, although their extent is unknown. A regression of the number of newspapers related to the number of men employed in printing has the implication at the vertical intercept of a fraction of a newspaper. This indicates at least some publishing activity.

Enterprising publishers and newspapermen, as we have seen in chapter 3, were anxious to create a reading public for their sales. Moreover, by 1830, newspaper editors were able to take advantage of both packet and road postal routes to distribute their publications to areas well outside their immediate village or city areas. Nonetheless, it must be said that they were dependent on population density for marketing their materials, and one would expect that a decent profit was more difficult to attain in low-density areas. Conversely, population density itself would be affected by an influx of commercial activity, although, in the case of printed materials, that activity was not so labor-intensive as was the building of canals and roads, for instance. It would seem, then, that the commercial activity associated with the production of printed materials was dependent upon population density and that this dependency did restrict the availability of published materials in sparsely populated areas. Likewise, this very restriction placed more of a burden upon individual families migrating to such areas to bring with them the needed materials to promote literacy and learning. The point was well illustrated by Mrs. Sedgwick's "Puzzled Housewife," a serial which ran in the 1842 *Cincinnati Enquirer,* where she remarked of the difficulties in educating her children amidst frontier conditions, "When I know that the material wants of my family are provided for, I devote myself to the intellectual education of my children; and here, faraway from schools and masters, I pour into their minds the knowledge I acquired in my youth."[37] This, no doubt, was sage advice for the enterprising Yankee moving westward. Those families in which parents were illiterate might be doubly disadvantaged when they "pulled up stakes" to move toward the frontier. In areas where low population density accompanied by high illiteracy had been the rule for generations, the same dilemma would persist in a vicious cycle which linked low population density, little publishing and printing activity, and low literacy levels.

Finally, the relationship between urbanity and illiteracy might be illustrated by examining a special, separate sample of 11,645 individual white families drawn from the census for the southern United States—a region which, as we have seen, generally exhibited a high rate of illiteracy. The proportion of southern families who were illiterate in 1840 was .29 for heads of families in the agricultural sector and .11 for those in the nonagricultural sector. There was undoubtedly a greater proportion of young nonfarmers in the South in 1840 than there had been forty to fifty years earlier. The proportion of heads of families in the nonagricultural sector of the South in 1840 was .16 and .17 for those aged twenty to twenty-nine and thirty to thirty-nine, respectively. For those sixty to sixty-nine and seventy and up, the proportions were .10 and .07.[38] It is possible that there was a tendency for people to shift to farming in old age, although it is unlikely that such a trend would be enough to counterbalance the shift of the young to nonagricultural pursuits. The shift to the urban or quasi-urban sector of the economy was accompanied by a reduction in illiteracy. The illiteracy rate among heads of families for those aged twenty to thirty-nine engaged in agriculture was .30; for those in nonagricultural pursuits it was .09. Among the forty to fifty-nine age-group illiteracy rates were .28 and .13 for those engaged in agricultural and nonagricultural pursuits, while for those aged 60 and over the illiteracy rates were .32 and .20, respectively, for the agricultural and nonagricultural occupations. The rates not only indicate the differences over time for the agricultural and nonagricultural sectors of the economy, but show a decrease in illiteracy within the urban sector. The development of common schools within urban areas undoubtedly contributed to this increase in literacy among urban dwellers.

Personal and Demographic Characteristics
of Illiterates
Wealth and Illiteracy

From the fact that illiteracy was strongly and inversely related to indices of development, we now move to the question of whether or not literacy and wealth were related at the family and individual levels. In our southern data, one major exception seemed to mitigate against the positive relationship between literacy and economic development in the aggregate—the advantages of wealth at the family level. For our sample from the South, we must hypothesize that in the absence of sufficient schooling in the immediate area of residency, the wealthy would have sufficient resources to purchase materials published at distant points and shipped with great care and expense, and to hire tutors or send their children to schools out of the area. We would expect to find, then, that wealth and literacy would be positively related and that differentials in wealth would be accompanied by differentials in literacy. The causal relationships presumed to exist here would be that wealth contributed to literacy by making it possible to procure the tools of literacy, namely, books and schools.

Table 5.10 The Proportion of White Male Families in the South in 1840 Who Were Illiterate (IL), Classified by the Number of Slaves Owned per White Family

Number of Slaves per White Family	Proportion of Families Illiterate		
	All	Agriculture	Nonagriculture
0	.350	.38	.15
1	.176	.22	.06
2	.146	.18	.03
3-4	.139	.15	.02
4-9	.119	.13	.02
10-19	.098	.10	.02
20 and up	.045	.05	.00

Source: The sample of 11,645.

When the proportion of white families in the South in 1840 who were illiterate is cross-classified by number of slaves owned and subclassified by nonagricultural and agricultural pursuits, the pattern is quite obvious, as seen in table 5.10. For those with no slaves, the proportion of illiterate families was .35 overall, .38 for those engaged in agriculture, and .15 for those not engaged in agriculture. For families owning five to nine slaves, the proportions were .12 (overall), .13 (agricultural), and .02 (nonagricultural). The proportion of illiterate families among those having twenty or more slaves was .045 overall, .05 for the agriculturalists, and .00 for the nonagriculturalists. Even though four to five of every one hundred families comprised one or more adults unable to read and write, it is quite clear that the wealthy possessed a literacy that the poor did not.[39] The relationship persists in agricultural and nonagricultural settings alike.

The 1860 and 1870 censuses enable us to study the Civil War and its aftermath, which saw as violent a redistribution of wealth as we have experienced in the United States. The questions which arise regarding this violent decade are (1) was there a stronger negative association between wealth and illiteracy in 1870 than in 1860, and (2) were the less wealthy classes more likely to be uneducated after the war? The extreme case of a meritocracy would be one with the uneducated, if not the least capable, at the bottom of the economic ladder and the educated at the top. Michael Young has created the hypothetical nightmare that those with no ability would remain essentially at the bottom from generation to generation. A few of the children at the bottom might rise and a few of the progeny of the

Table 5.11 Cumulative Proportions of Illiterates, Classified by Age and the
Cumulative Proportions of Wealthholders (N_w) for Free Males in
1860 and White Adult Males in 1870 in the United States

N_w	1860				1870			
	All	20-29	30-39	40-99	All	20-29	30-39	40-99
.10	.03	.03	.00	.02	.03	.06	.04	.03
.20	.08	.12	.03	.06	.09	.13	.10	.05
.30	.12	.28	.08	.11	.15	.22	.13	.11
.40	.23	.41	.15	.17	.25	.35	.22	.19
.50	.36	.62	.35	.22	.37	.45	.33	.26
.60	.46	.70	.41	.34	.52	.55	.44	.38
.70	.65	.77	.57	.44	.63	.66	.59	.52
1.00	1.00	1.00	1.00	1.00	1.00	1.00	1.00	1.00
G	.18	.04	.25	.34	.16	.11	.22	.28

Source: A sample of 4,833 for 1860 and 9,125 for 1870 drawn from the census
manuscripts.

meritorious might retrogress, but the relationship would be stable.[40] We
will investigate the intricate relationships in this connection.

If we array or sort all males from highest to lowest on the basis of
wealth, we can then count the number of illiterates between or above
given wealth levels. As seen in table 5.11, the top 10 percent of wealthholders in 1860 and 1870 comprised enough illiterate persons to account
for 3 percent of the male illiterates.[41] If illiteracy bore no relationship to
wealth, that is, if illiterates were randomly distributed along the wealth
scale, we would have about 10 percent. The top 20 percent of wealthholders in 1860 had 8.0 percent of the illiterates. There were 36 percent
above the median wealth value. Approximately 30 to 35 percent had no
wealth, and we can randomly distribute illiterates in this range. If there
had been no association between the cumulative proportions of illiterates
(IL_w) and the cumulative proportions of wealthholders (N_w), then IL_w and
N_w would have been about the same at all levels, and the Gini coefficient
of concentration *(G)* would have been zero; the Lorenz curve would
have been an undulating diagonal line. If there were perfect meritocratic
correlation, all illiterates would have been at the bottom and the Gini
coefficient would have been approximately 1.0. The Gini coefficient of
.185 indicates the extent of the correlation in the spectrum between .0 and
1.0.

The comparison between 1860 and 1870 reveals that there was no
strengthening of the meritocratic system in this decade but, rather, a
weakening. There was actually a greater proportion of illiterates in the top
decile range, (.033 instead of .029) and the Gini coefficient was less (.164
instead of .185). The results could be perplexing in an initial analysis. It
might have been presumed that a society based more on urban wealth, a
society with the North now dominating the economy, would have a

Table 5.12 Cumulative Proportions of Illiterates (IL$_W$), Classified by Cumulative
Proportions of Wealthholders (N$_w$) for the North and South for Free
Adult Males in 1860 and White Adult Males in 1870

N$_w$	IL$_w$ North		IL$_w$ South	
	Free Adult Males, 1860	White Adult Males, 1870	Free Adult Males, 1860	White Adult Males, 1870
.10	.023	.030	.007	.042
.20	.092	.090	.060	.106
.30	.123	.149	.100	.181
.40	.223	.232	.207	.290
.50	.339	.345	.360	.421
.60	.438	.474	.473	.549
.70	.631	.600	.639	.663
1.00	1.000	1.000	1.000	1.000
G	.200	.196	.203	.117

Source: A sample of 4,833 for 1860 and 9,125 for 1870 drawn from the census
manuscripts.

stronger positive correlation between literacy and wealth. A glance at the
regional data in table 5.12, however, indicates that the disruption was
largely a southern phenomenon. The meritocratic system of 1860 in the
South had been dramatically scrambled by 1870 so that correlation between wealth and illiteracy was only half as strong as before. There was
no more dramatic a change than in the top decile ranges; the established
wealth groups with their private tutors and academies institutionalized for
decades had been altered.

In the emerging northern economy in the United States in 1870, there
were stronger wealth-literacy correlations in the urban than in the rural
areas; the native born in urban areas had the highest Gini coefficients of
any group as shown below:

	North	South
Rural	.186	.156
Urban	.206	.146

Compared with the era of thirty years earlier, the ability to read and write
had undoubtedly become an even more important asset in commercial
and business activity than in farming. Contractual relations were more
sophisticated, and the rise in importance of the executory contract in
commerce and business dealings further disadvantaged the illiterate person. As seen in tables 5.11 and 5.12 literacy was also an important determinant of economic advancement during the individual's life cycle, a
fact which lent support to school reformers' claims that literacy through
schooling enhanced upward economic mobility.[42] Table 5.11 shows that
age and illiteracy were related in the context of wealth. More younger
illiterate men (ages twenty to twenty-nine and thirty to thirty-nine) were

able to achieve an economic standing in the top percentiles of wealth than those men forty and over. The brawn or strength of these younger men no doubt served them well and helped to offset any disadvantage due to lower levels of education, but the gradations in the percentile groups are clear. For example, the top 10 percent of wealthholders included 6 percent of the illiterates aged twenty to twenty-nine, 4 percent aged thirty to thirty-nine, and 3 percent aged forty to forty-nine. The same linear relationship is evident in each successive group for 1870. For 1860, the relationship is not so strong but is still very much in evidence. The nation's economy still made it possible for roughly 40 percent of the illiterates to obtain a fair beginning standard of living, and it was still possible for a young unlettered man to have, for instance, several hundred or thousand dollars in savings so that he could easily have more than the median wealth of his age-group. It demanded more literacy skill, however, to remain at or to rise above the median wealth among older individuals, so that the progress in the economic life cycle of the illiterate became more limited.

Fertility and Illiteracy

Aside from the advantages of wealth, only two conditions would seem capable of breaking the low population density, high illiteracy pattern: (1) a high fertility rate combined with a low death rate and little migration, which would gradually increase population density to a point which made printing and publishing a viable commercial activity, and (2) direct intervention by superior governmental authority in the affairs of communities experiencing such a pattern. The former case would represent a slow, evolutionary, and uncertain process of "self-correction," and might be considered as a possible counterfactual alternative to the intense activities of educational reformers in mid-nineteenth-century United States.

We may begin our discussion of illiteracy and fertility by examining a subsample for the southern United States. Here, fertility rates for illiterates were substantially higher than for literates in 1840 as shown in table 5.13. The fertility rate was one and two-thirds to almost twice as great in the class with the largest illiteracy rate as compared with the class with the least illiteracy. To test the relationship between fertility and illiteracy for the country as a whole, we may, in turn, use data from the 1870 census, which enables us to treat the individual rather than the county as the microcomponent for study.[43]

Three basic questions arise regarding the subject of fertility in 1870. (1) Did illiterate males marry earlier in life than literates? (2) If so, did it follow that illiterate fathers were younger when their first children were born? (3) Did this group father more children than did a group with at least some education? The answers to all of these questions are important because they help us to better understand how illiteracy was perpetuated

Table 5.13 Fertility in Southern Counties in 1840, Classified by Illiteracy

Illiteracy Class (lower class limit)	Proportion Illiterate, Adult White Males, 20 and Older	Number of White Children Aged 0-9 per Adult White Woman Aged 15-49
.001-	.019	1.19
.05-	.072	1.41
.10-	.149	1.57
.20-	.242	1.61
.30-	.338	1.67
.40-	.446	1.67
.50-	.539	1.74
.60-	.637	1.77

Source: United States Census, 1840, for 1,161 counties reporting illiteracy.

and, thus, how illiteracy might be eliminated. The numbers of illiterates in our sample are not large enough to allow study of the subset of married individuals for age classifications of the young. We may consider, however, all males, either married or unmarried, and the proportions having at least one child living in the home. This proportion is shown below in a subsample of 9,125 from the census of 1870:

Age Class	North		South	
	Lit.	Illit.	Lit.	Illit.
20–29	.305	.295	.377	.520
30–39	.707	.762	.810	.893
40–99	.749	.732	.812	.815

The demographic pattern of the life cycle of adult males could be portrayed first with a line representing the probability of marriage at any given age, followed by a line representing the probability of having one or more children living at home. The peak in the latter curve was about .75 (see table 5.14, age class forty and up) in the North, so at best it was only a three-quarters truth that children were in the home to do the reading and

Table 5.14 The Proportion of Adult White Males in the United States in 1870 Who Were Married (MAR), Classified by Literacy, Age, and Residence

Age Class	MAR North		MAR South	
	Lit.	Illit.	Lit.	Illit.
20-24	.16	.15	.23	.36
25-29	.49	.47	.58	.74
30-39	.71	.76	.81	.89
40 and up	.75	.73	.81	.81

Source: The sample of 9,125.

Note: The minimum cell sample size is 54.

Table 5.15   The Average Number of Children Living with an Adult White
Male Twenty and Older (CHIN), Classified by Age and
Residence of Adult Males in the United States, 1870

Age Class	CHIN North		CHIN South	
	Lit	Illit.	Lit.	Illit.
20-29	.51	.53	.64	1.01
30-39	2.04	2.50	2.62	3.31
40 and up	2.51	2.74	3.14	3.33

Source: The sample of 9,125.

writing for the illiterate parent. We note from table 5.14 that there was a greater tendency for illiterates, as compared with others, to have children when the husband was in his thirties, while the reverse was true after he was in his forties. In the northern sector this phenomenon was not attributable to earlier marriage. The figures in table 5.15 demonstrate significant differences only in the South. There the illiterates clearly had a higher probability of being married in the age span from twenty to forty. The figures for the North show small and mixed results, due largely to small sample sizes for the illiterate groups. At best, we can conclude that there was no difference in the timing of marriage in the nonslave states. Still, there is no question that the fertility rate of illiterates was significantly larger than that of literates not only in the South, but also in the North. The fact that marriage rates in the North did not differ between the two groups—literate and illiterate—had a bearing on the result that there was little difference in fertility for the age-group twenty to twenty-nine, but does not alter the overall finding that fertility was greater among illiterates. Thus, we see in table 5.15 that the average number of children living with an adult white male twenty years of age or older was greater for illiterates than for literates.

Differences in fertility were associated with occupation and nativity as well as region. Fertility was one-third to over half-again as large for farmers as for nonfarmers, and the same pattern prevailed essentially for literates as for illiterates except that the latter had 5 to 20 percent *more* children for each classification. In the North, fertility rates were also one-third to half-again as large for foreign born as for native born. Table 5.16 illustrates these findings. Within the foreign born group, illiterates also had higher fertility ratios, a finding consonant with that of Hareven and Vinovskis in their study of child bearing in Salem and Lynn, Massachusetts. Their findings for these urban communities in Essex County showed that "the fertility ratios of illiterate foreign-born women were 19.2 percent higher than those of literate foreign-born women." Literacy, they conclude, "was an important determinant of fertility" even when controlling for the occupation of the husband.[44]

A child was of greater economic value to an illiterate person if he or she

Table 5.16   The Average Number of Children of Adult White Males
in the United States in 1870 (CHIN), Classified by
Occupation and Nativity

	CHIN North		CHIN South	
	Lit.	Illit.	Lit.	Illit.
All	1.71	2.03	2.12	2.50
Native born	1.59	1.91	2.15	2.54
Farmers	1.89	2.32	2.41	2.64
Nonfarmers	1.32	1.40	1.58	2.19*
Foreign born	1.94	2.11	1.96	1.96*
Farmers	2.40	2.59	2.09	...
Nonfarmers	1.76	1.95	1.93	...

Source: The sample of 9,125.

*Includes only twenty-three cases.

remained in the nuclear family or in the immediate vicinity, particularly
if he or she became lettered. The earnings of children could also be of
greater importance to illiterate families if the latter tended to have less
income and wealth. From table 5.17 it is apparent that illiterate families
tended to keep their children out of school more than literate families.
Thus, the heritage of illiteracy possessed by the parent was transmitted to
the child in the form of neglect of schooling. As we have seen in chapter 4,
however, there is evidence that the neglect of children's schooling by
illiterate parents was most acute with older children in the family. The

Table 5.17   The Average Number of Children in School (SCHN), the
Average Proportion of Children in School (SCHIP), and
the Proportion of Men with at Least One Child in School
(SCHCHI) for all Free Adult Males in 1860 and Adult
White Males in 1870 in the United States, Classified by
Literacy

Age Class of Adult Male	Literate		Illiterate	
	1860	1870	1860	1870
		SCHN		
20-29	.04	.04	.03	.01
30-39	.86	.72	.60	.51
40-99	1.37	1.10	1.34	.90
		SCHIP		
20-29	.01	.01	.01	.01
30-39	.25	.19	.15	.15
40-99	.32	.28	.29	.21
		SCHCHI		
20-29	.13	.10	.04	.06
30-39	.40	.33	.31	.27
40-99	.49	.43	.43	.35

Source: Samples of 4,833 in 1860 and 9,125 in 1870.

Table 5.18   The Proportion of Children Attending School during
             the Year 1870 in the North (SCH), Classified by
             Order of Birth in the Family

Order of Birth in the Family	SCH of All Children		SCH of Children of Illiterate Fathers	
	Age 5-9	Age 15-19	Age 5-9	Age 15-19
Oldest child	.46	.42	.34	.35
Second oldest	.59	.43	.41	
Third oldest	.60	.45	.54	
Fourth oldest	.61	.55	.61	.40
Fifth or higher order	.55	.57	.36	

Source: The sample of 11,360.

Note: The sample of 903 children of illiterates includes only 119
of age fifteen to nineteen.

third, fourth, or fifth child in the family was more likely to attend school
and to attend for a greater number of years. This link between order of
birth and school attendance was present among children of literates as
well, but it is clear that the older children of illiterate fathers were at a
severe disadvantage relative to children of literate fathers. For younger
siblings the situation was improved and we might infer that the older
children could help their younger siblings by providing part of the wages
necessary for family sustenance. The process is observable in table 5.18
for various classifications of children. It might take more children for this
process to operate among illiterates, but it was nonetheless one possible
way in which family size might help, in the long run, to decrease illiteracy.
Ironically, such a method was dependent upon the sacrifice of the older
child in hopes that the younger might transcend the pattern of illiteracy
prevailing in the family.

Mobility and Intergenerational Illiteracy

Census data provide only one rather insensitive test on geographic immobility: is the state of residence the same as the state of birth? This
proves to be a difficult measure to employ in frontier states since most
individuals would show mobility by this test. It is obvious that all foreign
born would show mobility, so we must measure for this characteristic
only in the native born portion of the sample. The figures for 1870 given in
table 5.19 do illustrate less mobility among illiterates, but the difference is
far from large, particularly in the North. On the other hand, immobility
among southern illiterates is relatively large compared with that of northern illiterates. If we look at mobility among illiterates by cross-classifying
by occupation, differences also appear which indicate that among nonfarmers (most of whom are presumed to reside in urban areas) who were
illiterate, immobility was quite high. This was true in both the North and
the South, and is in contrast to the findings of Graff on illiterate persons in

Table 5.19 The Proportion of Adult Men of Native Birth Whose
Residence and Nativity State Were the Same (IMM),
Classified by Age-Group, Literacy, and Area in the
United States, 1870

Age Class	IMM All		IMM North		IMM South	
	Lit.	Illit.	Lit.	Illit.	Lit.	Illit.
20-39	.578	.639	.583	.640	.567	.639
20 and up	.521	.571	.525	.531	.501	.593
All	.556	.609	.562	.591	.542	.619

Source: The sample of 9,125.

urban Ontario. Among illiterate farmers, on the other hand, immobility
was less, thus suggesting that the condition of being illiterate for the urban
dweller was more likely to be a deterrent to improved economic status
insofar as that status depended upon the individual's being able to re-
locate.[45] The cognizance of employment alternatives or of promising
business opportunities would be limited to the medium of word of mouth
for the illiterate, and we would expect this to translate into less mobility.
Presumably, the longer the state of immobility persisted, the greater the
likelihood the illiterate would be isolated from the possibilities for reloca-
tion. Thus, a vicious cycle of illiteracy, immobility, and lack of economic
opportunity could become a feature of the life situation of the illiterate
individual. This syndrome, as we might label it, was very possibly the
situation in counties of very high illiteracy rates.[46]

To examine this cycle more closely, we turn to the Cumberland Plateau
of Appalachia, where, in 1840, three of the ten counties with the highest
illiteracy rates were located; in 1850, four of the counties with the highest
illiteracy rates were located in this region. One of these counties, Pike
County, was the land of the feuding Hatfields and McCoys. Another was
"Bloody Breathitt," which had earned an international reputation for its
murderous activity. These counties are in a mountainous region which has
very poor farmland. There are narrow strips of fertile land in the valley
bottoms, but their width would be only one hundred feet, at a maximum,
and, more likely, from twenty-five to fifty feet wide. Literature describing
the region stresses that the activity of the first settlers was largely hunting
and fishing. Caudill asserts that these people were the progeny of the
lowest socioeconomic classes in England, Scotland, and Ireland, who
were unlettered for the most part and were likely to have been orphans,
debtors, and other social outcasts.[47] Their story might well have been one
which saw cynical, angry, and penniless outcasts come to America as
indentured servants and finally escape to freedom in eastern Kentucky. If
these people had arrived in the fertile lands of northern Illinois and Iowa,
one can presume that they would have become part of the mainstream of
the developing country. As it was, they managed to survive by sub-

sistence farming after hunting became more difficult and saw little need to shift from the pattern of general illiteracy.

If the grandparents and great-grandparents of many Pike County illiterates in 1840 also had been illiterate, it is not surprising that this county had 852 illiterates twenty-one years and older among its 1,231 whites twenty and older in 1840. We cannot prove that the original state of illiteracy existed, but we can find many reasons why it should have been perpetuated. The twenty-five children enrolled in a small, one-room school in Pike County, for instance, accounted for less than 2 percent of the county's school-aged population in 1840. Such schools operated but one or two months a year, and then under extreme hardship.[48] The long, painful transition to literacy began only after 1840 in Kentucky. No districts had adopted the state recommendations for schooling in 1841 and 1842. Four had adopted them in 1843, seven in 1844, ten in 1845, sixteen in 1850, and fifty-eight by 1860.

Possibly just as important as the general absence of schooling in the years before mid-century was the fact that the entire labor force of Pike County was classified as agricultural, while Kentucky as a whole had 13 percent of its labor force in commerce and manufacturing. One local historian of Pike County remembers his grandfather's having said that in one year in the 1870s he had handled only six dollars and some odd cents in cash and that three dollars of it had been for taxes on his farm property. There was no economic goad to learn to read about products, materials, or machines. Moreover, there was no newspaper reported in the entire plateau, which now comprises nineteen counties.[49]

In attempting to better understand the illiteracy level of this one county, a study of mobility among illiterates and literates was made. The hypothesis was that illiterates would be more likely to remain in the county of birth while literates, being better informed, would leave a county with restricted economic and cultural advantages. A limited test of the hypothesis was performed by drawing a 10 percent sample of males twenty-one and over in Pike County for 1860.[50] The results are shown below:

	Number	Proportion
Kentucky born:		
Illiterate	49	.63
Literate	29	.37
	78	1.00
Virginia and North Carolina born:		
Illiterate	44	.60
Literate	29	.40
	73	1.00

The difference in the illiteracy proportion between the two birth groups is statistically significant from the standpoint of sampling error but unimportant in a practical sense. We are unable to say that the unlettered condition in the county was because of its complete isolation. Half the adults were from other states, and their illiteracy rate was as high as those born in the county. The homogeneity arose only because people with similar cultural and economic proclivities were willing to enter the county.

Since mobility seems to be insufficient to explain why the particular county of Pike continued to have such a high illiteracy rate, it would seem advantageous to study intergenerational illiteracy. Some idea of this can be obtained by studying families having children over twenty years of age still living with the family. A sample of forty-one Pike families in 1860 with nuclear children twenty-one and over had twenty-two illiterate fathers; 70 percent of these had one or more illiterate children, but four of these might be explained by the fact that the mothers were illiterate. This very small sample can only be suggestive, but it does seem that intergenerational illiteracy ties were very strong in an area in which schooling and institutions promoting literacy were so limited.

Our data from the census of 1870 tend to support the contention that in situations where schooling was severely restricted because of depressed economic conditions and a lack of social concentration, intergenerational illiteracy would be a common pattern. In our sample of men twenty and older, we have a small group of 569 who were still living with their parents, and we may look for some clues about illiteracy from this group, since we know the illiteracy of the parents and the 569 sons. It is important to note in these cases that the son is past the age at which he would most likely have become literate, that is, about age eleven if school attendance had been regular. (Of course, there would be exceptions, as some older individuals learned to read and others forgot how.) The data for this small but interesting group are given in table 5.20. We note first that the preponderance of illiterate sons had illiterate parents. The sample is too small for us to say that a son was more likely to have been illiterate if the

Table 5.20   The Illiteracy Rate (IL) of Sons Twenty and Older Living with Their Parents, for White Families in 1870 in the United States

Literacy Class of Sons	Number in Sample	Proportion with Illiterate Fathers	Proportion with Illiterate Mothers	Proportion with Either Parent, or Both, Illiterate
Literate	528	.04	.04	.06
Illiterate	41	.81	.76	.88
	569			

Source: The sample of 9,125 adult males, including our 569 cases.

father *rather* than the mother was unlettered. The number of fathers in the sample who were unlearned was fifty-two, and from these data we can compute a transition matrix from one generation to the next, as in table 5.21.

Table 5.21   The Probability That a Father Would Have Literate or Illiterate Children, Based on the Father's Literacy, for White Families in the United States in 1870

	Son Literate	Son Illiterate	Total
Literate father	.99	.01	1.00
Illiterate father	.37	.63	1.00

Source: The sample of 569 sons in nuclear families.

A matrix of this type leads, ultimately, to a stable number of literates, with 97 percent literate and 3 percent illiterate. This may not be far from the proportion of persons today who essentially are markers as adults. Certainly the matrix of table 5.21 is a contrivance, since we do not know about the illiterates or literates who had left their nuclear families. Yet the proportion of sons who were illiterate (.07) was just about the same as that for all adult white males (.08) of age twenty to twenty-nine.

Schooling would alter the bottom row of the table, enhancing the probability of literacy. The extreme position would be one where the bottom row vector was also (.99, .01). To move it even to (.5, .5) would shorten the number of generations necessary to bring society to a more egalitarian position with respect to literacy.

Conclusion

One of our major concerns in this chapter has been to establish some basic socioeconomic, geographic, and demographic parameters for discussing the causes of illiteracy in mid-nineteenth-century United States. This, in turn, has provided us with a context for interpreting the impact of the public common school as a form of cultural intervention and has led us to examine briefly the experiences of illiterates when dealing with day-to-day problematic situations. Thus, for instance, we have noted that the experiences of illiterate persons using written legal instruments indicate that their lack of reading and writing skills placed them at a disadvantage in financial dealings. While they were not necessarily divorced from the mainstream of American society, the absence of literacy skills placed them in a position of dependency. In dealing with the causes of illiteracy, we have attempted to avoid any singular explanation of illiteracy and any simplistic causal model, for it seems unlikely that such a model could offer much in the way of explanation. Instead, we have suggested numerous factors (as well as indicators of illiteracy) which, taken together, made it imperative in the eyes of school reformers to proceed with zeal in their interventionist activities.

Several trends in illiteracy are worth reviewing. First, it is evident that illiteracy rates dropped substantially between 1800 and 1840. From a rate of approximately 25 percent illiteracy in 1800, the rate dropped to between 3 and 9 percent in 1840 in the North; from 40 to 50 percent illiteracy in the South in 1800, the rate decreased to .19 in 1840. During this period, newspapermen, printers, and authors of common school textbooks had made strenuous efforts to promote an ideology of literacy highlighting the social utility of literacy, the importance of literacy to proper behavior, and the social and economic benefits of literacy to the individual. Common school reformers had likewise promoted this ideology, and in the last fifteen years of this period made a concerted effort to strengthen common schools in their respective states; they had not, however, attained the "systematization " of common schools. Thus, while common schooling was a popular idea prior to 1840 and efforts to extend the influence of the common school had been successful, the systematization itself (signaled, but not accomplished, by the coming of many state superintendencies of education in the late 1830s and the 1840s) should not be viewed as a major reason for the reduction of illiteracy rates in the first forty years of the nineteenth century. Kaestle and Vinovskis, in fact, have asserted that educational institutions of the late eighteenth century and early nineteenth century had the capacity "to increase the extent of schooling in the decades prior to the common school 'revival.' "[51]

The number of schools per county was a very sensitive indicator with respect to literacy, and this, in itself, is sufficient reason to infer that increased school attendance prior to systematization was a crucial factor in raising literacy rates. Moreover, it is likely that this indicator took its force from a concerted attempt on the part of media to promote education rather than any actual state-wide systematization of common schooling. Promotors behind the network of print had become increasingly sophisticated in their techniques for production and distribution of print materials in the first forty years of the nineteenth century. The major issues emerging from efforts at common school reform in the North by the late 1830s were issues over both the quality of literacy and the extent to which schooling reached all ethnic groups and socioeconomic levels of the population. This, in turn, was reflected in the concerns of reformers over school attendance. If the social utility of schooling were to be demonstrated, the great majority of youth would be required to come under its influence. Kaestle and Vinovskis have noted of school attendance in

Massachusetts that "it was the quality and amount of rural schooling that worried reformers."[52] In the urban areas of Massachusetts, non-attendance was the major problem seen by reformers, and the common school attempt to educate the young of immigrants was the dramatic case in point. In the South, however, the problem of basic literacy was more pronounced, so that efforts at school reform here were forced to deal more with questions of basic literacy than in the North.

It is apparent that even by 1840 great disparities in literacy rates at the county level still existed. Gini coefficients of .63 for 1840 and .52 for 1850 attest to this. County inequality for 1870, however, had dropped substantially to .34. Regional North-South differences were still strong, undoubtedly because of the persistence of a historical pattern but also because different labor patterns resulted in different literacy needs. Thus, it would seem that the discipline of the factory, the shop, and the merchant was different from that of the land in terms of literacy and that these differences were translated into different occupational skills relative to literacy. Moreover, literacy as a socializing experience for the young came to be increasingly associated with school experiences, thus tying literacy and the socializing experience of the school together. As we have seen, the functionality or dysfunctionality of such experiences became a major concern in establishing the purpose of the school with regard to youthful prospects for upward social and economic mobility. A perfect meritocratic correlation was not in evidence, with all illiterate persons clustered at the lower end of the wealth distribution; that there was a preponderence of illiterates at lower wealth levels was quite evident, however. Mobility, as has been observed, was still available for the illiterate, but it was becoming more difficult by 1870 for the unlettered individual to rise above the median wealth level and still more difficult to stay above that level. Thus, relative to the literate person, downward mobility was a distinct possibility for the illiterate.

Population density (urbanity) was still a strategic factor in illiteracy rates as new county formation was not keeping pace with the increase in population. This held true regardless of region. Commercial and manufacturing activity, too, was an important indicator of literacy levels as evidenced in our analysis of county per capita wealth figures. These two indicators, along with the strong positive association between schooling and literacy, certainly suggest that urbanity and an aggregate increase in wealth associated with commercial and manufacturing activity made educational facilities more available. Increased aggregate wealth in a community, however, did not guarantee increased school attendance among all socioeconomic groups in a community.[53] As we have seen in chapter 4, family wealth and ethnicity were mediating variables in extending schooling to all children.

Our mathematical formulation of illiteracy for adults is applicable after 1870 in the North only in attenuated form. Public schooling at the elementary level was an important counterinfluence to occupation, residence, wealth, and ethnicity in the achievement of literacy. Our regression analysis using county-level data has shown that the number of schools was of paramount importance in reducing illiteracy rates. Basic training in reading and writing was an economic good which was brought into the public sector and made somewhat less costly for young children and their parents, even though it was far from being a free good. This meant that basic education, which is an economic good just as food, clothing, and shelter are, became much less unequally distributed among families and children than it formerly had been. We have seen previously, however, that education at the intermediate and, more demonstrably, the high school level was still strongly unequal in its distribution. Our mathematical formulation might be considered by 1870 to apply more aptly in the North to secondary schooling, as occupational and wealth levels reassert themselves as important influences. Students of inequality have observed a recurring theme in our history: the decreasing inequality in the relative distribution of values of consumer expenditures for any specific good. That is particularly true in the case of clothing and housing, and we see that it was occurring with basic literacy *a fortiori* between 1840 and 1870.[54]

Within the context of commercial and manufacturing activity, the entrepreneurial values and the promotional efforts of enterprising publishers and printers were important factors in the spread of literacy, and these had greater impact in areas of high population density, where market conditions were more favorable. In areas of lower population density, on the other hand, entrepreneurial activities were not so easy to undertake. Editors, as we have seen in chapter 4, could achieve surprising circulation figures in low-population-density areas, but the demographic limitations were still there, so that the high population density, high literacy pattern remains. It is probable, however, that urban-rural differences in literacy would have been more accentuated had the motive for profit not been so conspicuous. This motive, moreover, was certainly aided by improvements in printing technology and the flurry of internal improvements (roads and canals) beginning in the 1820s.

Certain personal and individual attributes have emerged as important in the discussion of illiteracy rates. Sex differences were in evidence, as they were in colonial America, and it would be expected that these differences reflected different labor patterns between men and women. Work patterns in rural areas probably mitigated against equality of literacy for women. For women of foreign birth, traditional social and familial roles helped depress literacy rates. Still, it is clear that women were moving toward equality of literacy with men, particularly in urban areas. Schooling was critical to this reduction in inequality, since instruction for boys and girls was not substantially different in the common school during the years that students usually achieved basic literacy. Whether the trend toward equality of literacy was also evident at high levels of literacy is another question and one that could perhaps be answered by examining high school attendance rates following the Civil War.

Finally, our data on fertility among literates and illiterates, as well as our findings on intergenerational illiteracy, suggest that the counterfactual alternative of nonintervention through the process of schooling might have gradually resulted in increasing literacy rates. On the one hand, fertility rates were higher among illiterates, and this probably made its impact on literacy by making it more difficult to school the young of the illiterate. This, however, was related to order of birth within the family and resulted in greater opportunities for younger children but demonstrably fewer opportunities for the eldest offspring. Greater fertility, it would seem, was one way the illiterate family of lower wealth could compensate for their economic difficulties; however, this very compensation, in the long run, had the effect of giving the youngest child a better chance of attending school, since he (not likely she) had the advantage of the family's wealth accumulation over a longer period of time.

Intergenerational illiteracy was a common pattern, as our data from 1840 and 1870 indicate. This, in turn, was reinforced by the lower school attendance levels of children of illiterate parents. The heritage of illiteracy was thus perpetuated through the lack of schooling. In areas where illiteracy and geographic immobility were linked in a subculture of illiteracy, the problem was magnified. This pattern, while certainly an obstacle to the achievement of literacy among new generations, did not condemn families to illiteracy forever. A transition matrix using 1870 data leads us to believe that illiteracy would, in the long run, be reduced. Schooling, of course, would speed up the process of achieving literacy, and this was the reformer's aim. Clearly, if educational reformers were committed to modernization through literacy, a slow, let-nature-take-its-course attitude was not viable. In the minds of educational reformers, the synthesis of evangelical Protestantism with the Victorian commitment to modernization made universal, mass literacy a cultural imperative which could not tolerate the slow, feeble steps of nature, an imperative which demanded that schooling be used as a civilizing force among the unlettered.

Six

Conclusion

By mid-nineteenth century basic literacy had become a cultural imperative in the United States. Evangelical Protestant morality, a fervent nationalism, and an ethic of capitalism which recognized the commercial value of a literate public had made literacy a high-priority social cause. Literacy was viewed as both a prerequisite to proper socialization among the young and an asset in the forward march of democracy. Those with a thirst for profit to be realized from the sale of printed materials willingly linked their private ambitions to the more benevolent cause of public enlightenment through literacy. In the hands of zealous reformers who associated literacy with social amelioration, the cause of literacy achieved a certain urgency in the face of changing social and economic realities in nineteenth-century America, where a new cultural diversity and an emerging industrial economy threatened the traditional family structure inherited from the eighteenth century. For the individual who was the object of reform, literacy became one way of mapping a problematic social reality.

The normative question of whether literacy itself was to be valued had been settled by the end of the eighteenth century, although reformers knew well the dangers of print presented to young minds without a guiding hand. An ideology of literacy carried forward from the eighteenth century and associated primarily with the spiritual well-being of individual and community alike had been further developed within the contexts of nationalism and the ethic of economic self-improvement. Collectively, literacy clearly was considered part of the social cement which helped to guarantee social stability and adherence to cherished social and political norms. The function of literacy was seen as integrative; its value was to be assessed in terms of social cohesion. Individually, literacy was one attribute which helped to make the good man, that is, it was part of being virtuous, and the better man was the man who would improve his skills in reading and writing. The ideology of literacy promoted by printers, textbook authors, and newspapermen also viewed literacy skills as important in the achievement of economic success. Not only were literacy and schooling functionally linked, but both were seen as part of the formula for upward economic mobility. The illiterate person was commonly the disadvantaged one and less likely to make his way upward than the literate individual. It is important to note, however, that illiterate persons were not, in fact, "marginal" persons in the sense that they were alienated from the normal economic or social behaviors of most people. In pockets of very high illiteracy, where illiteracy itself constituted a cultural proclivity, this separation from the social mainstream was the case, but, in general, the illiterate person was "dependent" without being marginal.

The rhetoric of reform between 1830 and 1870, while it probably did exaggerate the importance of literacy in achieving economic success, nonetheless reflected the increasing importance of literacy in upward economic mobility. By 1870 there was evidence of a causal relationship between literacy and wealth. While illiteracy was emerging as an obstacle to economic mobility, it was not a severe enough one to prevent about 40 percent of the illiterate population from obtaining a fair beginning standard of living. Yet despite the reality of economic mobility for the illiterate person, the chances of greater upward economic mobility were better for the literate person. This was less true among the young, aged twenty to twenty-nine, whose physical strength could compensate for their lack of literacy skills; but by the middle years of the life cycle, upward economic mobility was restricted by illiteracy.

The period between 1787 and 1870 was characterized by rapid institutional development to accommodate and popularize an ideology of literacy. The production of imprints increased more rapidly than the population, attesting to the increasing importance of printed materials in the economy of the nation. Labor force participation in printing itself testified to the increasing human resources being committed to literacy and to the many individuals who had a direct investment in the popularization of print. As would be expected, however, this output varied from region to region (most notably along North-South and East-West vectors), but it is important that, in general, increased literacy rates accompanied increased paper production and publishing activity. The establishment of a communications network and the rise in literacy rates in nineteenth-century America were linked to both publishing activity and other indices of development including per capita wealth in manufacturing, improved acreage, and cash values per acre.

We have emphasized throughout and developed in mathematical fashion the basic causative link between population density (urbanity) and the

diffusion of basic literacy. There is little question that areas of high population density committed more resources per capita to the promotion of
literacy. (The impact of these resources, however, was dependent upon
other factors including ethnicity, wealth, and occupation.) Yet urbanity
was sometimes a function of geography and terrain as in the case of the
East (high literacy)–West (low literacy) gradient, which reflected the
settlement of the American West and the absence of what Lockridge
terms "social concentration" in frontier areas. In cases of dramatically
high illiteracy rates such as that of the Appalachian plateau, terrain was
surely an obstacle to achieving the population density necessary to provide the economic base (including a ready market for printed materials)
for sustaining a communications network based on print. In areas of low
population density, difficulties in the merchandizing of print strained the
entrepreneurial zeal of local newspaper editors and booksellers. It was in
areas of high population density that greater aggregate wealth helped to
create a viable communications network which included benevolent literacy and library associations, newspaper and book publishing, and book-
selling per se. Moreover, it was in areas of relatively high population
density that schooling flourished, and, as was evident in our regression
analysis of county variations in illiteracy rates, schooling was an important causative factor in reducing illiteracy. The exceptional area dispersion in illiteracy rates for 1840 ($G = .64$) had abated somewhat by 1850,
but the dramatic inverse relationship between illiteracy rates and population density remained for counties having population ranges from ten to
thirty thousand. By 1870 area dispersion in illiteracy had been reduced
considerably, and it is likely, along with the prodigious efforts at common
school reform, that technological improvements in the printing industry
and the rapid improvements in transportation between 1820 and 1850
helped reduce the high positive correlation between urbanity and literacy.

A model for the diffusion of literacy must be tempered by the realities of
macroeconomic conditions. If America in 1787 had had levels of per
capita wealth and income that existed a century later, it might immediately have embarked on an expanded system of public education
such as that which arose after 1830. The inadequacy of a tax base was still
very much in evidence in the 1830s in those states with the highest illiteracy rates. Education may be deemed an economic good just as clothing or
shelter, but it naturally arises after basic needs have generally been
satisfied. The fact that younger children in illiterate families were more
likely to attend school suggests the importance of a hierarchy of economic
goods and the opportunity costs of education.

The rise in basic literacy in the nineteenth century may be construed
as having diminished the economic inequality of the nation. The decrease
in the variability of this economic good is similar to that experienced

with clothing as dress became more uniform in quality and quantity; the decrease in the relative variability of housing values as distributed among families has been a continuing process since 1787. Public education did not make literacy a free good, however, except perhaps at the most rudimentary level. The reality that income was the alternative to schooling for those aged fifteen to nineteen permeates our statistical data and suggests the continuing process of inequality at higher levels as more basic needs are satisfied.

Between 1820 and 1870, educational reformers and promoters of mass literacy who attempted the building of institutions to popularize and increase literary consumption faced numerous obstacles other than sparseness of population. Their one distinct advantage, however, was the presence of an ideology of literacy inherited from the late eighteenth and early nineteenth centuries. Reformers seemed to anticipate only minor problems in shifting from a religious to a civic model for literacy. Protestantism and nationalism were natural allies in the early nineteenth century and were part of a similar cultural vision. In fact, for those who took the forming of a nation as the logical extension of building a city upon a hill, the reconciling of the spiritual and civic purposes of literacy proved an easy task. Beyond this logic which synthesized the religious and the civil dimensions of literacy, however, lay formidable social realities. To properly socialize the young through the medium of print, to properly raise the consciousness of the unconverted was an easily avowed goal. To pursue a policy of cultural intervention and to overcome the demographic, social, and economic obstacles to such socialization was quite another matter.

Both home and school were the objects of reform by newspaper editors, publishers, and educational reformers. The problems in making these two institutions the targets for persuasive tactics were different, however. Clearly the home with its traditional role in child rearing and socialization could not be abandoned simply because it was proving inadequate to the task of teaching basic literacy. In fact, there was good reason for reformers to appeal to the familiar picture of the young child learning to read under parental guidance. Home and school were seen in a symbiotic relationship. There is some evidence to demonstrate that books were more prevalent in families than among the unmarried, and this reinforced the belief that the home could help carry the burden to teach basic literacy. Appeals to self-help were also common as editors painted the image of farmers and apprentices spending their leisure time reading in front of the open hearth. (These appeals were also accompanied by suggestions to join social and apprentice libraries, where the selection of books would be greater.) On the negative side, though, was the disturbing fact of intergenerational illiteracy particularly among the poor. Clearly there was the possibility that illiteracy was perpetuated by the migration of illiterates with similar cultural proclivities to regions already characterized by high rates of illiteracy. This would, of course, have the effect of contributing to greater intergenerational illiteracy and creating pockets of high illiteracy. Even had reformers realized (which they probably did not) that high fertility rates accompanied by low death rates might, in the long run, increase population density to a point where schooling and the marketing of print materials were economically feasible, it was imperative in their eyes that this slow, evolutionary process be altered to keep pace with the advance of an industrial economy. Thus, the choice to intervene in the illiteracy syndrome took the form of a cultural imperative which sought to facilitate by imposition the socialization of children of both native and foreign born illiterate parents. The missionary zeal which characterized evangelical Protestantism was carried forth by common school advocates in a moral crusade against illiteracy, an important part of which was the strategy of cultural intervention through common school reform.

Given the choice to make the common school the major institution for the achievement of basic literacy, the problem for reformers was twofold. First, the problem of legitimizing such a choice among the population in general was an immediate one. As we are often reminded, the problem was a substantive one involving the content of the curriculum and reading texts; moreover, it was a problem which led to increasing religious strife by mid-century. Not everyone was a willing participant in common school reform, including dissident Protestants as well as Roman Catholics. Educational reformers, however, were in command of a powerful and readily available tool in the form of the newspaper. Not only were newspapers widely distributed, but editors themselves often had a vested interest in both literacy and schooling, in the case of the latter because they commonly served as distributors and compilers of school texts. In the case of the former, they usually considered themselves as protectors of the public intelligence and as arbiters of good taste.

Early superintendents of common schools recognized the newspaper editor as a natural ally in the fight for an extended common school system. Samuel Lewis of Ohio, for example, solicited county auditors to prepare articles for newspapers because he believed that "editors would insert an article once a week for the good of Education."[1] Educational reform groups such as the Western Literary Institute of Cincinnati also took an active part in legitimizing the choice to intervene, through schooling, in the process of child rearing. Such groups did not have the large audience that newspaper editors were accustomed to, but they were influential in legislative circles where the legal requirements of school districting, certification of teachers, and allowable tax support were being framed. Among teachers themselves, there was little convincing to be done with respect to the importance of reading. Reading, along with spelling, had been a cherished part of the curriculum, and, as we have illustrated, pedagogy was preoccupied with these skills. There were many who thought that reading was improperly taught in the public common schools, but this itself only served to bring before the public the great reading debate of the 1840s. The school itself was the forum for the debate, and the attention focused on the subject of reading instruction served to re-emphasize the importance of literacy in socializing the young.

In the long run, problems associated with legitimacy and the quality of reading instruction were secondary compared with the social and economic obstacles to equality of literacy. Because wealth, ethnicity, and occupation were important factors influencing literacy, no quick metamorphosis of the population could be expected. Thus, the urgency of the reformer met head on with the social and economic determinants of illiteracy. Moreover, the achievement of basic literacy, reformers realized, was an adaptive behavior required of the illiterate. Thus, it was the expectation of those who would transform the unlettered that the latter would internalize and express a system of values shared by the literate. Instruction in literacy was not simply a technical matter of decoding symbols; rather, it was a way of transforming the world view of the unlettered, including a willingness to subject oneself to the authority of print.

The basic causal linkage between urbanity and literacy certainly was a concern for educational reformers, who attempted to advance the cause of literacy in sparsely settled regions of the United States. The impact of an ideology of literacy, insofar as that impact was related to population density, was determined by indices of economic development, and for the most part lay outside the reformer's reach. Problems stemming from the association of literacy with occupation, ethnicity, and individual wealth, on the other hand, appeared more amenable to eradication, and it was to these basic factors that reformers gave most of their attention.

As they had been in colonial America, occupational differences in literacy rates were certainly evident in the first two decades of the nineteenth century. Thus, reformers who led the crusade against illiteracy were faced with an occupational-illiteracy hierarchy which saw the highest illiteracy rates among laborers, with farmers occupying the middle ground and skilled labor being the most literate. This hierarchy persisted, but it is imperative that we realize that the actual decline in illiteracy rates of about 17 percent between 1820 and 1870 was experienced in general. In absolute terms, for example, laborers remained more illiterate than farmers between 1850 and 1870, but both experienced a rapid rise in literacy during these decades. The efforts, then, of those who addressed themselves to the plight of the farmer by urging him to occupy his spare time with reading and to the plight of the mechanic and apprentice by financing libraries for these special groups did not alter the occupational hierarchy of literacy, but probably prevented the gaps from becoming greater. More important than these voluntaristic efforts at social amelioration, however, was the increasing volume of legislation directed at organizing more efficient common school systems. From the efforts of the 1820s toward "enabling" legislation to the more rigorous attempts from 1837 to 1870 to control the fortunes of local school districts through state financial pressure, the common school systems of various states gradually succeeded in bringing most children from ages five to fourteen into the environment of the common school. There were, unquestionably, still great inequalities in years of schooling in all regions of the country in 1860 with the greatest differences appearing along the North-South vector. Enrollment patterns in the North were not differentiated by father's occupation (farm and nonfarm) until after age fourteen. Despite this dramatic success in bringing children into the common school to achieve basic literacy, an occupational hierarchy of literacy still persisted into the late nineteenth century. The configuration of the hierarchy had partially changed, however. In the North, literacy rates among skilled laborers were still higher than for farmers and laborers; however, unskilled laborers in both the North and South had achieved parity with farmers—a fact which reflected the intensity of common school reform in urban areas.

Ethnicity and nativity, like occupation, were strongly related to patterns of illiteracy, and this remained true until 1850. By 1870, however, foreign born and native born men had generally achieved similar literacy rates. Among foreign born women there was greater disparity, and illiteracy rates for foreign born women in the North were two to four times as large as for native born women. While native born women (particularly in urban areas) were rapidly achieving equality of literacy with native born men, traditional female and familial roles among foreign born women acted to curb equality of literacy between foreign born men and women. There were also disparities in illiteracy rates among specified ethnic groups. Canadian male immigrants had very high illiteracy rates even by 1870 (.25), and Irish male immigrants were also high with a rate of .18. German, English, and Welsh males were at about the same level (about 5 percent illiterate) as those born in the United States. By the 1890s, however, there was little difference in illiteracy rates for the native born and foreign born, and the reason, in all probability, was to be found in the efforts of school reformers to undertake the acculturation of immigrant children in the public common schools. The primary motivation for reformers, if we are to judge by their rhetoric, in persuading the children of foreign born parents and grandparents to attend school was to accelerate the process of acculturation through basic literacy and the socializing influence of native born peers. It was a fact that children of the foreign born—those of Irish born parentage, for example—did enroll in proportions as great as or greater than children of those born in the United States in age-group five to nine. Between the ages of ten and fourteen Irish and German children also achieved high enrollment proportions (.78 and .77, respectively), although these were not as great as the .84 proportion of children of United States born parents in the same age-group. By ages fifteen to nineteen, however, enrollment proportions for children of the foreign born dropped dramatically compared with children of the native born. This drop, which began in the ten to fourteen age-group but was accentuated from ages fifteen to nineteen, cannot, however, be attributed primarily to the effects of nativity and ethnicity. As we have noted, it was the factor of wealth which played the most important role in the enrollment of older children in both farm and nonfarm sectors and among the children of the native as well as the foreign born. Thus, in the years during which basic literacy was acquired (ages six through eleven) children of the foreign born received the advantages of schooling; moreover, the actual achievement of literacy among enrolled children was little affected by ethnicity. At the same time, there was a cruel irony in this achievement. It is clear that parents of these children expected basic literacy to be a gateway to upward economic mobility. Yet the widespread achievement of basic literacy made it increasingly a poor measure to be used in the process of social and economic selection. Following the lead of some school officials in the late 1860s, schoolmen increasingly realized that they must look closely at the different levels of literacy achieved through schooling. They perceived, likewise, that it was possible to create a hierarchy of achievement in literacy and to apply that hierarchy for purposes of internal (school) selection as well as to suggest that this academic selection might be applied to future social and economic selection. Social and economic advantages which had been related to basic literacy would then become associated with particular levels of literacy beyond the bare minimum. Thus, school attendance between the years of fifteen and nineteen was to become increasingly important in economic and social selection. As we have noted, the factor of wealth operated to deny advanced schooling to children of both the native born and foreign born, but was more pronounced among the foreign born in urban areas, where reformers made their greatest efforts.

The interaction of ethnicity and wealth in school enrollments of children born to immigrants of the major ethnic groups in the United States was one manifestation of the persistent relationship of wealth to literacy which is so evident from the colonial period forward. Certainly it was easier to procure books, buy newspapers, and subscribe to libraries if one was not among the poor. As we have noted, the ownership of more than three books was a function of wealth, although the ownership of from one to three books was common and not related to level of wealth. It is also evident that newspaper and library subscriptions demanded a considerable sacrifice of wages for the common laborer. Thus, in these cases, wealth may be said to be a cause of higher levels of literacy. Whether literacy, in turn, contributed to greater wealth accumulation is a different but related question. Professional and commercial occupations demanded a higher level of literacy, and to this extent it may be said that literacy was necessary to procure the increased income afforded by these activities. While upward economic mobility was still possible for the illiterate by 1870, it is evident that among older individuals, higher literacy skills were required to remain at or rise above the median wealth line. Thus, as we have noted, economic advancement of the illiterate was limited in comparison to that of the literate individual.

By 1800 the level of illiteracy was between 30 and 40 percent for those who occupied the lower half of the wealth distribution. This rate probably declined moderately until 1830, at which point it began to decline rapidly, especially between 1840 and 1860. As of 1860, the top 10 percent of all male wealthholders included 2.9 percent of all male illiterates; the top 50 percent of wealthholders had 7.8 percent of the illiterates. Certainly, a meritocratic system existed in 1860 and 1870, although the severity of its structure had lessened from thirty years previous. Common school reforms between 1830 and 1870 had contributed to moderating the strong link between low wealth and high illiteracy found in the first half of the nineteenth century, but the meritocratic relationship between wealth and literacy was still much in evidence. Reformers had been unable to prevent (and perhaps they had no intention of preventing) the impact of wealth on achieving higher levels of literacy through more advanced schooling. It was this basic fact which helped to perpetuate a wealth-literacy hierarchy and denied to the poor an equal chance for upward economic mobility. Like the occupational-literacy hierarchy which characterized nineteenth-century America, the wealth-literacy hierarchy remained a socioeconomic reality. While reformers had demonstrated that equality of basic literacy could be achieved and that literacy and economic success were positively and meaningfully related, a meritocratic social structure based upon literacy persisted.

Notes

Chapter 1

1. Horace Mason, "Fundamental Education and Functional Literacy--Problems and Possibilities," Convergence 6 (1973):57. Harvey J. Graff has spoken to the problem of linking literacy to modernization in his recent work The Literacy Myth (New York, 1979). His distinction between skills and values accompanying literacy is a useful one. The "complex of attitudinal changes" which represent a possible link between literacy, school, and modernization, says Graff, are "a result of the acquisition and possession of literacy, but perhaps [modernization] is more directly the result of the processes that accompany the dissemination of that ability: the values and organization of the school. This duality is not often recognized, but may comprise the essence of schooling's contribution to development and modernization" (p. 9).

2. See Harvey J. Graff, "Notes on Methods for Studying Literacy from the Manuscript Census," Historical Methods Newsletter 5 (Dec. 1971):11-16, for suggestions in using census manuscripts.

3. See Maris A. Vinovskis, "Trends in Massachusetts Education, 1826-1860," History of Education Quarterly 12 (Winter 1972):501-29, for an analysis of these problems. For a comprehensive treatment of school attendance in Massachusetts, see Carl F. Kaestle and Maris A. Vinovskis, Education and Social Change in Nineteenth-Century Massachusetts: Quantitative Studies, Final Research Report, 31 Dec. 1976, National Institute of Education, Grant NE-G-00-3-0068, Project 3-0825.

4. The problem of operational definition has been discussed by Richard T. Murphy of ETS in "Changing Demands and Definitions of Literacy Assessment" (Functional Literacy Conference, Indiana University, 29 June 1979). While Murphy's discussion of operational definitions is valuable, he vastly underestimates the difficulties associated with the concept of literacy itself.

5. Bouzid Hammiche gives the function-nonfunction distinction a slightly different interpretation. He stresses that functional literacy is "defined by its methodological characteristics, in that, taught while actually at work, a man studies and learns in his own concrete environment and is enabled to improve his working capacity." The stress on learning in the work environment rather than for it is undoubtedly occasioned by Hammiche's concern with adult education ("Functional Literacy and Educational Revolution," in Leon Bataille [ed.], A Turning Point for Literacy [New York, 1976], p. 119).

6. Graff, Literacy Myth, pp. 3-4.

7. Quoted in David Harman, "Literacy: An Overview," Harvard Educational Review 40 (May 1970):227.

8. William S. Gray, The Teaching of Reading and Writing (Paris, 1956), p. 19, quoted in UNESCO, World Illiteracy at Mid-Century, a Statistical Study (Paris, 1957), p. 20.

9. UNESCO, World Illiteracy at Mid-Century, p. 19.
10. National Center for Education Statistics, The Condition of Education (Washington, 1976), pp. 60-61.
11. J. R. Clammer, Literacy and Social Change (Leiden, 1976), p. 6.
12. The Statistics of the Population of the United States, Ninth Census, vol. 1 (Washington, 1872), p. xxx.
13. Harvey Graff, "Towards a Meaning of Literacy: Literacy and Social Structure in Hamilton, Ontario," History of Education Quarterly 12 (Fall 1972): 418.
14. Kenneth A. Lockridge, Literacy in Colonial New England (New York, 1974), p. 7.
15. UNESCO, The Experimental World Literacy Programme: A Critical Assessment (Paris, 1976), p. 118.
16. Graff, Literacy Myth, pp. 53-54.
17. Cynthia Brown, "Literacy in 30 Hours: Paulo Freire's Process in Northeast Brazil," Social Policy 5 (July/Aug. 1974):25.
18. Lucien Febvre and Henri-Jean Martin, The Coming of the Book: The Impact of Printing, 1450-1800, trans. David Gerard, ed. Geoffrey Nowell-Smith and David Wootton (London and Atlantic Highlands, N. J., 1976), p. 294.
19. Richard D. Altick, The English Common Reader: A Social History of the Mass Reading Public, 1800-1900 (Chicago, 1957), p. 72.
20. Ibid., pp. 72, 73.
21. Peter L. Berger, "Consciousness Raising: To Whom--By Whom?" Social Policy 5 (Sept./Oct. 1974):40. Graff has used the concept of "hegemony" to conceptualize the phenomenon on a sociological level. More specifically, the concept of "hegemony" expresses a theory of the sociology of knowledge. In dealing with nineteenth-century school promotors in Canada he notes that the hegemony "which was to obtain from correct and proper moral schooling, therefore, represents the social order in which one way of life and pattern of behavior becomes dominant; in which one concept of reality is diffused throughout society in its institutional and private functions" (Literacy Myth, p. 34).
22. Sylvia Scribner and Michael Cole, "Literacy without Schooling: Testing for Intellectual Effects," Harvard Educational Review 48 (November 1978): 451.
23. Ibid., pp. 451-52.
24. Berger, "Consciousness Raising," p. 40.
25. Barbara Finkelstein, "Pedagogy as Intrusion: Teaching Values in Popular Primary Schools in Nineteenth-Century America," History of Childhood Quarterly 2 (Winter 1975):349-78.
26. Talcott Parsons, "Culture and Social System Revisited," in Louis Schneider and Charles M. Bonjean (eds.), The Idea of Culture in the Social Sciences (Cambridge, 1973), p. 36.
27. Richard D. Heyman, "A Theoretical Look at Knowledge, Schools, and Social Change," Comparative Education Review 18 (Oct. 1974):414.
28. Jack Goody and Ian Watt, "Literate Culture: Some General Considerations," in Robert Disch (ed.), The Future of Literacy (Englewood Cliffs, 1973), p. 53.
29. Heyman, "A Theoretical Look," p. 414.
30. John McLeish, Evangelical Religion and Popular Education (London, 1969), p. 20.
31. Altick, English Common Reader, p. 32.
32. McLeish, Evangelical Religion, p. 20.
33. Ibid., p. 46.
34. Ibid., p. 19.
35. Ibid., p. 20.
36. Ibid., p. 93.
37. Ibid., p. 93.
38. Ibid., p. 55.
39. Ibid., p. 56.
40. Ibid., p. 59.
41. Altick, English Common Reader, pp. 73-76. Febvre and Martin, Coming of the Book, p. 192.

42. Altick, English Common Reader, p. 76.
43. Ibid., p. 75. R. K. Webb, The British Working Class Reader 1790-1848: Literacy and Social Tension (London, 1955), p. 16.
44. Altick, English Common Reader, p. 73.
45. Webb, British Working Class Reader, p. 26.
46. Altick, English Common Reader, p. 76.
47. Ibid., pp. 99-100.
48. S. Scott Miyakawa, Protestants and Pioneers (Chicago, 1964), p. 110.
49. Robert W. Lynn and Elliott Wright, The Big Little School: Sunday Child of American Protestantism (New York, 1971), p. 13.
50. For Great Britain, notes Altick, "we must not overestimate the number of literates whom the Sunday Schools produced . . .; no high degree of literacy can be imparted in once-a-week classes." "Nevertheless," he continues, "the Sunday Schools did swell the total of the nation's literates, both directly and by sharpening popular interest in reading, so that there was considerable home study on the part of adults. Children who acquired some rudimentary skill in the art often shared it with their elders" (Altick, English Common Reader, p. 68).
51. Clifford S. Griffin, "Religious Benevolence as Social Control, 1815-1860," Mississippi Valley Historical Review 44 (Dec. 1957):424.
52. The relationship between Sunday schools and literacy has been treated in Thomas W. Laqueur's excellent work Religion and Respectability: Sunday Schools and English Working Class Culture, 1780-1850 (New Haven, 1976). "Secular instruction in [British] Sunday schools," notes Laqueur, "must be seen against the background of a society in which the facilities for mass popular education were still in their infancy. Cultural as well as economic factors determined that the formal schooling available to a great part of the population was only one-third of what is today considered sufficient to ensure functional literacy" (p. 102). "For most students the Sunday schools added three, four or five years of part-time education to a very limited and discontinuous period of weekday schooling, sometimes amounting to no more than a few months in a dame's school; for a minority it had to take the place of all full-time instruction" (p. 101).
53. Carl F. Kaestle, The Evolution of an Urban School System: New York City, 1750-1850 (Cambridge, Mass., 1973), p. 121.
54. Edwin Wilbur Rice, The Sunday-School Movement and the American Sunday-School Union, 1780-1917 (Philadelphia, 1917), p. 46.
55. Ibid.
56. Ibid., p. 76.
57. Lynn and Wright, Bit Little School, p. 29.
58. The phrase is that of John Hutchison, who argues that the essential feature of religious language, and hence that of religion and faith, is its communication of a "total or comprehensive life orientation" and that statements of religion and faith may be "interpreted as orientation statements" (John A. Hutchison, Language and Faith: Studies in Sign, Symbol, and Meaning [Philadelphia, 1968], p. 101).
59. G. S. Osborne, Scottish and English Schools: A Comparative Survey of the Past Fifty Years (Pittsburgh, 1966), p. 4. James Scotland, The History of Scottish Education, vol. 1 (London, 1969), pp. 47-48.
60. Lockridge, Literacy in Colonial New England, p. 99.
61. Egil Johansson, "Summary," En Studie Med Kvantitativa Metoder Av Folkundervisningen I Bygdea Socken, 1845-1873 (Umea, 1972).
62. Quoted in Harvey J. Graff, "Literacy and Social Structure in the Nineteenth-Century City," Ph.D. dissertation, University of Toronto, 1975, p. 392.
63. Daniel P. Resnick and Lauren B. Resnick, "The Nature of Literacy: An Historical Exploration," Harvard Educational Review 47 (Aug. 1977):374.
64. Richard Pratte, Ideology and Education (New York, 1977).
65. Timothy L. Smith, "Protestant Schooling and American Nationality, 1800-1850," Journal of American History 53 (Mar. 1967):680.
66. Resnick and Resnick, "Nature of Literacy," p. 384. David Tyack, "The Kingdom of God and the Common School: Protestant Ministers and the Educational Awakening in the West," Harvard Educational Review 36 (Fall 1966):447-69.

67. Stanley K. Schultz, The Culture Factory: Boston Public Schools, 1789-1860 (New York, 1973), p. 69.
68. H. Harbaugh, "Parochial or Christian Schools," Mercersburg Quarterly Review 5 (Jan. 1853):33.
69. Rev. George Mull, "Morality in the Public Schools," Reformed Quarterly Review 29, n.s. 4 (Oct. 1882):472-73.
70. Tyack, "Kingdom of God and the Common School," p. 466.
71. Daniel Walker Howe (ed.), Victorian America (Philadelphia, 1976), pp. 11-12.
72. John Fletcher Clews Harrison, The Early Victorians, 1832-1851 (New York, 1971), p. 135.
73. Goody and Watt, "Literate Culture," p. 53.
74. Howe, Victorian America, p. 24.
75. Francois Furet and Jacques Ozouf, Lire et écrire (Paris, 1977).
76. Roger S. Schofield, "Illiteracy in Pre-Industrial England: The Work of the Cambridge Group for the History of Population and Social Structure," in Egil Johansson (ed.), Literacy and Society in a Historical Perspective--A Conference Report, Educational Reports, Umea, no. 2 (Umea, 1973), p. 13.
77. David Cressy, "Educational Opportunity in Tudor and Stuart England," History of Education Quarterly 16 (Fall 1976):314. See also idem, "Levels of Illiteracy in England, 1530-1730," Historical Journal 20 (1977): 23, and idem, "Literacy in Seventeenth-Century England: More Evidence," Journal of Interdisciplinary History 8(Summer 1977):147-48.
78. Furet and Ozouf, Lire et écrire, p. 351.
79. Lockridge, Literacy in Colonial New England, p. 55.
80. Graff, Literacy Myth, pp. 115, 80.
81. Ibid., p. 72.
82. Lockridge, Literacy in Colonial New England, p. 55.
83. Edward Stevens, "Wealth and Culture on the American Frontier," paper presented at the spring meeting of the Ohio Academy of History, Columbus, 21 Apr. 1979.
84. See Albert Fishlow, "The American Common School Revival: Fact or Fancy," in Henry Rosovsky (ed.), Industrialization in Two Systems (New York, 1966), pp. 40-67.
85. Selwyn K. Troen, "Popular Education in Nineteenth-Century St. Louis," History of Education Quarterly 13 (Spring 1973):33. Idem, The Public and the Schools (Columbia, Mo., 1975).
86. Albert Fishlow, "Levels of Nineteenth-Century American Investment in Education," Journal of Economic History 26 (Dec. 1966): 418-36. Lewis C. Solmon, "Opportunity Costs and Models of Schooling in the Nineteenth Century," Southern Economic Journal 37 (July 1970): 66-83. Lee Soltow and Edward Stevens, "Economic Aspects of School Participation in Mid-Nineteenth-Century United States," Journal of Interdisciplinary History 8 (Autumn 1977): 221-43.
87. Kaestle and Vinovskis, Education and Social Change in Nineteenth-Century Massachusetts, pp. 86-87.
88. See Robert A. Carlson, The Quest for Conformity: Americanization through Education (New York, 1975).
89. Edward Stevens and Lee Soltow, "Quantitative Factors in the Acculturation of Immigrant Children in Mid-Nineteenth-Century United States," paper presented at the meeting of the American Educational Research Association, Toronto, Apr. 1978.

Chapter 2

1. Lawrence Cremin, American Education:The Colonial Experience, 1607-1783. (New York, 1970), p. 124.
2. Quoted in Edmund S. Morgan, The Puritan Family, rev. ed. (New York, 1966), pp. 88-89.
3. Bernard Bailyn, Education in the Forming of American Society, reprinted ed. (New York, 1960), p. 26.
4. Marcus Jernegan, Laboring and Dependent Classes in Colonial America, reprinted ed. (New York, 1965), p. 112.
5. Duke De La Rochefoucault Liancourt, Travels through the United States of North America (London, 1799), p. 277.
6. Ibid., p. 334.

7. Ibid. For the nineteenth century, see, for instance, Harvey J. Graff, "'Pauperism, Misery, and Vice': Illiteracy and Criminality in the Nineteenth Century," Journal of Social History 2 (1978): 245-68.

8. James T. Adams, Provincial Society 1690-1763, ed. Arthur M. Schesinger and Dixon R. Fox (New York, 1927), p. 132.

9. Jernegan, Laboring and Dependent Classes in Colonial America, p. 111.

10. Gottlieb Mittelberger, Journey to Pennsylvania, ed. Oscar Handlin and John Clive (Cambridge, Mass., 1960), p. 47.

11. Ibid., p. 53.

12. Jon Teaford, "The Transformation of Massachusetts Education," History of Education Quarterly 10 (Fall 1970): 298.

13. Mittelberger, Journey to Pennsylvania, p. 43.

14. Select Cases of the Mayor's Court of New York City, 1674-1784, ed. Richard B. Morris, American Legal Records 2 (Washington, D. C., 1935): 29-30.

15. Jernegan, Laboring and Dependent Classes in Colonial America, p. 91.

16. Ibid., pp. 104-6.

17. Acts of the State of Ohio, vol. 4 (Chillicothe, 1805; reprinted by Laning Co., Norwalk, Ohio, 1901), Fourth Session of the General Assembly, pp. 72-73.

18. "Indentures of Apprenticeship, 1694-5--1707-8," Collections of the New York Historical Society, vol. 18 (1885), pp. 565-622; "Indentures of Apprentices, 1718-1729," vol. 42 (1909-11), pp. 113-99. The indentures, most of which were completed on forms, are not reprinted in full in these publications. The editors of the 1694-1708 records, however, do make a special point of noting the provision for education, e.g., "Usual form, except that master further agrees 'to allow him Evening Schooling Every winter from Christmas as is Customary.'" In the records for 1718-1727 provisions for education are mentioned so frequently that while indentures are not reprinted in full, the trend toward greater inclusion of educational provisions is unmistakable.

19. "The Indentures of Managers of the House of Employment in Philadelphia County in 1798, Administered under the Form of the Act of Assembly for the Relief of the Poor," book B, folio 9, microfilm 980136, Indentures, Loose Papers, Almshouses, Guardians of the Poor, Philadelphia County, 1795-1806, Genealogical Society of Salt Lake City.

20. Collections of the New York Historical Society 18 (1885): 593, 598.

21. "The Indentures of Managers of the House of Employment in Philadelphia County in 1798"; Indenture, Daniel Porter to Wm. Thompson Cooper for 3 years, 8 Jan. 1798.

22. Kenneth A. Lockridge, Literacy in Colonial New England (New York, 1974), pp. 19-39.

23. Lawrence Stone, "Literacy and Education in England, 1640-1900," Past and Present 42 (Feb. 1969):98.

24. David Cressy, "Levels of Illiteracy in England, 1530-1730," Historical Journal 20 (1977): 11.

25. We established a procedure for estimating differences in illiteracy among the living and dead and those with and without wealth. The data for 1870 indicate that illiteracy for those with wealth was 10.1 percent less than illiteracy for all adult males, but that for deceased with wealth it was but 2.0 percent less than that for all adult males. The inference is that the illiteracy rate obtained from wills in New Hampshire, for instance, may very well have been similar to that for all living adult males. In this case, the upward bias of the will data arises from the fact that the deceased had an average age greater than that of the living together with the fact that older people tended to have higher illiteracy rates; the downward bias arose from the fact that people with wills and wealth tended to have lower illiteracy. The two biases tended in fact to almost counterbalance each other. The effects are illustrated in the following table, which gives the illiteracy rate in the United States in 1870 of deceased males having wealth as estimated from data for the living:

Age		Living Males	Deceased Males
		All with Positive	All with Positive
Age	All	Wealth	Wealth
(1)	(2)	(3)	(4)
20-29	.082	.072	.072
30-39	.078	.065	.065
40-49	.087	.076	.076
50-59	.104	.095	.095
60-69	.102	.093	.093
70-99	.109	.106	.106
20-99	.087	.078	.085
Average			
Age	38.4	42.1	50.7

(Col. 2 gives the illiteracy rates of 9,125 adult white males. Col. 3 gives the rates of 5,764 of the col. 2 men reporting positive wealth. Col. 4 is obtained from the 5,764 of col. 3 by applying 1865 age-specific death rates in Massachusetts [the probability times a frequency of 1] for eight age classes, 20-29, . . . , 80-99. Source: The manuscripts of the 1870 census and Historical Statistics of the United States, series B, pp. 163-75.)

    26. In New Hampshire, one of the problems was the fee for the administration of estates, which could amount to 5 percent of a fifty-pound estate (Probate Records of the Province of New Hampshire, ed. Albert Batchellor, vol. 1, pp. xii, xvii). It is imperative that we realize that the validity of a sample from wills rests on the assumption that such documents are a random sample of the distribution of wealth of the deceased; this is not likely to be the case, and they probably underrepresent those with little or no wealth. The census of New Hampshire in 1767 counted 1,230 men sixty years of age and older and 5,740 above sixteen years in the state. The annual number of wills and administered estates of males between 1755 and 1760 averaged about 1.4 percent of this number. This is a low representation as judged from the death rate in Massachusetts of .0164 for males twenty and older in the period 1860-65 (see Documents and Records of New Hampshire, vol. 6 (1776-83), p. 170; Historical Statistics of the United States, series B, pp. 163-75; and Lockridge, Literacy in Colonial New England, p. 123). If only one-third of the deceased are accounted for by wills, for instance, and if they are representative of the top two-thirds of the total wealth distribution, then we can correct for the underrepresentation in the following manner. We know from the 1860 and 1870 census data that the illiteracy rate for those men with wealth above the thirty-third decile was only 90 percent of that for all men. We might estimate, then, that our New Hampshire figures should be multiplied by about 1.1 to arrive at the state levels of illiteracy.

    27. Probate Records of the Province of New Hampshire, vol. 1, p. xii.

    28. The number of testate cases considered for the four curves in figure 2.1 are as follows:

	Maine	New Hampshire	Essex County	Hartford County
1641-59	. . .	11	76	56
1660-79	36	67	238	87
1680-99	37	74	22	185
1700-19	43	133	. . .	198
1720-39	75	191	. . .	354
1740-60	83	650	. . .	245

    29. Cremin, American Education, p. 192; Adams, Provincial Society, p. 133.

    30. Sumner Chilton Powell, Puritan Village (New York, 1965). Studies such as David Galenson's "Literacy and the Social Origins of Some Early Americans" (Historical Journal 22 [1979]:75-92) may help us to a better understanding of the levels of literacy among late seventeenth-century colonists. He has noted that indentured servants bound over for service in the American colonies "came in significant numbers from all levels of the broad segment of

English society known to contemporaries as the Commons, bounded at one end by the gentry, at the other by the paupers" (p. 91). Like other studies of literacy during this period, Galenson's shows levels of literacy to vary considerably by occupation.

31. James A. Henretta, The Evolution of American Society, 1700-1815 (Lexington, Mass., 1973), p. 22.

32. Adams, Provincial Society, p. 133.

33. Documents Relative to the Colonial History of New York, the State of New York, Procured in Holland, England, and France, ed. E. B. Callaghan, vol. 4 (Albany, 1856), pp. 933-39.

34. Ibid., pp. 1005-9.

35. Archives of Maryland, "Proceedings and Acts," vol. 7, pp. 521-55.

36. Documents and Records of New Hampshire, vol. 8 (1776-83), pp. 204, 266-69. Originals are in the New Hampshire State Archives.

37. Colonial Records of North Carolina, ed. Walter Clark (Raleigh, 1886, and New York, AMS Reprint, 1968), vol. 22, pp. 169, 173, 179.

38. Documents Relative to the Colonial History of New York, vol. 3, pp. 834-41.

39. The equation specified is log T = -.49 + .44 log P, where N = 11 for decadal figures from 1670 to 1770 and R^2 = .98. The equation is roughly consistent with the number of towns and cities in Connecticut in 1970. The town data are obtained from the annual fiscal reports in Public Records of Connecticut, vols. 1-13. These were transcribed and edited in accordance with a resolution of the General Assembly by J. Hammon Trumbull (Hartford, 1852). Populations are from Historical Statistics of the United States, series Z, p. 8.

40. Historical Statistics of the United States, series P, pp. 43-72.

41. Rush Welter, The Mind of America, 1820-1860 (New York, 1975), p. 311.

42. State Commissioner of Common Schools, Ohio, Annual Report, 1867 (Columbus, 1868), p. 40.

43. Records of the Colony of Rhode Island and Providence Plantations, vol. 1 (Providence, 1856), p. 14.

44. Ibid., p. 31.

45. Records of the Governor and Company of the Massachusetts Bay in New England (Boston, 1854), p. 358. Other charts are given in Kenneth A. Lockridge, Literacy in Colonial New England (New York, 1974).

46. Documents Relative to the Colonial History of the State of New York, vol. 1 (Albany, 1856), pp. 191-93.

47. Archives of Maryland, Judicial and Testamentary Business of the Provincial Court, 1637-1650, "Proceedings and Acts of the General Assembly, 1637/8-1664," ed. William Browne (Baltimore, 1887), p. 28.

48. Ibid., pp. 29-31.

49. Documents Relative to the Colonial History of the State of New York, vol. 14 (Albany, 1883), pp. 24-25.

50. Archives of Maryland, "Proceedings of the County Courts of Kent, 1648-1676, Talbot, 1662-1674, and Somerset, 1665-1668, Counties," vol. 54, Court Series 7 (Baltimore, 1937), pp. 4-5.

51. Archives of Maryland, Judicial and Testamentary Business, vol. 54, pp. 3-64, 465-549. Ibid., vol. 54, pp. 4, 5, 238, 485, 604. Ibid., vol. 53, pp. 44-270. Duplicated names have been eliminated in almost all cases.

52. Documents Relative to the Colonial History of New York, vol. 14, p. 7.

53. Ibid., pp. 7-8.

54. Ibid., pp. 361-63, 552; vol. 3, p. 926.

55. Records of the Colony of New Plymouth in New England, ed. Nathaniel B. Shurtleff (Boston, 1855), vol. 3, pp. 15-16, vol. 4, p. 130.

56. Leon de Valinger, Jr. (ed.), "Court Records of Kent County, Delaware, 1680-1705," in American Legal Records, vol. 8 (Washington, D. C., 1959), pp. 347-48.

57. Archives of Maryland, "Proceedings of the County Courts," vol. 54, pp. 4, 5, 238, 485, 604.

58. "Records of the Suffolk County Court, 1671-1680," Publications of the Colonial Society of Massachusetts, vol. 29 (Boston, 1933), pp. 276-77.

59. Lockridge, Literacy in Colonial New England, p. 37.

60. Ibid., pp. 52-55.

61. Samuel Knox, "An Essay on the Best System of Liberal Education" essay presented to the American Philosophical Society, 1798, Early American Imprints, no. 35690, pp. 5-6.

62. Academicus to Thomas Jefferson, "Plan for the Education of Youth," c. Jan. 1797, submitted to the Philosophical Society of Philadelphia, 1797, Archives no. 10, American Philosophical Society Library, Philadelphia.

63. Samuel Harrison Smith, "Remarks on Education," essay presented to the American Philosophical Society, 1798, Early American Imprints, no. 34558, p. 66.

64. Rush Welter, Popular Education and Democratic Thought in America (New York, 1962), p. 27.

65. Knox, "Essay on the Best System of Liberal Education," p. 23.

66. Edward Frank Humphrey, Nationalism and Religion in America, 1774-1789 (Boston, 1924), p. 503.

67. Cedric B. Cowing, The Great Awakening and the American Revolution: Colonial Thought in the Eighteenth Century (Chicago, 1971), p. 203.

68. Ibid., pp. 203, 222-23.

69. Benjamin Rush, "A Plan for the Establishment of Public Schools and the Diffusion of Knowledge in Pennsylvania," in Wilson Smith (ed.), Theories of Education in Early America, 1655-1819 (New York, 1973), p. 246.

70. Ibid., pp. 246, 244.

71. De Witt Clinton, "To the Public Address of the Trustees of the Society for Establishing a Free School in the City of New York, for the Education of Such Poor Children as Do Not Belong to, or Are Not Provided by Any Religious Society," New York Evening Post, 21 May 1805 in Wilson Smith (ed.), Theories of Education in Early America, 1655-1819 (New York, 1973), p. 342.

72. Ibid., pp. 354, 352.

73. Timothy L. Smith, "Protestant Schooling and American Nationality, 1800-1850," Journal of American History 53 (Mar. 1967):680.

74. Edward Stevens, "Wealth and Culture on the American Frontier," paper presented at the spring meeting of the Ohio Academy of History, Columbus, 21 Apr. 1979.

75. United States Statutes at Large, 1789-99, Fourth Congress, Session I, chap. 36, 1796, pp. 477-78. We are indebted to Captain Ira Dye for general instructions. Seamen were enrolled at ports other than Philadelphia, but the recorded dates are less complete.

76. The sample size for states are Massachusetts (N = 155), Connecticut (N = 99), New Hampshire, Vermont, and Maine (N = 111), New York (N = 281), New Jersey (N = 96), Pennsylvania (N = 193), and North Carolina (N = 126).

77. Figures for illiteracy among selected occupational groups are as follows:

Occupation	IL 1799-1829	IL 1830-94	Sample Size 1799-1829
Blacksmith	.38	.29	90
Carpenter	.25	.15	101
Farmer	.46	.28	587
Laborer	.54	.30	285
Shoemaker	.37	.03	116
Other	.37	.14	623
All	.42	.21	1,802

78. Collections of the New York Historical Society 18 (1885):565-622; 42 (1909-1911):113-99.

79. See Egil Johansson, The History of Literacy in Sweden in Comparison with Some Other Countries, Educational Reports, Umea, no. 12 (Umea, 1977), and Egil Johansson (ed.), Literacy and Society in a Historical Perspective--A Conference Report, Educational Reports, Umea, no. 2 (Umea, 1973); Kenneth Lockridge, Literacy in Colonial New England (New York, 1971); and Harvey J. Graff, The Literacy Myth: Literacy and Social Structure in the Nineteenth-Century City (New York: 1979). Wiebe has noted that systematization in education was not a fact (except perhaps in Boston) but a model. State officials and educational reformers with a vision of a cohesive American republic were keepers of that model, he remarks, and they assumed that "community leaders everywhere shared the same ethical system, the same dedication to public

service and the same aspirations to unity." In a decentralized nation of oc-
casional communication, he continues, the state administrator "articulated the
norms of common-school education against which isolated communities could
gauge their accomplishments" (Robert H. Wiebe, "The Social Functions of
Public Education," American Quarterly 21 [Summer 1969]:149-51). Wiebe's
remarks serve to remind us that we must proceed with caution in applying
the concept of system to nineteenth-century common school education, yet we
should keep in mind that from Massachusetts to the Midwest, educational
legislation affecting school districting, curriculum, teacher standards, and
the organization of graded schools brought stability to the educational process.
Schultz has remarked that "the graded school was to be one of the chief
tools used in the process of manufacturing good Americans" (Stanley K. Schultz,
The Culture Factory:Boston Public Schools, 1789-1860 [New York, 1973], p.
131). One cannot say that the administrative machinery was sufficient by mid-
century to bring a high degree of efficiency to the system, yet systematization
was a mark of mid-nineteenth-century educational reform.
    80. Lockridge, Literacy in Colonial New England, p. 52.

Chapter 3

    1. Egil Johansson, The History of Literacy in Sweden in Comparison with
Some Other Countries, Educational Reports, Umea, no. 12 (Umea, 1977), pp. 7-9.
    2. M. Seliger, Ideology and Politics (New York, 1976), p. 120.
    3. Richard Pratte, Ideology and Education (New York, 1977), p. 225.
    4. Clifford Geertz, "Ideology as a Cultural System," in David E.
Apter (ed.), Ideology and Discontent (London, 1964), p. 64.
    5. Harvey J. Graff, The Literacy Myth (New York, 1979), p. 29.
    6. Seliger, Ideology and Politics, p. 106.
    7. Pratte, Ideology and Education, p. 226.
    8. Geoffrey H. Bantock, The Implications of Literacy (Leicester, 1966),
pp. 7, 11.
    9. Egil Johansson (ed.), Literacy and Society in a Historical Perspective--
A Conference Report, Educational Reports, Umea, no. 2 (Umea, 1973);
Johansson, History of Literacy in Sweden.
    10. Michael Katz's The Irony of Early School Reform (Boston, 1970) has
made extensive use of the concept of ideology in treating pedagogical innovation
as it occurred in nineteenth-century New England. In his analysis of mid-
nineteenth-century educational reform in Massachusetts, Katz has noted that
"schoolmen assumed that the unfavorable influence of society upon personality
was to be countered by the inculcation of a restraint based upon sublimation,
a substitution of 'higher' for 'lower' pleasures" (p. 120).
    11. Michalina Vaughn and Margaret S. Archer, Social Conflict and
Educational Change in England and France, 1789-1848 (Cambridge, 1971), p. 20.
    12. Edward Pessen, Most Uncommon Jacksonians (Albany, 1967), p. 186.
    13. Rush Welter, The Mind of America, 1820-1860 (New York, 1975),
p. 261.
    14. Joseph Story, "A Discourse Pronounced at Cambridge, before the
Phi Beta Kappa Society," 31 Aug. 1826, in E. B. Williston (comp.), Eloquence
of the United States, vol. 5 (Middleton, Conn., 1827), pp. 419-20.
    15. "Memorial of a Number of Citizens of Boston to the Senate and House
of Representatives," 13 Feb. 1832, American State Papers, Class VII (Washington,
1834), p. 341.
    16. Athens Mirror and Literary Register, Athens, Ohio 23 Sept. 1826,
4:2.
    17. Huron Reflector, Norwalk, Ohio, 25 Mar. 1851, 4:2.
    18. Athens Mirror and Literary Register, Athens, Ohio, 2 Aug. 1828, 4:4;
Athens Messenger, Athens, Ohio, 10 May 1850, 1:2.
    19. Cleveland Herald and Gazette, Cleveland, Ohio, 7 Sept. 1839, 3:1,
reprinted in Annals of Cleveland, vol. 22, no. 532, p. 70.
    20. Monica Kiefer, American Children through Their Books, 1700-1835
(Philadelphia, 1948), p. 63.
    21. Ruth Miller Elson, Guardians of Tradition (Lincoln, Nebr. 1964), p.
338; Kiefer, American Children through Their Books, p. 72.
    22. Anne Scott Macleod, A Moral Tale (Hamden, Conn., 1975), p. 158.
    23. Zanesville City Times, Zanesville, Ohio, 3 Mar. 1855, 1:4.

24. [W. Dunlap], The Child's New Play-Thing: Being a Spelling-Book Intended to Make the Learning to Read, a Diversion instead of a Task Consisting of a New-Invented Alphabet for Children (Philadelphia, 1763); [Isaiah Thomas], Tom Thumb's Playbook: To Teach Children Their letters as Soon as They Can Speak Being a New and Pleasant Method to Allure Little Ones in the First Principles of Learning (Boston, 1761); Noah Webster, The American Spelling Book: Containing an Easy Standard of Pronunciation Being the First Part of a Grammatical Institute of the English Language, 2d ed. (Boston, 1790), p. 57.

25. S. Hays, Stories for Little Children, part 1 (Philadelphia, 1812), p. 12.

26. Nathan Guilford, The Western Spelling Book, Designed for the Use of Common Schools (Cincinnati, 1831), p. 92.

27. Athens Mirror and Literary Register, Athens, Ohio, 8 Nov. 1828, 1:5.

28. Webster, American Spelling Book, p. 66; [Josiah Townsend], A Letter to Children and Young Persons, Particularly Such as Attend Sunday Schools or Other Charity Schools (Halifax, 1809), p. 10.

29. William H. McGuffey, McGuffey's Eclectic First Reader (Cincinnati, 1836), pp. 26-27.

30. The Mother's Gift; or, a Present for All Little Boys Who Wish to Be Good (Philadelphia, 1791), p. 47.

31. Mrs. Anna Letitia Barbauld, Lessons for Children from Two to Four Years Old (Philadelphia, 1788), p. 7.

32. William H. McGuffey, McGuffey's New Primary Reader (Cincinnati, 1864), p. 9.

33. Western Spy and Literary Cadet, Cincinnati, Ohio, 24 Mar. 1821, 2:1.

34. Ibid., 21 Apr. 1821, 2:1.

35. Ibid., 12 May 1821, 2:1.

36. Data for the study were gathered from 1,118 estate inventories of two Ohio counties: Washington County, which included the city of Marietta and had 20 percent of Ohio's population in 1800, and Athens County. Both counties were significant in the development of the main artery to the American West, the Ohio River Valley. From an economic standpoint, Athens County remained less developed than Marietta and Washington County; for this reason, it is useful for comparative purposes in analysis. The Athens County sample (414) represents all inventoried estates from 1831 (the first on record) to 1859. The Washington County sample (704) represents all inventoried estates from 1790 to 1823. Because the number of inventories grew so large during the last half of the period under study, about one-third (sampling every tenth page of the probate records) of the inventories are included for Washington County between 1824 and 1859. The sample is preponderantly male, with females constituting only 5 percent of the inventories. Where it was possible to exclude inventories of persons with guardians, this was done, since the wealth of these deceased is not comparable with those of adults. Generally, then, the sample consists of white males, aged twenty and over.

If we use a figure of 2 percent for the death rate among white males twenty and over, the sample represents between 15 and 17 percent of those dying in a given year. This figure is considerably lower than the 40 percent figure of Smith and Lockridge, and reflects the fact that (1) in a frontier region geographic mobility was greater than in the Boston area, (2) the enforcement of statutes relating to inventories was more difficult in these early years of the frontier, (3) some nonitemized inventories were excluded from the sample since they were of no use in ascertaining book ownership or the percentages on various consumer items used for analysis, and (4) appraisements, which are similar to inventories but are used only for sale of the estate, were excluded, since items inventoried in estates are sometimes not found in the appraisements. When appraisements and inventories are added, with no repetition of names, the sample represents 30 percent of the dying.

Available cemetery records enable us to approximate the age distribution of the dying for a subsample of 106 from Athens County. As expected, the greater number of deaths occurred between ages 30 and 69, with 49 percent of the total dying between ages 40 and 60. The median age at death was 49.5. Assuming that very little wealth was actually accumulated during the first twenty-five years of life, this means that the data are capturing the accumulation of

wealth during a period of approximately twenty-five years prior to death.
Thus, for our earlier data in Washington County, most of the accumulation oc-
curred from 1765 to 1790. For the later death date of 1855, for instance, we
can expect most of the wealth to have accumulated from 1830 to 1855.
Excellent discussions of biases in probate data are given in Gary B.
Nash, "Urban Wealth and Poverty in Pre-Revolutionary America," Journal of
Interdisciplinary History 6 (Spring 1976): 545-84; Daniel Scott Smith, "Underregistration and Bias in Probate Records: An Analysis of Data from Eighteenth-
Century Hingham, Massachusetts," William and Mary Quarterly 32 (Jan. 1975):
100-110; Gloria L. Main, "The Correction of Biases in Colonial American Probate
Records," Historical Methods Newsletter 8 (Dec. 1974):10-28. See also a note
by Kenneth Lockridge, "A Communication," William and Mary Quarterly 25 (July
1968):516-17.
        37.   The mean personal estate values, in dollars, of book owners and
non-book owners from the sample of 1,118 (see table 3.1) are tabulated below:

	Athens County			Washington County		
	Book Owners	Non-Book Owners	Ratio	Book Owners	Non-Book Owners	Ratio
1790-99	...	...	...	285	232	1.2
1800-09	...	...	...	853	457	1.9
1810-19	712	170	4.2	860	456	1.9
1820-29	407	219	1.8	942	292	3.2
1830-39	390	320	1.2	1113	538	2.1
1840-49	905	494	1.8	1903	1213	1.6
1850-59	1197	721	1.7	1325	910	1.4
1790-1859	840	467	1.8	1220	645	1.9

        38.   Asa Lyman, The American Reader: Containing Elegant Selections in
Prose and Poetry, 2d ed. (Portland, Me., 1811), p. 294.
        39.   Anthony Benezet, The Pennsylvania Spelling Book; or, Youth's
Friendly Instructor and Monitor (Philadelphia, 1779), p. 5.
        40.   Kiefer, American Children through Their Books, p. 86.
        41.   Samuel Wood, The New York Reader, No. 1, Adapted to the Capacities
of the Younger Class of Learners (New York, 1812), p. 123.
        42.   Webster, American Spelling Book, pp. 56, 65.
        43.   A. Pickett and John W. Pickett, The New Juvenile Spelling Book and
Rudimental Reader (Cincinnati, 1837), p. 52.
        44.   McGuffey, McGuffey's Eclectic First Reader, p. 51.
        45.   The Child's Instructor (Philadelphia, 1808), in Clifton Johnson, Old-
Time Schools and School-Books (New York, 1917), p. 237.
        46.   Barbauld, Lessons for Children from Two to Four Years Old, p. 9.
        47.   The Good Child's Delight; or, the Road to Knowledge in Short,
Entertaining Lessons of One and Two Syllables (Philadelphia, 1795), pp. 29-32.
        48.   Charles W. Sanders, Sanders' Spelling Book Containing a Minute and
Comprehensive System of Introductory Orthography (Cleveland, 1844), pp. 66-
67.
        49.   Webster, American Spelling Book, p. 57.
        50.   William H. McGuffey, McGuffey's Newly Revised Eclectic Second Reader
(Cincinnati, 1853), p. 10.
        51.   William H. McGuffey, McGuffey's Eclectic Third Reader (Cincinnati,
1848), p. 61.
        52.   Daniel Crandall, The Columbian Spelling-Book: Containing the Elements
of the English Language (Cooperstown, 1820), p. 38.
        53.   Zanesville Gazette, Zanesville, Ohio, 7 Mar. 1838, 1:1.
        54.   Athens Mirror and Literary Register, Athens, Ohio, 15 Mar. 1828, 1:4;
8 Nov. 1828, 1:5.
        55.   "A Word to Apprentices," Child's Newspaper, Cincinnati, Ohio, 7
Jan. 1834, 4:2.
        56.   Reprinted in Zanesville Gazette, Zanesville, Ohio, 24 Dec. 1836,
1:5-6.
        57.   Huron Reflector, Norwalk, Ohio, 23 July 1839, 1:5.
        58.   Ohio Journal of Education (Columbus, 1856), p. 97.
        59.   Louis B. Wright, Culture on the Moving Frontier (Bloomington, Ind.,
1955), p. 236.

60. W. T. Barry, Post Office Department, to William Russel, Committee on the Post Office and Post Roads, House of Representatives, in American State Papers, Class VII, vol. 1 (Washington, 1834), p. 339. An 1828 resolution of one Mr. Verplanck of New York to the House of Representatives to reduce the rate of postage on periodical publications, for instance, noted that "the high postage of these publications . . . was an obstacle in the way of the prosecution of many benevolent plans" including those involving "the purposes of general education." Resolution of Mr. Verplanck of New York, 21 Dec. 1829, in Register of Debates of Congress, part 2, vol. 13, p. 479.

61. American State Papers, Class VII (Washington, 1834), p. 183.

62. Richard D. Brown, "The Emergence of Urban Society in Massachusetts, 1760-1820," Journal of American History 61 (June 1974):44.

63. Cleveland Herald, Cleveland, Ohio, 4 Mar. 1841, 3:1, reprinted in Annals of Cleveland, vol. 23, no. 366, p. 59.

64. Benjamin Franklin, Autobiography, in John Tebbel, A History of Book Publishing in the United States, vol. 1 (New York, 1972), p. 156.

65. Tebbel, History of Book Publishing, pp. 160-61.

66. Uriah P. James Papers, "Catalog" (1852), "Catalog" (1840), Collection 198, Ohio Historical Society.

67. Ellen Shaffer, "The Children's Books of the American Sunday-School Union," Book Collector 17 (Oct. 1966): 23.

68. Tebbel, History of Book Publishing, p. 514.

69. Samuel Williams Papers, Box 15, Folder 1, Collection 148, Ohio Historical Society.

70. F—ratios for all types of books were measured at the .01 level of significance before and after 1830.

71. United States Department of Commerce, Historical Statistics of the United States, part 1 (Washington, 1975), pp. 163, 468.

72. Western Spy and Literary Cadet, Cincinnati, Ohio, 13 Jan. 1821, 2:3.

73. Ibid., 10 Feb. 1821, 2:5.

74. Ibid., 14 Apr. 1821, 2:2.

75. Ohio Republican, Zanesville, Ohio, 5 Jan. 1833, 3:3.

76. Huron Reflector, Norwalk, Ohio, 12 Mar. 1833, 3:6; Ohio Argus, Lebanon, Ohio, 4 Jan. 1833, 4:4.

77. Ibid.

78. Dorothy V. Martin, "A History of the Library Movement in Ohio to 1850 with a Special Study of Cincinnati's Library Development," master's thesis, Ohio State University, 1935, p. 77.

79. Paul Kaufman, "The Community Library: A Chapter in English Social History," Transactions of the American Philosophical Society, n.s., part 7, 57 (1967):24.

80. Using subscriber records of four of these organizations in conjunction with tax duplicates, Stevens is currently investigating membership-wealth patterns of social libraries. Comparative distributions of the number of acres owned by members of each library compared with the local county populations are given below:

Name of Association, Date	Percentage of the Total Acres Owned by Members (Local County Populations) above Selected Percentiles		
	90	70	50
Chillicothe, 1812	.66(.61)	.82(.84)	.91(.93)
Columbus, 1816	.38(.33)	.72(.69)	.92(.91)
Mentor, 1825	.31(.59)	.62(.78)	.79(.89)
Mentor, 1834	.31(.51)	.63(.74)	.86(.88)
Western, 1825	.31(.59)	.58(.79)	.79(.90)
Western, 1834	.28(.48)	.54(.76)	.71(.87)
Western, 1844	.24(.45)	.57(.69)	.77(.84)

Source: The several subscriber lists and county tax duplicates.

81. "Catalog of Books in the Farmer's Library" (1827), University of Rochester, Special Collections; "Catalog of Books in the Chillicothe Library" (1804), John Kerr Papers, 1788-1844, Container 3, Western Reserve Historical Society; "Catalog of Books Belonging to the Western Library Association," vol. 1, Ohio Historical Society.

82. Graff, Literacy Myth, p. 240.
83. Tenth Annual Report, Eastern State Penitentiary, Pennsylvania (Philadelphia, 1839), p. 9.
84. Michael B. Katz, The Irony of Early School Reform (Boston, 1968), p. 184.

Chapter 4

1. S. M. Hamilton (ed.), Writings of James Monroe, vol. 3, 6 Dec. 1801, pp. 306-7, quoted in Harry Ammon, James Monroe: The Quest for National Identity (New York, 1971), p. 177.
2. Ibid.
3. William Manning, The Key to Liberty, Shewing the Causes Why a Free Government Has Always Failed, and a Remidy Against It (Billerica, Mass., 1822), pp. 19-21, 35-36, quoted in Robert H. Bremner (ed.), Children and Youth in America, vol. 1 (Cambridge, Mass., 1970), p. 229.
4. Timothy Dwight, A Discourse on Some Events of the Last Century, address delivered in New Haven, 7 Jan. 1801, at Yale (New Haven, 1801).
5. Samuel Miller, "A Sketch of the Revolutions and Improvements in Science, Arts, and Literature in America," from Brief Retrospect of the Eighteenth Century (1803), reprinted in William and Mary Quarterly 10 (Jan. 1953): 612.
6. Cleveland Register, Cleveland, Ohio, 15 Sept. 1818, 4:2-3, reprinted in Annals of Cleveland, vol. 1, no. 267, p. 109.
7. Ohio Republican, Zanesville, Ohio, 22 June 1833, 2:1-2.
8. Thomas Jefferson, Notes on the State of Virginia, "Query XIV," reprinted in Gordon C. Lee (ed.), Crusade against Ignorance: Thomas Jefferson on Education (New York, 1961), p. 94.
9. Hiram Orcutt, Hints to Common School Teachers, Parents, and Pupils (Rutland, Vt. 1859), p. 131.
10. Lawrence A. Cremin, Traditions of American Education (New York, 1977), p. 56.
11. Most standard texts on the history of American education contain accounts of the moral mission of the schools. We mention three recent accounts of special interest: Carl F. Kaestle, The Evolution of an Urban School System: New York City, 1750-1850 (Cambridge, Mass., 1973), chap. 4; Stanley K. Schultz, The Culture Factory: Boston Public Schools, 1789-1860 (New York, 1973), chap. 5; and David Tyack, The One Best System: A History of American Urban Education (Cambridge, Mass., 1974).
12. Rowland Berthoff, An Unsettled People (New York, 1971), p. 210.
13. "Report of the Working Men's Committee," as appearing in the Working Man's Advocate, New York, 6 Mar. 1830, and abstracted from the Mechanics' Free Press, Philadelphia, Pa. See John R. Commons (ed.), A Documentary History of American Industrial Society, vol. 5 (Cleveland, 1910), p. 95.
14. Ulysses S. Grant, Personal Memoirs, vol. 1 (New York, 1885), pp. 21, 25.
15. For a review of these theories, their strengths, and their weaknesses, and an attempt to reconcile their seeming divergent themes, see Carl F. Kaestle, "Social Change, Discipline, and the Common School in Early Nineteenth-Century America," Journal of Interdisciplinary History 9 (Summer 1978):1-17.
16. State Commissioner of Common Schools, Ohio, Annual Report, 1863 (Columbus, 1864), p. 17-18.
17. Edward Jarvis, "The Value of Common School Education to Common Labor," Circular of Information of the Bureau of Education, no. 3 (Washington, 1879), p. 27.
18. Carl F. Kaestle and Maris A. Vinovskis, Education and Social Change in Nineteenth-Century Massachusetts: Quantitative Studies, Final Research Report, 31 Dec. 1976, National Institute of Education, Grant NE-G-00-3-0068, Project 3-0825, pp. 81-82.
19. Ibid., pp. 27, 82, 85.
20. Harvey J. Graff, "Literacy and Social Structure in the Nineteenth-Century City," Ph.D. dissertation, University of Toronto, 1975; Michael B. Katz, "Who Went to School?" History of Education Quarterly 12 (Fall 1972): 432-54.
21. Ohio Commissioner, Annual Report, 1863, pp. 17-18.

22. Superintendent of Public Instruction, Forty-Seventh Annual Report (Harrisburg, 1880), p. xvii.

23. Daniel Calhoun, The Intelligence of a People (Princeton, N. J., 1973), pp. 201-2. For a description and analysis of the ways in which America coped with the inadequacies of social institutions inherited from colonial times, see also David Rothman, The Discovery of the Asylum (Boston, 1971).

24. Schultz, Culture Factory, p. 72.

25. Quoted in Michael M. Gordon, Assimilation in American Life (New York, 1964), p. 116.

26. Lee Soltow, Men and Wealth in the United States, 1850-1870 (New Haven, 1975), p. 175. The Gini coefficient (G) is an overall measure of relative inequality. G = 0 represents perfect equality; G = 1 represents perfect inequality. If all real estate values were equal, G would equal 0.

27. Ibid., pp. 180, 183.

28. Ibid., pp. 178-79.

29. Richard Pratte, Ideology and Education (New York, 1977), p. 138.

30. Lockean empiricism had for some time been the basis for an environmentalist approach to pedagogy which made it possible for teachers to see the child as a creature moulded by the "sensations" of his environment. Locke's tabula rasa conception of the infant mind, however, had also encouraged teachers to view the student's mind as a container to be filled with knowledge. Pestalozzian theory had taken the sensationalism of Locke and extended it to teaching methodology. Thus, Pestalozzi developed his doctrine of Anschauung, or direct, concrete observation. In his school, notes Kilpatrick of Pestalozzi, "no word was to be used for any purpose until adequate Anschauung had preceded. The thing or the distinction must somehow be seen or felt or otherwise observed in the concrete" (William H. Kilpatrick, introduction to Heinrich Pestalozzi, The Education of Man: Aphorisms [New York, 1951], pp. viii-ix). John M. Keagy in his Pestalozzian Primer (Harrisburg, 1827) attempted to apply these principles to the teaching of reading. Horace Mann, as well, advocated the "whole word" method of teaching reading in which children began with whole words whose meaning and pronunciation they already knew. This, it was argued, was naturally interesting and more pleasurable to children and resulted in more effective learning (Robert L. Church and Michael O. Sedlak, Education in the United States [New York, 1976], p. 97).

31. Western Spy and Literary Cadet, Cincinnati, Ohio, 24 Mar. 1821, 2:2.

32. Ibid.

33. Keagy, Pestalozzian Primer, p. 10.

34. Ibid., p. 12.

35. Charles Royce, "Instruction in Phonetics," Ohio Journal of Education 2 (1853): 351-52.

36. Alonzo Potter, The School and the School Master (Boston, 1843), p. 424.

37. Mrs. M. Bakewell, The Mother's Practical Guide in the Early Training of Her Children (London, 1836), pp. 39, 41, 94, 106.

38. Kaestle and Vinovskis, Education and Social Change in Nineteenth-Century Massachusetts, p. 211; Charles Northend, Obstacles to the Greater Success of Common Schools (Boston, 1844), p. 15.

39. The American Primer Calculated for the Instruction of Young Children (Norfolk, 1803), p. 26.

40. Warren Burton (ed.), The District School as It Was (New York, 1928), pp. 21-22.

41. Clifton Johnson, The Country School (New York, 1907), p. 52.

42. Daniel Crandall, The Columbian Spelling-Book: Containing the Elements of The English Language (Cooperstown, N. Y., 1820), p. 94.

43. William McGuffey, McGuffey's New First Eclectic Reader (Cincinnati, 1857, 1864), pp. 20, 66.

44. The school districts sampled included the following: Districts 3 and 5, Perry Township, Columbiana Co., Ohio, 1840-52 (Mss. 578 in Western Reserve Historical Society, Cleveland, Ohio); District 5, Butler Township, Columbiana Co., Ohio, 1846-60 (Mss. 908 in Western Reserve Historical Society); District 1, Sullivan Township, Ashland Co., Ohio, 1847-53 (Mss. 1208 in Western Reserve Historical Society); Districts 1, 2, 3, 4, 6, 8, 9, and 10, Bainbridge Township, Geauga Co., Ohio, 1875-76 (Mss. 3405 in Western Reserve Historical Society);

District 6, Springfield Township, Hamilton Co., Ohio, 1844-45 (Mss. qA6495, RMU, Ross County Historical Society, Chillicothe, Ohio); Greenfield Union School, Highland Co., Ohio, 1859-67 ("Teacher Ledger," Ross County Historical Society); District 5, Twinsburg, Summit Co., Ohio, 1847-56 (Mss. T92, Hudson Historical Society, Hudson, Ohio).

45. The age and sex distribution for the subsample of 1,106 is below. For figure 4.1, ages twenty-one to twenty-seven were omitted.

Age	Males (N)	Sample Size Females (N)	Total (N)	Percent
3	0	2	2	.2
4	18	13	31	2.8
5	18	23	41	3.7
6	22	34	56	5.1
7	45	29	74	6.7
8	49	31	80	7.2
9	45	40	85	7.7
10	65	63	128	11.6
11	48	59	107	9.7
12	59	68	127	11.5
13	43	49	92	8.3
14	40	34	74	6.7
15	30	22	52	4.7
16	31	17	48	4.3
17	18	14	32	2.9
18	26	15	41	3.7
19	10	11	21	1.9
20	4	3	7	.6
21-27	6	2	8	.7
Total	577	529	1106	100.0

46. The age and sex distribution for the subsample of 333 is below. For figure 4.2, ages 16 to 18 were omitted.

Age	Males (N)	Sample Size Females (N)	Total (N)	Percent
3	1	1	2	.6
4	7	13	20	6.0
5	11	21	32	9.6
6	21	19	40	12.0
7	20	21	41	12.3
8	24	23	47	14.1
9	10	18	28	8.4
10	18	21	39	11.7
11	13	8	21	6.3
12	5	18	23	6.9
13	6	15	21	6.3
14	1	6	7	2.1
15	0	4	4	1.2
16-18	1	7	8	2.5
Total	138	195	333	100.0

47. Alice M. Earle, Child Life in Colonial Days (New York, 1927), p. 74.

48. Clifton Johnson, Old-Time Schools and School-Books (New York, 1917), p. 293; Peter A. Soderbergh, "'Old School Days' on the Middle Border, 1849-1859: The Mary Payne Beard Letters," History of Education Quarterly 8 (Winter 1968): 501.

49. Ohio Journal of Education 2 (1853): 8. This latter condition might well have been the motivation for a series of problems and answers entitled "Youth's Corner" which appeared periodically from the latter 1840s to the early 1860s in at least two Ohio newspapers. "Youth's Corner" might well be cited as one of the more fascinating attempts of newspapers to engage adolescents in

mental culture. The series generally was devoted to arithmetical and mathematical exercises, although problems regarding geography and history, and even a debate on the advantages and disadvantages of trial by jury were among the features to which young minds were asked to respond.

50. Pennsylvania School Journal 32 (1884):358.

51. Johnson, Old-Time Schools, p. 40.

52. David P. Page, Theory and Practice of Teaching (Syracuse, N. Y., 1847), p. 23.

53. Ibid.

54. Jacob Abbott, Rollo's Correspondence (Philadelphia, 1850), pp. 21, 31.

55. Sara Worthington King Family Papers, Box 2, Folder 1, Letters of Thomas W. King, Dec. 1827 to 12 Mar. 1835, Ohio Historical Society, Columbus, Ohio.

56. William Henry Seward Collection, Special Collections, University of Rochester, Rochester, N. Y.

57. Both Troen and Vinovskis have pointed to the difficulty of breaking down school attendance data by attendance/age or attendance/age/subject. See Selwyn K. Troen, "Popular Education in Nineteenth-Century St. Louis," History of Education Quarterly 13 (Spring 1973): 23-40, and The Public and the Schools (Columbia, Mo., 1975); also Maris A. Vinovskis, "Trends in Massachusetts Education, 1826-1860," History of Education Quarterly 12 (Winter 1972):501-29.

58. The entire Ohio sample included 2,694 cases, with ages ranging from three to twenty; 2,288 of these provided both age and attendance information. The mean number of days attended for all cases was 49.5. Age and attendance figures (median and Gini coefficient) for the three periods in figures 4.4 and 4.5 are listed in detail below.

Figure 4.4

				Attendance					
	1840-49			1850-59			1860-69		
Age	N	Median	G	N	Median	G	N	Median	G
3	4	39.5	.28	0	...	...	2	43.5	.30
4	20	46.	.29	19	26.5	.39	3	50.5	.16
5	38	45.5	.24	16	53.5	.38	11	54.8	.22
6	56	48.	.27	27	48.5	.29	16	55.	.23
7	74	56.	.23	25	59.	.26	12	47.	.24
8	67	55.5	.25	39	51.8	.32	16	62.	.18
9	69	51.8	.27	41	56.3	.34	18	57.	.31
10	72	51.5	.31	50	50.	.34	36	52.5	.47
11	80	48.5	.31	60	52.	.40	29	55.8	.34
12	82	52.	.29	62	62.	.35	29	46.3	.33
13	81	51.3	.33	39	47.	.34	25	66.5	.22
14	64	50.	.31	26	47.	.40	19	45.	.34
15	51	43.	.35	18	45.5	.38	5	71.5	.03
16	42	43.5	.30	12	58.	.21	8	58.	.13
17	31	45.	.27	9	52.	.13	6	31.	.21
18	18	42.5	.23	11	51.	.25	14	44.5	.26
19	3	20.5	.14	5	65.	.30	6	28.5	.19
20	0	...	...	0	...	...	3	59.5	.22

Figure 4.5

Attendance

Age	1840-49			1850-59		
	N	Median	G	N	Median	G
3	2	50.	.46	0	...	...
4	14	49.5	.32	5	59.8	.35
5	17	41.	.32	19	47.5	.33
6	89	65.	.37	7	53.3	.14
7	90	77.	.34	15	47.	.27
8	79	72.3	.32	20	50.	.27
9	51	72.5	.36	13	52.8	.26
10	59	58.8	.40	29	38.8	.27
11	25	57.	.31	17	32.	.42
12	23	40.	.28	26	50.	.30
13	18	36.5	.40	19	47.8	.32
14	21	45.5	.25	10	34.5	.24
15	15	50.5	.18	10	45.	.18
16	10	60.5	.31	1	80.	0
17	10	33.	.22	5	55.8	.31

(Source: as in note 44.)
    The entire Rochester, New York, sample included 1,450 cases, ranging in age from five to eighteen; 1,334 of these included both age and attendance data. The mean number of days attended for all cases was 112. Age and attendance figures (median and Gini coefficient) for the two periods in figure 4.6 are listed in detail below.

Figure 4.6

Attendance

Age	1861-69			1870-74		
	N	Median	G	N	Median	G
5	98	58.	.40	22	88.	.36
6	110	134.	.30	33	87.	.39
7	107	134.	.30	35	116.	.38
8	101	153.	.23	35	127.	.32
9	101	137.	.32	30	146.	.29
10	87	129.	.32	41	168.	.25
11	98	128.	.32	41	168.	.20
12	95	132.	.26	46	129.	.35
13	67	124.	.28	31	125.	.30
14	63	77.	.37	23	123.	.31
15	27	102.	.39	14	130.	.27
16	17	105.	.32	4	123.	.42
17	3	85.	.17	2	35.	.04
18	2	94.	.08	1	81.	...

(Source: Public School no. 10, "Annual Registers," City of Rochester, New York.)
    59. For Ohio winter terms, the regression equations with standardized B's (rounded to the nearest hundredth) and zero intercept, where Y = attendance, X_1 = age, and Z_1 = sex, were, for 1840-49, $Y = .44X_1 + .35Z_1X_1 - .34X_1^2 - .62Z_1X_1^2$; for 1850-59, $Y = .53X_1 - .57X_1^2$; for 1860-69, $Y = .66X_1 - .82X_1^2$. For Ohio summer terms, the equations were, for 1840-49, $Y = .33X_1 + .18X_1^2 - .16Z_1X_1^2$; for 1850-59, $Y = .70X_1 - 1.28X_1^2 + .41Z_1X_1^2$. For Rochester, New York, September-June terms, the regression equations with normalized B's (rounded to the nearest hundredth) and zero intercept, where Y = attendance and X_1 = age, were for 1861-69, $Y = 1.08X_1 - 1.09X_1^2$; for 1870-75, $Y = .89X_1 - .87X_1^2$. All R^2 were significant at the .01 level. They were as follows:

	R^2	F-ratio
Winter (Ohio)		
1840-49	.06	7.01
1850-59	.01	3.95
1860-69	.04	11.40
Summer (Ohio)		
1840-49	.09	7.22
1850-59	.12	11.87
Rochester		
1861-69	.03	12.10
1870-74	.02	6.11

60.   Kaestle and Vinovskis, Education and Social Change in Nineteenth-Century Massachusetts, p. 262.

61.   Isabel V. Sawhill, "Economic Perspectives on the Family," in Alice Rossi, Jerome Kagan, and Tamara Hareven (eds.), The Family (New York, 1978), p. 117.

62.   Kaestle and Vinovskis have noted that for younger children ages four to eight school attendance was "an age-specific phenomenon" (Kaestle and Vinovskis, Education and Social Change in Nineteenth-Century Massachusetts, p. 261).

63.   Geal Grover Norris, Autobiographical Account, 1855, Mss. 3243, Western Reserve Historical Society, Cleveland, Ohio, p. 9.

64.   For ages five and six, the regression equations and R^2 values, respectively, were as follows, where Y = achievement in reading and X_1 = attendance in days: $Y = 61.16 + .17X_1$, $R^2 = .55$ and $Y = 71.66 + .17X_1$, $R^2 = .50$. For age seven, the number of students (four) in the subsample was so small that even an R^2 of .51 was insignificant; however, it is likely that with only twice this number, the F-ratio would be significant. (Source: Public School no. 10, "Record of Promotions, 1871-1879," City of Rochester, New York.)

65.   The assumption is made on the basis of a report cited in the Pennsylvania School Journal (32 [1884]:358), which notes that it has been customary to have recitations four times a day in reading. The following schedule (or program) was published, noting that it "may easily be adapted to the wants of almost any country school":

Hours	Minutes	Classes
9	10	Roll call and opening exercises
9-10	10	Reading, chart class
9-20	15	Reading, D
9-35	15	Reading, C
9-50	20	Arithmetic, B
10-10	20	Arithmetic, A
10-30	15	RECESS
10-45	10	Language, chart class
10-55	15	Arithmetic, C & D
11-10	15	Reading, B
11-25	15	History
11-40	20	Writing (two classes)
12	60	NOON
1	20	Roll call. Geography, B (A & C)
1-20	10	Number, chart class
1-30	10	Reading, D
1-40	10	Reading, C
1-50	20	Reading, A
2-10	15	Language, C (B & D)
2-25	15	RECESS
2-40	10	Reading, chart class
2-50	20	Grammar, A
3-10	20	Geography, C & D
3-30	20	Spelling (two classes)
3-50	10	Closing exercises

66. John A. Nietz, Old Text Books (Pittsburgh, 1961), p. 77.
67. "Annual Report of the School Commissioner for the Year 1854,"
Public Document no. 6, Annual Reports Made to the Governor of Ohio for the
Year 1854 (Columbus, 1855), pp. 210-13. Subsequent reports did not include
data on scholars able to read and write. Perhaps this was because the
literacy figures were somewhat embarrassing. Of the total scholars enrolled
in public schools, only 66 percent could read and write (ibid., pp. 222-23).
68. For each year the hours of reading instruction assumed for a child
equals mean days attendance/year times hours of reading instruction/day. Two
hours of reading instruction per day are assumed for children ages five to
eight; one hour per day is assumed for children ages nine to eleven.
69. Kaestle and Vinovskis, Education and Social Change in Nineteenth-
Century Massachusetts, pp. 260-61.
70. Samples of 4,517 children, ages five to nineteen, in 1860 and 6,872
children (including 1.4 percent nonwhite), ages five to nineteen, in 1870, in
nuclear families.
71. The proportion of children in school in northern states whose
fathers were native born was as follows:

Age Class of Father	North		South	
			Free	White
	1860	1870	1860	1870
20-29	.02	.02	0	0
30-39	.32	.22	.16	.13
40-99	.37	.31	.24	.20

72. Samples were taken with a "spin procedure." In the spin procedure
a given spot is designated on the microfilm reader. The film is attached and
half-turns are made with the feeder arm. If the entry line with the spot
marked a male twenty or older, the various members of the family were recorded
including the wife, children, servants, farm laborers, and others. This was a
sample of families and not households, with only one of several possible families
in the house being chosen. Only entries associated with the adult male were
considered. The spin procedure is described in detail in Soltow, Men and
Wealth.
Family data were recorded for 10,235 adult males twenty and older in
1870. We generally exclude 596 of these cases since they represented sons
twenty and older living in families with fathers also twenty and older. To
include these cases would give undue weight to families with more than one
adult male. The remaining 9,639 units accounted for 38,360 persons including
9,639 adult male heads or single adult males, 18,769 children, 677 servants,
421 farm laborers, and 1,431 others. Of the 9,639 we find 7,979 in families
of size two or more, 7,423 with a wife present, and 6,222 with at least one
child.
A similar but smaller sample was drawn from the 1860 microfilm consisting of 4,833 free males twenty and older and 4,522 after eliminating those
where the son appeared in the entry line with the designated spot on the
microfilm reader. In this case we account for 3,738 families of size two or
more, 3,493 with the wife present, and 3,085 with children. The total number
of persons in these families was 19,213. It is generally found advisable to
consider only the 9,125 white adult males in 1870 in making comparisons with
the 4,833 cases in 1860.
73. Church and Sedlak, Education in the United States, p. 121.
74. John Payne, "March 20, 1835," Diary (Ohio Historical Society Collections, Columbus, Ohio).
75. E. G. West notes that "it is now a recognized world-wide phenomenon
that absenteeism from schools is more common in agricultural areas, whether
their education is compulsory or not, and whether they have state schooling
or private schooling." He adds, however, that "periodic absence from nineteenth-century schools was . . . not necessarily a sign of parental negligence.
It could have been the result of a judicious weighing of the expected sacrifice
in family income against the expected educational benefits" (E. G. West,
Education and the Industrial Revolution [New York, 1975], pp. 35-36). The
older farm boy of the 1860s in the United States may thus have found a way to
"have his cake and eat it too."

76. One other alternative is leisure, but this alternative has generally been ignored in models of schooling and the formation of human capital. Rather, the choice "has been assumed to be a school or work choice. If leisure is valued, the decision becomes a choice between three ways of spending time." See Lewis C. Solmon, "Opportunity Costs and Models of Schooling in the Nineteenth Century," Southern Economic Journal 37 (July 1970):67.

77. John Modell, "Patterns of Consumption, Acculturation, and Family Income Strategies in Late Nineteenth-Century America," in Tamara K. Hareven and Maris A. Vinovskis (eds.), Family and Population in Nineteenth-Century America (Princeton, 1978), pp. 230-31.

78. Stephan Thernstrom, Poverty and Progress: Social Mobility in a Nineteenth-Century City (New York, 1969), p. 22.

79. Bureau of Labor Statistics, Ohio, Second Annual Report, 1878 (Columbus, 1879), p. 56.

80. Ibid.

81. Ibid., p. 54.

82. Compendium of the Ninth Census of the United States, p. 797. For the entire population of males, the numbers of age-group 12-15.5 were 16 percent of the numbers in the age-group 15.5 and older.

83. Alexander J. Field, "Educational Reform and Manufacturing Development in Mid-Nineteenth Century Massachusetts," Ph.D. dissertation, Stanford University, 1974, p. 317.

84. Bureau of Labor Statistics, Ohio, Report, 1878, pp. 47, 151, 190.

85. See Michael B. Katz, The Irony of Early School Reform (Boston, 1968), and Church and Sedlak, Education in the United States.

86. For a discussion of socioeconomic factors in New York City which mitigated against both the rich and the poor attending public schools, see Kaestle, Evolution of an Urban School System, pp. 88-111.

87. Thernstrom, Poverty and Progress, p. 110.

88. Ibid.

89. Regression analysis indicates that partial correlation coefficients for nativity and wealth are about the same for age-groups fifteen to nineteen and ten to fourteen.

90. Jane Riblett Wilkie, "Social Status, Acculturation, and School Attendance in 1850 Boston,"Journal of Social History 11 (Winter 1977):180.

91. The problem of the acculturation and assimilation of ethnic groups in the American social order is exceedingly complex, for demographic factors (complex in themselves) are multiplied by the difficulties in assessing the status of ethnic groups as they build or transplant their own institutions and interact with already established ones.

92. The age distribution for the 1870 sample of 11,360 children is as follows:

Age	N
0-4	3,432
5-9	2,891
10-14	2,385
15-19	1,596
20 and up	1,056

93. See Robert V. Wells, "On the Dangers of Constructing Artificial Cohorts in Times of Rapid Social Change," Journal of Interdisciplinary History 9 (Summer 1978):103-10, on the problems of interpreting age-specific findings from cross-sectional analysis of census data.

94. Laurence Glasco, "Ethnicity and Family Structure in Nineteenth Century America: The Native-Born, Irish, and Germans of Buffalo, New York, 1855." Paper delivered at the Clark University Conference on the Family, Social Structure, and Social Change, 1972, p. 26. Glasco classifies households into four categories: nuclear, extended, augmented, and adult mixed. "A 'nuclear' household is composed solely of a conjugal or nuclear family, consisting of the family head plus a spouse and/or child(ren). An 'extended' household has a nuclear family as its basic module, plus one or more relatives. An 'augmented' household consists of either a nuclear or an extended family plus one or more non-related persons, usually boarders or lodgers. (In our classification here, we have excluded servants from consideration of household

structure.) Finally, the 'adult mixed' household is composed either of an isolated individual plus non-conjugal kin and/or non-relatives." For other recent studies of family structure, see John Demos, "Demography and Psychology in the Historical Study of Family Life: A Personal Life," in Peter Laslett and Richard Wall (eds.), Household and Family in Past Time (Cambridge, 1972); John Modell and Tamara K. Hareven, "Urbanization and the Malleable Household: An Examination of Boarding and Lodging in American Families," Journal of Marriage and the Family 35 (Aug. 1973):467-79; Robert V. Wells, "Demographic Change and the Life Cycle of American Families," in Theodore K. Rabb and Robert I. Rotberg (eds.), The Family in History (New York, 1973); Edward Shorter, The Making of the Modern Family (New York, 1975); Alice S. Rossi, Jerome Kagen, and Tamara K. Hareven (eds.), The Family (New York, 1978); Tamara K. Hareven (ed.), Family and Kin in Urban Communities, 1700-1930 (New York, 1977); and Hareven and Vinovskis, Family and Population in Nineteenth-Century America.

95. Jay P. Dolan has noted in his study of New York's Catholics that some ward (neighborhood) public elementary schools did not necessarily offend the "religious sensibilities of Catholics," that the presence of Catholic teachers and, in the case of the Germans, bilingual teaching both made the public schools satisfactory for Catholics (The Immigrant Church: New York's Irish and German Catholics, 1815-1865 [Baltimore, 1975], pp. 108, 119). For general works dealing with the Protestant-Catholic and the immigrant-native struggle, see Ray Allen Billington, The Protestant Crusade, 1800-1860 (New York, 1938), and John Higham, Strangers in the Land (New York, 1966). For the same issue as it erupted within the schools of two major cities, see Vincent P. Lannie, "Alienation in America: The Immigrant Catholic and Public Education in Pre-Civil War America," Review of Politics 32 (Oct. 1970):503-21; Vincent P. Lannie and Bernard C. Diethorn, "For the Honor and Glory of God: The Philadelphia Bible Riots of 1840," History of Education Quarterly 8 (Spring 1968):44-106; Joseph J. McCadden, "New York's School Crisis of 1840-1842: Its Irish Antecedents," Thought 41 (1966):561-88; and Colin Greer, The Great School Legend (New York, 1972).

96. Jay P. Dolan ("Immigrants in the City: New York's Irish and German Catholics," Church History 41 [Sept. 1972]: 362) emphasizes the group solidarity gained through extra-parochial organizations among the German and Irish Catholics of New York City. See also Dolan, Immigrant Church. Colman J. Barry, The Catholic Church and German Americans (Milwaukee, 1953), gives an account of the importance of preserving the native German language among German children. M. Justille McDonald remarks upon the close tie between the German language and German Catholicism as follows: "Priests and people firmly believed that: 'Mit der Sprache geht der Glaube'; hence, the establishment of German parishes and parochial schools" (History of the Irish in Wisconsin in the Nineteenth Century [Washington, D. C., 1954], p. 204). For a recent reconceptualization of the relationship between religion and ethnicity, see Harry S. Stout, "Ethnicity and Religion in America," Ethnicity 2 (June 1975): 204-24. Stout notes: "If ethnoreligious faith is an expression of ultimate allegiance, and the 'church' represents an institution conceived to maintain and perpetuate that allegiance, then the churches, sects, and denominations become as important as symbols of ethnic allegiance as they are for themselves. . . . Seen in such a light, the immigrant churches served the allegiance of the ethnic group at the expense of a prophetic message aimed at all sectors of society. . . . Schools were established under the aegis of the church and efforts were made to inculcate the group with ethnic values and faith in the ethnic heritage" (p. 207).

97. S. N. Eisenstadt, "Archetypal Patterns of Youth," in Erik H. Erikson (ed.), Youth: Change and Challenge (New York, 1963), p. 32.

98. For an account of the growth of the Irish national school system, see Norman Atkinson, Irish Education: A History of Educational Institutions (Dublin, 1969), pp. 90-120, and Donald H. Akenson, The Irish Education Experiment (London, 1970). The story of "hedge schools," an alternative school network which administered both the rudiments of learning and the classics to the poor and middle class, is summarized in P. J. Dowling, A History of Irish Education: A Study in Conflicting Loyalties (Cork, 1971), pp. 86-100. Explorations of the Irish and German ethnic experience are plentiful, and we cite only a few in addition to those already noted: Gordon, Assimilation in

American Life; Emmet H. Rothan, The German Catholic Immigrant in the United States, 1830-1860 (Washington, D. C., 1946); Andrew M. Greeley, That Most Distressful Nation (Chicago, 1972); Lawrence J. McCaffrey, "The Conservative Image of Irish-America," Ethnicity 2 (Sept. 1975):271-80.

99. McDonald, History of the Irish in Wisconsin, p. 219.

100. Carlo M. Cipolla, Literacy and Development in the West (Baltimore, 1969), pp. 73, 127, 115. See also Census of Ireland, 1901, part 2, General Report, p. 151.

101. Ruth Miller Elson, Guardians of Tradition: American Schoolbooks of the Nineteenth Century (Lincoln, Nebr., 1964), pp. 144, 123-28, 143-46.

102. Graff has noted that "age specific profiles of . . . children reveal that not only did fewer children of illiterates attend school, but that they attended for fewer years" (Graff, Literacy Myth, p. 169).

103. In this sample no distinction can be made between Irish fathers who were Catholic and those who were Protestant. It is noted, however, that in Ontario, Canada, in 1871 the illiteracy rate for those of Irish origin who were Catholic was .20, while for those of Irish origin who were Protestant it was .08 (from an unpublished sample of 5,386 adult males drawn from the Ontario census manuscripts of 1871 by Lee Soltow).

104. The observation of John Francis Maguire in 1868 that the "land was the grand resource of the Irish emigrant, as well as the safest and surest means of his advancement" might well have been correct for those immigrant laborers on the canals and railroads of Ohio and Illinois, who earned enough to purchase the first farm (The Irish in America [London, 1868], reprint edition by Arno Press, 1969, p. 237, and Marcus Lee Hansen, The Immigrant in American History [Cambridge, Mass., 1940], p. 165). For the urban dweller, however, such hopes were frustrated and soon exhausted. For the young of the impoverished immigrant who were expected to balance the family budget, it is unlikely that the labor involved was carried out in the spirit of the self-made man, as it might have been for the native American (Oscar Handlin, Boston's Immigrants, 1790-1865 [Cambridge, Mass., 1941], p. 65, and Irvin G. Wyllie, The Self-Made Man in America [New Brunswick, New Jersey, 1954], passim). In a study of labor market discrimination in Waltham, Massachusetts, in 1850, H. M. Gitelman notes that Irish men and boys were assigned the types of positions which did not offer promotion opportunities ("No Irish Need Apply: Patterns of and Responses to Ethnic Discrimination in the Labor Market," Labor History 14 [Winter 1973]: 56-68). For a recent analysis of "changes in the distribution of the male labor force" in Philadelphia between 1850 and 1880, see Bruce Laurie, Theodore Hershberg, and George Alter, "Immigrants and Industry: The Philadelphia Experience, 1850-1880," Journal of Social History 9 (Winter 1975):219-48.

105. For the foreign born father, foreign born child category, N = 75, 136, 126, and 120 for the age-groups zero to four, five to nine, ten to fourteen, and fifteen to nineteen, respectively.

106. William V. Shannon, The American Irish (New York, 1963), p. 37.

107. Ibid.

108. Lannie and Diethorn, "For the Honor and Glory of God," passim; McCadden, "New York's School Crisis of 1840-1842," passim.

109. Dolan, Immigrant Church, p. 105.

110. McDonald, History of the Irish in Wisconsin, p. 219.

111. A general measure of school enrollment for each country has been derived by standardizing for age. The total northern populations in each of the three age-groups have been used as weights applied to the SCH rates in the three age columns. This may be interpreted as the proportion of those aged five to nineteen enrolled in school if each ethnic group had the age composition of the population as a whole. One troublesome feature in dealing with nuclear children is that we do not consider children who have left their families, particularly those fifteen and over. Some evidence that this is not a substantial problem stems from the fact that the ratio of the population fifteen to nineteen relative to that ten to fourteen is roughly the same for all ethnic groups. These were .54, .70, .66, .49, .75, .63, and .92, respectively, for the groups Ireland, Germany, England, Canada, the Northeast, the Northwest, and the South for our data. The reported figures by census authorities considering nuclear and nonnuclear children gave a ratio of .84 for the United States. About 20 percent of children fifteen to nineteen are outside the

nuclear families in 1870. It must be remembered that an ethnic study for two or three generations must be limited to nuclear family data.

112. Wilkie, "Social Status, Acculturation, and School Attendance in 1850 Boston," p. 181.

113. George Stetson, Literacy and Crime in Massachusetts and the Necessity for Moral and Industrial Training in the Public Schools, copy from the Andover Review (Boston, 1886) in the Widener Library, Harvard University, p. 23.

Chapter 5

1. Pennsylvania did have a law in 1833 stating that a will must be signed unless prevented by last illness. It necessitated an act of 1848 to validate the use of the mark (Lee's Estate [1887] 5 Pa. Co., 396).

2. Sir William Blackstone, Knight, Commentaries on the Laws of England in Four Books, book 2, ed. William Draper Lewis (Philadelphia, 1900), pp. 304-5.

3. Thoroughgood v. Cole (1582), 2 Rep., 9. For another early case see Shulter's Case (1655), 12 Rep., 90.

4. Thomas Hemphill et al. v. James Hemphill et al. (1830), 13 N.C., 255-56. On a laissez-faire concept of contract law, see Morton J. Horwitz, "The Historical Foundations of Modern Contract Law," Harvard Law Review 87 (Mar. 1974):917-56, and P. S. Atiyah, The Rise and Fall of Freedom of Contract (Oxford, 1979).

5. Clifton v. Murray (1849), 7 Ga., 564.

6. Nathaniel Atwood v. James Cobb (1834), 15 Mass., 227.

7. Taylor v. Atchison (1870), 54 Ill., 196.

8. Walker v. Ebert (1871), 29 Wis., 194.

9. Bauer and others v. Roth and another (1833), Pa. Reports, 4 Rawle, 83.

10. Thomas Hemphill et al. v. James Hemphill et al. (1830), 13 N.C., 255.

11. Charles Stewart Davies, "An Address Delivered on Commemoration of Fryeburg," 9 May 1825, Portland, Me., reprinted in Joseph L. Blau (ed.), Social Theories of Jacksonian Democracy (Indianapolis, 1954), p. 46.

12. Francis Wright, "A Course of Popular Lectures," N. Y., 1829, reprinted in Blau, Social Theories, pp. 285-87.

13. "Report on Returns of Children Employed in Factories," Commonwealth of Massachusetts, Senate, 14 June 1825, reprinted in John R. Commons (ed.), A Documentary History of American Industrial Society, vol. 5 (Cleveland, 1910), p. 59.

14. Mechanics' Free Press, 21 Aug. 1830, 2:3-4, reprinted in Commons, Documentary History, p. 62.

15. "Testimony," Journal of the Senate of the Commonwealth of Pennsylvania, vol. 2 (5 Dec. 1837), p. 281.

16. From "Questions Addressed to Candidates for the State Legislature" by the Working Men's Party of Philadelphia, reprinted in Commons, Documentary History, p. 102.

17. "Education and the Prevention of Crime," Twelfth Annual Report of the Inspectors of the Eastern Penitentiary, Pennsylvania (Philadelphia, 1840), p. 10.

18. Michael B. Katz, The Irony of Early School Reform (Boston, 1970), p. 184.

19. Daily True Democrat, 11 Feb. 1851, 2:4, reprinted in Annals of Cleveland, vol. 34, no. 1477.

20. Cleveland Leader, 5 Dec. 1863, 1:1, reprinted in Annals of Cleveland, vol. 46, no. 1223, p. 218.

21. Cleveland Leader, 3 May 1864, 2:1; 19 May 1864, 2:2, reprinted in Annals of Cleveland, vol. 47, nos. 565-66, p. 57.

22. Athens Messenger, 30 Apr. 1868, 4:5.

23. The population of the reporting counties was 6.2 million. A factor of 1.04 is used to adjust for the population exactly twenty years of age.

24. Bureau of the Census, "Illiteracy in the United States, Nov. 1969," Current Population Reports, series P-20, no. 217, 1971.

25. Norvell Northcutt, Adult Functional Competency: A Summary (Austin, 1975).

26. To standardize for age only accentuates the differences, since women were 4.5 years younger in 1860 and 4.8 years younger in 1870. The upward trend in illiteracy with advancing age thus makes the differences larger.

27. Census of 1890, Miscellaneous, vol. 2, part 2, pp. 330-31; Census of 1870, vol. 1, p. 396. The sex/illiteracy ratios for whites twenty-one and up in 1850 and 1860 were 1.47 and 1.41, respectively. The 1890 ratios are computed without considering total population sizes. The number of native born females was slightly less than that for males in each age class, for 1890. See Historical Statistics of the United States, series A, pp. 119-34.

28. First Annual Report of the Commissioners of Common Schools in Connecticut (Hartford, 1839), p. 12.

29. Charles L. Coon, The Beginnings of Public Education in North Carolina: A Documentary History, 1790-1840 (Raleigh, 1908), pp. 431-35, 548-53.

30. Western Spy, Cincinnati, Ohio, 28 July 1821, 1:2.

31. Western Herald, Steubenville, Ohio, 20 May 1808, 3:3.

32. R. S. Schofield, "The Measurement of Literacy in Pre-Industrial England," in Jack Goody (ed.), Literacy in Traditional Societies (Cambridge, 1968), p. 315.

33. The coefficient would be zero if all counties had the same IL rate and would be 1.0 if all illiterates were in only one county.

34. Curiously, literacy data were reported in more detail than were general populations for the counties. County counts are given for both white and colored males twenty-one and older who could not read or write, and for the total male population twenty-one and older. An estimate of the white (and colored) male populations twenty-one and older was made using white-colored ratios for the male population zero and older.

35. There is an element of the regression fallacy in tracing only extreme examples. Some counties conceivably retrogressed, but the general relative inequality did diminish.

36. If there were no association between the two variables IL and size, G would be zero; if there were perfect association, G would be a little less than 1.0. If a population were 10 percent illiterate and if all the illiterates lived in the most sparsely populated areas, the Lorenz curve would be horizontal for 90 percent of the range and G would be .95.

37. Mrs. Sedgwick, "The Puzzled Housewife," Daily Cincinnati Enquirer, Cincinnati, Ohio, 12 July 1842, 2:5-6.

38. The migration of the young to urban sectors of the economy is displayed in tabular form as follows:

Age	Proportion of Heads in Nonagricultural Sector
20-29	.16
30-39	.17
40-49	.15
50-59	.12
60-69	.10
70 and up	.07

39. A similar conclusion is reached by Harvey J. Graff, who asserts that the "poverty of illiterates stands out dramatically among the patterns of wealthholding" (The Literacy Myth [New York, 1979], p. 84). A cross-cultural perspective may be added by noting a recently published table by Nicolas for Savoie, France, for the periods 1721-25 and 1781-85. This table demonstrates the strong direct relationship of the size of the dowry and the probability of having a full signature for both the groom and the bride. The evidence may be the best elaborate expression of illiteracy and wealth that we now have for the eighteenth century. (Jean Nicolas, La savoie au 18e siècle, noblesse et bourgeoise, vol. 2 [Paris, 1979], pp. 930-31.)

40. Michael Young, The Rise of Meritocracy (Baltimore, 1958).

41. The notation is $(\overline{N_w, IL_w})$ = (.10, .029).

42. Our conclusions do not necessarily run counter to Graff, who asserts that ascriptive characteristics such as birth, inheritance, and structural inequality were of greater importance to economic rewards than were educational achievement and literacy. There were undoubtedly structural inequalities, and the accidents of birth cannot be dismissed. Yet the real point is whether

or not the fact of being literate modified the effects of these factors. Our data suggest that it did. (Graff, Literacy Myth, pp. 71, 84.)

43. For the period prior to 1870, see Don R. Leet, Population Pressure and Human Fertility Response, Ohio, 1810-1860 (New York, 1978). Leet found for Ohio that "illiteracy could prove to be a variable with a small but significant influence on fertility differentials" (p. 233).

44. Tamara K. Hareven and Maris A. Vinovskis, "Patterns of Childbearing in Late Nineteenth-Century America: The Determinants of Marital Fertility in Five Massachusetts Towns in 1880," in Tamara K. Hareven and Maris A. Vinovskis (eds.), Family and Population in Nineteenth-Century America (Princeton, 1978), pp. 113, 123.

45. The classifications by illiteracy and occupation of the immobility of native born adult white males in 1870 given in the following table reveal one anomaly--illiterates in the farm sector in the North were slightly less mobile than literates. (The standard error of the immobile proportion for illiterates is .5 percent.) No ready explanation is forthcoming for this phenomenon aside from the fact that they were, on the average, four years older than their literate counterparts.

Occupation Class	All Lit.	All Illit.	North Lit.	North Illit.	South Lit.	South Illit.
Farmer	.54	.59	.54	.50	.56	.62
Nonfarmer	.57	.66	.59	.70	.50	.62

(Note that three of the illiteracy cells have frequencies of 100 or less. Source: the sample of 9,125.) Our findings run contrary to those of Graff, who found that "illiterates were more mobile, more transient men and women, and the differences stand regardless of ethnicity, age, sex, life cycle, marital status, or economic position" (Literacy Myth, p. 123).

46. The counties with the highest illiteracy rates in the nation in 1840 and 1850 are listed below.

County and State	IL	White Population 20 and up	Children in School
1840			
Houston, Georgia	.76	1,828	446
Pike, Kentucky	.72	1,231	23
Harlan, Kentucky	.70	1,040	0
Breathitt, Kentucky	.69	733	0
Ware, Georgia	.65	754	478
Campbell, Tennessee	.64	2,066	56
Fentress, Tennessee	.63	1,273	0
Wayne, North Carolina	.62	2,895	213
Yancey, North Carolina	.62	2,096	30
Appling, Georgia	.61	626	55
1850			
Kittson, Minnesota	.87	437	2
Martin, Indiana	.69	2,266	1,678
Letcher, Kentucky	.69	870	351
Pike, Kentucky	.69	1,970	276
Ozark, Missouri	.66	792	159
Clay, Kentucky	.66	1,787	303
St. Mary's Maryland	.65	2,872	1,782
Perry, Kentucky	.64	1,080	276
Vermillion, Louisiana	.63	922	138
Los Angeles, California	.63	1,738	9

47. Harry Caudill, Night Comes to the Cumberlands (Boston, 1962), pp. 5-7.

48. Herbert Click, "History of Education in Pike County, Kentucky," M.A. thesis, University of Kentucky, 1930; Tybee Oliver, "Elementary and Secondary Education in Kentucky Prior to 1860," M.A. thesis, University of Chicago, 1912.

49. The average valuation of property per taxpayer in Pike County in 1840 was but one-quarter of that for the state (Auditor's Office, "A Statement of the Revenue for the Year 1840," Frankfort, Kentucky, Legislative Documents,

Dec. 1840 Session, p. 18). The number of taxpayers in the county was but 44 percent of the number of whites twenty and older recorded in the census. Inequality of property values was large.

50. Data were drawn from each tenth page of Dewey Honaker, <u>1860 Census of Pike County</u> (Pikesville, Kentucky, 1974), mimeographed.

51. Kaestle and Vinovskis, <u>Education and Social Change in Nineteenth-Century Massachusetts</u>, p. 30.

52. Ibid., p. 87.

53. Kaestle and Vinovskis have noted that "wealth of the community had very little impact on total school enrollment" (ibid., p. 98).

54. Lee Soltow, "Distribution of Income and Wealth," <u>Encyclopedia of American Economic History</u>, ed. Glenn Porter, vol. 3 (New York, 1980), pp. 1087-1119; Claudia B. Kidwell and Margaret C. Christman, <u>Suiting Everyone: The Democratization of Clothing in America</u> (Washington, 1974).

Conclusion

1. William G. Lewis, <u>Biography of Samuel Lewis</u> (Cincinnati, 1857), pp. 244-45.

Bibliography

Books, Essays, and Periodicals

Adams, James T. Provincial Society, 1690-1763. Ed. Arthur M. Schlesinger and Dixon R. Fox. New York: Macmillan Co., 1927.

Akenson, Donald H. The Irish Education Experiment. London: Routledge & Kegan Paul, 1970.

Altick, Richard D. The English Common Reader: A Social History of the Mass Reading Public, 1800-1900. Chicago: University of Chicago Press, 1957.

Ammon, Harry. James Monroe: The Quest for National Identity. New York: McGraw-Hill, 1971.

Apter, David E. (ed.). Ideology and Discontent. London: Free Press of Glencoe, 1964.

Atiyah, P. S. The Rise and Fall of Freedom of Contract. Oxford: Clarendon Press, 1979.

Atkinson, Norma. Irish Education: A History of Educational Institutions. Dublin: Allan Figgis, 1969.

Bailyn, Bernard. Education in the Forming of American Society. Reprinted ed. New York: Random House, Vintage Books, 1960.

Bakewell, Mrs. M. The Mother's Practical Guide in the Early Training of Her Children. London: Hamilton, Adams & Co., 1836.

Bantock, Geoffrey H. The Implications of Literacy. Leicester: Leicester University Press, 1966.

Barnard, Henry. Legal Provision Respecting Education and Employment of Children in Factories. Hartford, 1842, Library of American Civilization, no. 40086.

_____. "Subjects and Courses of Instruction in Cities." American Journal of Education 19 (1869):465-576.

Barry, Colman J. The Catholic Church and German Americans. Milwaukee: Bruce Publishing Co., 1953.

Barry, W. T. Post Office Department to Russel, William, Committee on the Post Office and Post Roads, House of Representatives. American State Papers, Class VII. Washington: GPO, 1834.

Bataille, Leon (ed.). A Turning Point for Literacy. New York: Pergamon Press, 1976.

Belok, Michael V. "The Courtesy Tradition and Early Schoolbooks." History of Education Quarterly 8 (Fall 1968):306-18.

Berger, Peter L. "Consciousness Raising: To Whom--By Whom?" Social Policy 5 (Sept./Oct. 1974):38-42.

Berthoff, Rowland. An Unsettled People. New York: Harper & Row, 1971.

Billington, Ray Allen. The Protestant Crusade, 1800-1860. New York: Macmillan Co., 1938.

229

Blackstone, Sir William, Knight. Commentaries on the Laws of England in Four Books. Vol. 2. Ed. William Draper Lewis. Philadelphia: Rees Welsh & Co., 1900.

Blau, Joseph L. (ed.). Social Theories of Jacksonian Democracy. Indianapolis: Bobbs-Merrill Co., 1954.

Bond, Beverley W., Jr. The Civilization of the Old Northwest. New York: Macmillan Co., 1934.

Bremner, Robert H. (ed.). Children and Youth in America. Vol. 1. Cambridge, Mass.: Harvard University Press, 1970.

Bridenbaugh, Carl. Cities in the Wilderness. New York: Knopf, 1955.

Bromage, Arthur. "The Political Implications of Illiteracy." Ph.D. thesis, Harvard University, 1928.

Brown, Cynthia. "Literacy in 30 Hours: Paulo Freire's Process in Northeast Brazil." Social Policy 5 (July/Aug. 1974): 25-32.

Brown, Richard D. "The Emergence of Urban Society in Massachusetts, 1760-1820." Journal of American History 61 (June 1974):29-51.

Bruchey, Stuart. The Roots of American Economic Growth, 1607-1861. New York: Harper & Row, 1965.

Bunker, Frank. Reorganization of the Public School System. Bulletin no. 8. United States Bureau of Education, 1916.

Burns, James A. "A History of Catholic Parochial Schools in the United States." Catholic University Bulletin 5 (Oct. 1906):434-52.

Burton, Warren. Helps to Education in the Homes of Our Country. Boston: Crosby & Nichols, 1863.

Burton, Warren (ed.). The District School as It Was. New York: Thomas Y. Crowell Co., 1928.

Calhoun, Daniel. The Intelligence of a People. Princeton, N. J.: Princeton University Press, 1973.

Carlson, Robert A. The Quest for Conformity: Americanization through Education. New York: Wiley, 1975.

Carpenter, Charles. History of American Schoolbooks. Philadelphia: University of Pennsylvania Press, 1963.

Caudill, Harry. Night Comes to the Cumberlands. Boston: Little, Brown, 1962.

Church, Robert L., and Michael W. Sedlak. Education in the United States. New York: Free Press, 1976.

Cipolla, Carlo M. Literacy and Development in the West. Baltimore: Penguin Books, 1969.

Clammer, J. R. Literacy and Social Change. Leiden: E. J. Brill, 1976.

Clark, Thomas D. "Building Libraries in the Early Ohio Valley." Journal of Library History 6 (Apr. 1971):101-19.

Click, Herbert. "History of Education in Pike County, Kentucky." M.A. thesis, University of Kentucky, 1930.

Clinton, De Witt. "To the Public. Address of the Trustees of the Society for Establishing a Free School in the City of New York, for the Education of Such Poor Children as Do Not Belong to, or Are Not Provided by Any Religious Society." New York Evening Post, 21 May 1805. In Wilson Smith (ed.), Theories of Education in Early America, 1655-1819, p. 342. New York, 1973.

Commons, John R. (ed.). A Documentary History of American Industrial Society. Vol. 5. Cleveland: Arthur H. Clark Co., 1910.

Coon, Charles L. The Beginnings of Public Education in North Carolina: A Documentary History, 1790-1840. Raleigh: Publications of the North Carolina Historical Commission, 1908.

Cowing, Cedric B. The Great Awakening and the American Revolution: Colonial Thought in the Eighteenth Century. Chicago: Rand McNally, 1971.

Cremin, Lawrence. American Education: The Colonial Experience, 1607-1786. New York: Harper & Row, 1970.

_____. Traditions of American Education. New York: Basic Books, 1977.

Cressy, David. "Educational Opportunity in Tudor and Stuart England." History of Education Quarterly 16 (Fall 1976):301-20.

_____. "Levels of Illiteracy in England, 1530-1730." Historical Journal 20 (1977):1-23.

_____. "Literacy in Seventeenth-Century England: More Evidence."
    Journal of Interdisciplinary History 8 (Summer 1977):141-50.
Curti, Merle. The Making of an American Community. Stanford, Calif.:
    Stanford University Press, 1959.
Demos, John. "Demography and Psychology in the Historical Study of Family
    Life: A Personal Life." In Household and Family in Past Time. Ed.
    Peter Laslett and Richard Wall. Cambridge: Cambridge University
    Press, 1972.
_____. "Developmental Perspectives on the History of Childhood." Journal
    of Interdisciplinary History 2 (Autumn 1971):315-28.
Disch, Robert (ed.). The Future of Literacy. Englewood Cliffs, N. J.:
    Prentice-Hall, 1973.
Dolan, Jay P. The Immigrant Church: New York's Irish and German Catholics,
    1815-1865. Baltimore: Johns Hopkins University Press, 1975.
_____. "Immigrants in the City: New York's Irish and German Catholics."
    Church History 41 (Sept. 1972):354-68.
Dowling, P. J. A History of Irish Education: A Study in Conflicting Loyalties.
    Cork, Ireland: Mercier Press, 1971.
Dunn, W. Ross. Education in Territorial Ohio. Ohio Archaeological and Histori-
    cal Publications, no. 35. Columbus: Ohio State Archaeological and
    Historical Society, 1926.
Dwight, Timothy. A Discourse on Some Events of the Last Century.
    Delivered in New Haven at Yale University, 7 Jan. 1801. New Haven:
    Ezra Read, 1801.
Earle, Alice M. Child Life in Colonial Days. New York: Macmillan Co.,
    1927.
Eisenstadt, S. N. "Archetypal Patterns of Youth." In Youth: Change
    and Challenge. Ed. Erik Erikson. New York: Basic Books, 1963.
Elson, Ruth Miller. Guardians of Tradition: American Schoolbooks of the Nine-
    teenth Century. Lincoln: University of Nebraska Press, 1964.
Febvre, Lucien, and Henri-Jean Martin. The Coming of the Book: The Impact
    of Printing, 1450-1800. Trans. David Gerard. Ed. Geoffrey Nowell-
    Smith and David Wooton. London and Atlantic Highlands, N. J.:
    Humanities Press, 1976.
Field, Alexander James. "Educational Expansion in Mid-Nineteenth Century
    Massachusetts: Human Capital Formation or Structural Reinforcement."
    Harvard Educational Review 46 (Nov. 1976):521-52.
_____. "Educational Reform and Manufacturing Development in Mid-Nineteenth
    Century Massachusetts." Ph.D. dissertation, Stanford University, 1974.
Finklestein, Barbara. "Pedagogy as Intrusion: Teaching Values in Popular
    Primary Schools in Nineteenth-Century America." History of Childhood
    Quarterly 2 (Winter 1975):349-78.
Fishlow, Albert. "Levels of Nineteenth-Century American Investment in
    Education." Journal of Economic History 26 (Dec., 1966):418-36.
_____. "The American Common School Revival: Fact or Fancy." In Industriali-
    zation in Two Systems. Ed. Henry Rosovsky. New York: Wiley, 1966.
Foote, John Parsons. The Schools of Cincinnati. Cincinnati: C. F. Bradley &
    Co., 1855.
Franklin, Benjamin. Autobiography and Other Writings. New York: New
    American Library, 1961.
Furet, Francois, and Jacques Ozouf. Lire et écrire. Paris: Aux Editions De
    Minuit, 1977.
Galenson, David. "Literacy and the Social Origins of Some Early Americans."
    Historical Journal 22 (1979):75-92.
Gitelman, H. M. "No Irish Need Apply: Patterns of and Responses to Ethnic
    Discrimination in the Labor Market." Labor History 14 (Winter 1973):
    56-68.
Glasco, Laurence. "Ethnicity and Family Structure in Nineteenth Century
    America: The Native Born, Irish, and Germans of Buffalo, New York,
    1855." Paper delivered at Clark University Conference on the Family,
    Social Structure, and Social Change, 1972.
Goody, Jack, and Ian Watt. "The Consequences of Literacy." Comparative
    Studies in Society and History 5 (1962):304-45.
Gordon, Michael M. Assimilation in American Life. New York: Oxford
    University Press, 1964.

Gould, Benjamin. Investigations in the Military and Anthropological Statistics of American Soldiers. New York: U. S. Sanitary Commission, 1869.

Graff, Harvey J. "Literacy and Social Structure in the Nineteenth-Century City." Ph.D. dissertation, University of Toronto, 1975.
_____. The Literacy Myth: Literacy and Social Structure in the Nineteenth-Century City. New York: Academic Press, 1979.
_____. "Notes on Methods for Studying Literacy from the Manuscript Census." Historical Methods Newsletter 5 (Dec. 1971):11-16.
_____. "'Pauperism, Misery, and Vice': Illiteracy and Criminality in the Nineteenth Century." Journal of Social History 2 (1978):245-68.
_____. "Towards a Meaning of Literacy: Literacy and Social Structure in Hamilton, Ontario." History of Education Quarterly 12 (Fall 1972): 411-31.

Grant, Ulysses S. Personal Memoirs. Vol. 1. New York: Charles L. Webster & Co., 1885.

Greeley, Andrew M. That Most Distressful Nation. Chicago: Quadrangle Books, 1972.

Greer, Colin. The Great School Legend. New York: Basic Books, 1972.

Greer, Colin (ed.). Divided Society: The Ethnic Experience in America. New York: Basic Books, 1974.

Greven, Philip J., Jr. Child-Rearing Concepts, 1628-1861. Itasca, Ill.: F. E. Peacock Publishers, 1973.

Griffin, Clifford S. "Religious Benevolence as Social Control, 1815-1860." Mississippi Valley Historical Review 44 (Dec. 1957):423-44.

Handlin, Oscar. Boston's Immigrants, 1790-1865. Cambridge, Mass.: Harvard University Press, 1941.

Hansen, Marcus Lee. The Immigrant in American History. Cambridge, Mass.: Harvard University Press, 1940.

Harbaugh, H. "Parochial or Christian Schools." Mercersburg Quarterly 5 (Jan. 1853):23-50.

Hareven, Tamara K. (ed.). Family and Kin in Urban Communities, 1700-1930. New York: New Viewpoints, 1977.

Hareven, Tamara K., and Maris A. Vinovskis (eds.). Family and Population in Nineteenth-Century America. Princeton, N. J.: Princeton University Press, 1978.

Harman, David. "Literacy: An Overview." Harvard Educational Review 40 (May 1970):226-43.

Harris, Michael H. "Books on the Frontier: The Extent and Nature of Book Ownership in Southern Indiana, 1800-1850." Library Quarterly 42 (Oct. 1972):416-29.

Harrison, John Fletcher Clews. The Early Victorians, 1832-1851. New York: Praeger, 1971.

Hart, Jim A. The Developing Views on the News, Editorial Syndrome, 1500-1800. Carbondale: Southern Illinois University Press, 1970.

Henretta, James A. The Evolution of American Society, 1700-1815. Lexington, Mass.: D. C. Heath & Co., 1973.

Henry, James. An Address upon Education and Common Schools. Albany: C. Van Benthuysen & Co., 1843.

Heyman, Richard D. "A Theoretical Look at Knowledge, Schools, and Social Change." Comparative Education Review 18 (Oct. 1974):411-18.

Higham, John. Strangers in the Land. New York: Antheneum, 1966.

Hofstadter, Richard. Anti-Intellectualism in American Life. New York: Knopf, 1963.

Horwitz, Morton J. "The Historical Foundations of Modern Contract Law." Harvard Law Review 87 (Mar. 1974):917-56.

Howe, Daniel Walker (ed.). Victorian America. Philadelphia: University of Pennsylvania Press, 1976.

Humphrey, Edward Frank. Nationalism and Religion in America, 1774-1789. Boston: Chipman Law Publishing Co., 1924.

Hunter, Miriam C. The One-Room Schools of Coshocton County, Ohio. Ann Arbor, Mich.: Brown-Brumfield, 1974.

Hutchinson, Edward P. Immigrants and Their Children, 1850-1950. New York: Wiley, 1956.

Hutchison, John A. Language and Faith: Studies in Sign, Symbol, and Meaning.
     Philadelphia: Westminster Press, 1968.
Jarvis, Edward. "The Value of Common School Education to Common Labor."
     Circular of Information of the Bureau of Education, no. 3. Washington:
     GPO, 1879.
Jernegan, Marcus. Laboring and Dependent Classes in Colonial America.
     Reprinted ed. New York: Frederick Ungar, 1965.
Johansson, Egil. En Studie Med Kvantitativa Metoder Av Folkundervisningen I
     Bygdea Socken, 1845-1873. Umea: Umea Universitet Pedagogiska
     Institutionen, 1972.
_____. The History of Literacy in Sweden in Comparison with Some Other
     Countries. Educational Reports, Umea, no. 12. Umea: Umea University
     and Umea School of Education, 1977.
Johansson, Egil (ed.). Literacy and Society in a Historical Perspective--A
     Conference Report. Educational Reports, Umea, no. 2. Umea: Umea
     University and Umea School of Education, 1973.
Johnson, Clifton. The Country School. New York: Thomas Y. Crowell &
     Co., 1907.
_____. Old-Time Schools and School-Books. New York: Macmillan Co., 1917.
Johnson, Elmer D. History of Libraries in the Western World. Metucken, N. J.:
     Scarecrow Press, 1970.
Johnson, Richard. "Educational Policy and Social Control in Early Victorian
     England." Past and Present 49 (Nov. 1970):96-119.
Kaestle, Carl F. "Social Change, Discipline, and the Common School in Early
     Nineteenth-Century America." Journal of Interdisciplinary History 9
     (Summer 1978):1-17.
_____. The Evolution of an Urban School System: New York City, 1750-1850.
     Cambridge, Mass.: Harvard University Press, 1973.
Kaestle, Carl F., and Maris A. Vinovskis. Education and Social Change in
     Nineteenth-Century Massachusetts: Quantitative Studies. Final Research
     Report, 31 Dec. 1976. National Institute of Education, Grant NE-G-00-3-
     0068, Project 3-0825.
Katz, Michael B. The Irony of Early School Reform. Boston: Beacon Press,
     1970.
_____. "Who Went to School?" History of Education Quarterly 12 (Fall
     1972):432-54.
Kaufman, Paul. "The Community Library: A Chapter in English Social History."
     Transactions of the American Philosophical Society, n.s., part 7, vol. 57
     (1967).
Kett, Joseph. "Adolescence and Youth in Nineteenth-Century America."
     Journal of Interdisciplinary History 11 (Autumn 1971):283-98.
Kidwell, Claudia B., and Margaret C. Christman. Suiting Everyone: The
     Democratization of Clothing in America. Washington: Smithsonian
     Institution Press, 1974.
Kiefer, Monica. American Children through their Books, 1700-1835. Philadelphia:
     University of Pennsylvania Press, 1948.
Kilpatrick, William H. Introduction to Pestalozzi, Heinrich, The Education of
     Man: Aphorisms. New York: Philosophical Library, 1951.
Knox, Samuel. "An Essay on the Best System of Liberal Education." Essay
     presented to the American Philosophical Society, 1798. Early American
     Imprints, no. 35690.
Kobre, Sidney. The Development of the Colonial Newspaper. Pittsburgh:
     Colonial Press, 1944.
Kuhn, Anne L. The Mother's Role in Childhood Education: New England
     Concepts, 1830-1860. New Haven: Yale University Press, 1947.
Liancourt, Duke De La Rochefoucault. Travels through the United States of
     North America. London, 1799.
Lannie, Vincent P. "Alienation in America: The Immigrant Catholic and Public
     Education in Pre-Civil War America." Review of Politics 32 (Oct. 1970):
     503-21.
Lannie, Vincent P., and Bernard C. Diethorn. "For the Honor and Glory of
     God: The Philadelphia Bible Riots of 1840." History of Education
     Quarterly 8 (Spring 1968):44-106.

Laqueur, Thomas Walter. Religion and Respectability: Sunday Schools and English Working Class Culture, 1780-1850. New Haven: Yale University Press, 1976.

Laurie, Bruce, Theodore Herschberg, and George Alter. "Immigrants and Industry: The Philadelphia Experience, 1850-1880." Journal of Social History 9 (Winter 1975):219-48.

Lee, Alfred M. The Daily Newspaper in America: The Evolution of a Social Instrument. New York: Macmillan Co., 1937.

Lee, Gordon C. (ed.). Crusade against Ignorance: Thomas Jefferson on Education. New York: Teachers College, Columbia University Press, 1961.

Leet, Don R. Population Pressure and Human Fertility Response, Ohio, 1810-1860. New York: Arno Press, 1978.

Lewis, William G. W. Biography of Samuel Lewis. Cincinnati: R. P. Thompson, 1857.

Lockridge, Kenneth. "A Communication." William and Mary Quarterly 25 (July 1968):516-17.

_____. Literacy in Colonial New England. New York: W. W. Norton & Co., 1974.

Lynn, Robert W., and Elliott Wright. The Big Little School. New York: Harper & Row, 1971.

McCadden, Joseph J. "New York's School Crisis of 1840-42: Its Irish Antecedents." Thought 41 (1966):561-88.

McCaffrey, Lawrence J. "The Conservative Image of Irish-America." Ethnicity 2 (Sept. 1975):271-80.

McDonald, M. Justille. History of the Irish in Wisconsin in the Nineteenth Century. Washington: Catholic University of America Press, 1954.

McLeish, John. Evangelical Religion and Popular Education. London: Methuen & Co., 1969.

Macleod, Anne Scott. A Moral Tale. Hamden, Conn.: Archron Books, 1975.

McMullen, Haynes. "The Use of Books in the Ohio Valley Before 1850." Journal of Library History 1 (Jan. 1966):43-56.

Maguire, John Francis. The Irish in America. London: Longmans, Green & Co., 1868. Reprint edition by Arno Press, 1969.

Main, Gloria L. "The Correction of Biases in Colonial American Probate Records." Historical Methods Newsletter 8 (Dec. 1974):10-28.

Main, Jackson Turner. The Social Structure of Revolutionary America. Princeton, N. J.: Princeton University Press, 1965.

Mann, Horace. Life and Works of Horace Mann. Vol. 5, Boston: Lee & Shepard, 1891.

Mansfield, Edward D. American Education: Its Principles and Elements. New York: A. S. Barnes & Co., 1851.

Martin, Dorothy V. "A History of the Library Movement in Ohio to 1850 with a Special Study of Cincinnati's Library Development." Master's thesis, Ohio State University, 1935.

Mason, Horace. "Fundamental Education and Functional Literacy--Problems and Possibilities." Convergence 6 (1973):55-61.

Miller, Samuel. "A Sketch of the Revolutions and Improvements in Science, Arts, and Literature in America." In Brief Retrospect of the Eighteenth Century (1803). Reprinted in William and Mary Quarterly 10 (Jan. 1953): 579-627.

Mittelberger, Gottlieb. Journey to Pennsylvania. Ed. Oscar Handlin and John Clive. Cambridge, Mass.: Harvard University Press, Belknap Press, 1960.

Miyakawa, S. Scott. Protestants and Pioneers. Chicago: University of Chicago Press, 1964.

Modell, John, and Tamara K. Hareven. "Urbanization and the Malleable Household: An Examination of Boarding and Lodging in American Families." Journal of Marriage and the Family 35 (Aug. 1973):467-79.

Morgan, Edmund S. The Puritan Family. Rev. ed. New York: Harper & Row, 1966.

Mott, Frank L. American Journalism: A History, 1690-1960. New York: Macmillan Co., 1962.

Mull, Rev. George. "Morality in the Public Schools." Reformed Quarterly Review 29, n.s. 4 (Oct. 1882):467-88.

Murphy, Richard T. "Changing Demands and Definitions of Literacy Assessment."
    Paper delivered at the Functional Literacy Conference, Indiana University,
    29 June 1979.
Nash, Gary B. "Urban Wealth and Poverty in Pre-Revolutionary America."
    Journal of Interdisciplinary History 6 (Spring 1976):545-84.
New-York Historical Society. The Burghers of New Amsterdam and the Freemen
    of New York, 1675-1866. Collections of the New-York Historical Society,
    vol. 18. New York: New-York Historical Society, 1885.
_____. Ledger Number 1. Chamberlain's Office Corporation of the City of New
    York, May 11, 1691 to November 12, 1699, and Indentures of Apprentices,
    Oct. 21, 1718 to August 7, 1727. Collections of the New-York Historical
    Society, vol. 42. New York: New-York Historical Society, 1909.
Nicolas, Jean. La savoie au 18e siècle, noblesse et bourgeoise. Vol. 2.
    Paris: Maloine, 1979.
Nietz, John A. Old Text Books. Pittsburgh: University of Pittsburgh
    Press, 1961.
Northcutt, Norvell. Adult Functional Competency: A Summary. Austin: Univer-
    sity of Texas, Division of Extension, 1975.
Northend, Charles. Obstacles to the Greater Success of Common Schools.
    Boston: William D. Ticknor, 1844.
Oliver, Tybee. "Elementary and Secondary Education in Kentucky prior to
    1860." M.A. thesis, University of Chicago, 1912.
Orcutt, Hiram. Hints to Common School Teachers, Parents, and Pupils.
    Rutland, Vt.: George A. Tuttle & Co., 1859.
_____. Reminiscences of School Life. Cambridge, Mass.: Harvard University
    Press, 1898.
Osborne, G. S. Scottish and English Schools: A Comparative Survey of the
    Past Fifty Years. Pittsburgh: University of Pittsburgh Press, 1966.
Page, David P. The Mutual Duties of Parents and Teachers. Boston: William
    D. Ticknor, 1838.
_____. Theory and Practice of Teaching. Syracuse, N.Y.: Hall & Dickson,
    1847.
Parsons, Talcott. "Culture and Social System Revisited." In The Idea of
    Culture in the Social Sciences. Ed. Louis Schneider and Charles M.
    Bonjean. Cambridge: University Press, 1973.
Pennsylvania School Journal 32 (1884):358.
Pessen, Edward. Most Uncommon Jacksonians. Albany: State University of
    New York Press, 1967.
Potter, Alonzo. The School and the School Master. Boston: W. B. Fowle &
    N. Capan, 1843.
Powell, Sumner Chilton. Puritan Village. New York: Doubleday & Co., Anchor
    Books, 1965.
Pratte, Richard. Ideology and Education. New York: David McKay Co., 1977.
Prescott, Thomas H. The Volume of the World. Columbus: J. & H. Miller,
    1851.
Rabb, Theodore K., and Robert I. Rotberg (eds.). The Family in History.
    New York: Harper & Row, 1973.
Reeder, R. R. Historical Development of School Readers. Columbia University
    Contributions to Philosophy, Psychology, and Education, vol. 8
    New York: Columbia University Press, 1900.
Reisner, Edward H. Nationalism and Education Since 1789. New York:
    Macmillan Co., 1922.
Resnick, Daniel P., and Lauren B. Resnick. "The Nature of Literacy: An
    Historical Exploration." Harvard Educational Review 47 (Aug. 1977):
    370-85.
Rice, Edwin Wilbur. The Sunday-School Movement and the American Sunday-
    School Union, 1780-1917. Philadelphia: American Sunday-School Union,
    1917.
Rossi, Alice S., Jerome Kagen, and Tamara K. Hareven (eds.). The Family.
    New York: W. W. Norton, 1978.
Rothan, Emmet H. The German Catholic Immigrant in the United States, 1830-
    1860. Washington: Catholic University of America Press, 1946.
Rothman, David. The Discovery of the Asylum. Boston: Little, Brown,
    1971.

Rush, Benjamin. "A Plan for the Establishment of Public Schools and the Diffusion of Knowledge in Pennsylvania." In Theories of Education in Early America, 1655-1819. Ed. Wilson Smith. New York: Bobbs-Merrill Co., 1973.

Sanderson, Michael. "Literacy and Social Mobility in the Industrial Revolution in England." Past and Present 56 (1972):75-104.

Schlesinger, Arthur M. Learning How to Behave: A Historical Study of American Etiquette Books. New York: Macmillan Co., 1947.

_____. Prelude to Independence: The Newspaper War on Britain, 1764-1776. New York: Knopf, 1966.

Schofield, R. S. "The Measurement of Literacy in Pre-Industrial England." In Literacy in Traditional Societies. Ed. Jack Goody. Cambridge: Cambridge University Press, 1968.

Schultz, Stanley K. The Culture Factory: Boston Public Schools, 1789-1860. New York: Oxford University Press, 1973.

Scotland, James. The History of Scottish Education. London: University of London Press, 1969.

Scribner, Sylvia, and Michael Cole. "Literacy without Schooling: Testing for Intellectual Effects." Harvard Educational Review 48 (Nov. 1978):448-61.

Select Cases of the Mayor's Court of New York City, 1674-1784. Ed. Richard B. Morris. American Legal Records, vol. 2. Washington: American Historical Association, 1935.

Seliger, M. Ideology and Politics. New York: Free Press, 1976.

Seybolt, Robert Francis. Apprenticeship and Apprenticeship Education in Colonial New England and New York. Teachers College, Columbia University Contributions to Education, no. 85. New York: Teachers College, Columbia University Press, 1917.

Shaffer, Ellen. "The Children's Books of the American Sunday-School Union." Book Collector 17 (Oct. 1966):21-28.

Shannon, William V. The American Irish. New York: Macmillan Co., 1963.

Shilling, D. C. Pioneer Schools and Schoolmasters. Ohio Archaeological and Historical Publications, no. 25. Columbus: Ohio State Archaeological and Historical Society, 1916.

Shorter, Edward. The Making of the Modern Family. New York: Basic Books, 1975.

Sloane, William. Children's Books in England and America in the Seventeenth Century. New York: King's Crown Press, 1955.

Smith, Daniel Scott. "Underregistration and Bias in Probate Records: An Analysis of Data from Eighteenth-Century Hingham, Massachusetts." William and Mary Quarterly 32 (Jan. 1975):100-110.

Smith, Samuel Harrison. "Remarks on Education." Essay presented to the American Philosophical Society, 1798. Early American Imprints, no. 34558.

Smith, Timothy L. "Protestant Schooling and American Nationality, 1800-1850." Journal of American History 53 (Mar. 1967):679-95.

Soderbergh, Peter A. "'Old School Days' on the Middle Border, 1849-1859: The Mary Payne Beard Letters." History of Education Quarterly 8 (Winter 1968):497-504.

Solmon, Lewis C. "Opportunity Costs and Models of Schooling in the Nineteenth Century." Southern Economic Journal 37 (July 1970):66-83.

Soltow, Lee. "Distribution of Income and Wealth." In Encyclopedia of American Economic History. Ed. Glenn Porter. Vol. 3. New York: Charles Scribner's Sons, 1980.

_____. Men and Wealth in the United States, 1850-1870. New Haven: Yale University Press, 1975.

Soltow, Lee, and Edward Stevens. "Economic Aspects of School Participation in Mid-Nineteenth-Century United States." Journal of Interdisciplinary History 8 (Autumn 1977):221-43.

Stephens, W. B. "Illiteracy and Schooling in the Provincial Towns, 1646-1870: A Comparative Approach." In Urban Education in the Nineteenth Century: Proceedings of the 1976 Annual Conference of the History of Education Society in Great Britain. Ed. D. A. Reeder. London: Taylor & Francis, 1977.

Stetson, George. Literacy and Crime in Massachusetts and the Necessity for Moral and Industrial Training in the Public Schools. Copy from The Andover Review. Boston, 1886 in the Widener Library, Harvard University.

Stevens, Edward. "Relationships of Social Library Membership, Wealth, and Literary Culture in Early Ohio." Forthcoming in The Journal of Library History.

_____. "Wealth and Literary Culture in the Old American West." Social Science History, forthcoming.

Stevens, Edward, and Lee Soltow. "Quantitative Factors in the Acculturation of Immigrant Children in Mid-Nineteenth Century United States." Paper delivered at the American Educational Research Association meeting in Toronto, 27-31 Mar. 1978.

Stone, Lawrence. "Literacy and Education in England, 1640-1900." Past and Present 42 (Feb. 1969):69-193.

Story, Joseph. "A Discourse Pronounced at Cambridge, before the Phi Beta Kappa Society, August 31, 1826." In Eloquence of the United States. Ed. E. B. Williston. Vol. 5. Middleton, Conn.: E. & H. Clark, 1827.

Stout, Harry S. "Ethnicity and Religion in America." Ethnicity 2 (June 1975):204-24.

Sutton, Walter. The Western Book Trade. Columbus: Ohio State University Press, 1961.

Teaford, Jon. "The Transformation of Massachusetts Education." History of Education Quarterly 10 (Fall 1970):287-307.

Tebbel, John. The Compact History of the American Newspaper. New York: Hawthorn Books, 1969.

_____. A History of Book Publishing in the United States. Vol. 1. New York: R. R. Bowker, 1972.

Thernstrom, Stephan. Poverty and Progress: Social Mobility in a Nineteenth Century City. New York: Atheneum, 1969.

Troen, Selwyn K. "Popular Education in Nineteenth-Century St. Louis." History of Education Quarterly 13 (Spring 1973):23-40.

_____. The Public and the Schools. Columbia: University of Missouri Press, 1975.

Tyack, David. "The Kingdom of God and the Common School: Protestant Ministers and the Educational Awakening in the West." Harvard Educational Review 36 (Fall 1966):447-69.

_____. The One Best System: A History of American Urban Education. Cambridge, Mass.: Harvard University Press, 1974.

UNESCO. The Experimental World Literacy Programme: A Critical Assessment. Paris: UNESCO, 1976.

_____. World Illiteracy at Mid-Century, a Statistical Study. Paris: UNESCO, 1957.

Vaughn, Michalina, and Margaret S. Archer. Social Conflict and Educational Change in England and France, 1789-1848. Cambridge: University Press, 1971.

Verplanck, Mr., of New York. "Resolution to the House of Representatives, December 21, 1829." Register of Debates of Congress. 21st Congress, 1st Session, vol. 6, part 1, p. 479.

Vinovskis, Maris A. "Trends in Massachusetts Education, 1826-1860." History of Education Quarterly 12 (Winter 1972):501-29.

Wadlin, Horace G. "Illiteracy in Massachusetts." In Sixty-Fifth Annual Report of the Board of Education, 1900-1901. Boston: Wright & Potter Printing Co., 1902.

Weatherford, John (ed.). "School and Other Days, 1859: Selections from the Diaries of Robert and Sylvester Bishop." Ohio Historical Quarterly 70 (Jan. 1961):58-63.

Webb, R. K. The British Working Class Reader, 1790-1848: Literacy and Social Tension. London: George Allen & Unwin, 1955.

_____. "Literacy among the Working Classes." Scottish Historical Review 33 (Feb. 1954):100-114.

Wells, Robert V. "Demographic Change and the Life Cycle of American Families." In The Family in History. Ed. Theodore K. Rabb and Robert I. Rotberg. New York: Harper & Row, 1973.

_____. "On the Dangers of Constructing Artificial Cohorts in Times of Rapid Social Change." Journal of Interdisciplinary History 9 (Summer 1978):103-10.

Welter, Rush. The Mind of America, 1820-1860. New York: Columbia University Press, 1975.

West, E. G. Education and the Industrial Revolution. New York: Harper & Row, 1975.

White, Emerson E. "The Country School Problem." In NEA Proceedings of the Thirteenth Annual Meeting of the National Council of Education. Asbury Park, N. J., 1894. St. Paul: Pioneer Press Co., 1895.

Wiebe, Robert H. "The Social Functions of Public Education." American Quarterly 21 (Summer 1969):147-64.

Wilkie, Jane Riblett. "Social Status, Acculturation, and School Attendance in 1850 Boston." Journal of Social History 11 (Winter 1977):179-92.

Williston, E. B. (ed.). Eloquence of the United States. Middleton, Conn.: E. & H. Clark, 1827.

Wright, Louis B. Culture on the Moving Frontier. Bloomington: Indiana University Press, 1955.

Wyllie, Irvin G. The Self-Made Man in America. New Brunswick, N. J.: Rutgers University Press, 1954.

Young, Michael. The Rise of Meritocracy. Baltimore: Penguin Books, 1958.

Documents, Manuscripts, and Unpublished Materials

Acts of the State of Ohio, vol. 4. Chillicothe, 1805. Reprinted by Lansing Co., Norwalk, Ohio, 1901. Fourth Session of the General Assembly.

Auditor's Office, Frankfort, Kentucky. "A Statement of the Revenue for the Year 1840." Legislative Documents. Dec. Session, 1840.

Archives of Maryland. "Proceedings of the County Courts of Kent, 1648-1676. Talbot, 1662-1674, and Somerset, 1665-1668, Counties." Vol. 54. Court Series 7. Baltimore, 1937.

Archives of Maryland, Judicial and Testamentary Business of the Provincial Court, 1637-1650. "Proceedings and Acts of the General Assembly, 1637/8-1664." Ed. William Browne. Baltimore, 1887.

Archives of Maryland. "Proceedings and Acts." Vol. 7.

American Digest. "Signatures." Century Index. St. Paul, 1902.

Academicus to Thomas Jefferson, 7 Jan. 1797. "Plan for the Education of Youth," c. 1797. Archives no. 10. Philadelphia, American Philosophical Society.

Bureau of Statistics of Labor and Agriculture, Pennsylvania. First Annual Report, 1872-73. Harrisburg, 1874.

Bureau of Census. "Illiteracy in the United States, Nov. 1969." Current Population Reports. Series P-20, no. 217, 1971.

Bureau of Labor Statistics, Ohio. Second Annual Report, 1878. Columbus, 1879.

"Catalog of Books Belonging to the Western Library Association." Vol. 1. Ohio Historical Society.

"Catalog of Books in the Farmer's Library (1827)." Special Collections. University of Rochester.

Census of Industry. "Manuscripts," Ohio and Wisconsin, 1870.

Census of Ireland, part 2. General Report, 1901.

Colonial Records of North Carolina. Ed. Walter Clark. Raleigh, 1886, and New York, AMS Reprint, 1968.

Commissioner of Common Schools, Connecticut. First Annual Report. Hartford, 1839.

Common School Journal. Various volumes.

Compendium of the Ninth Census of the United States. Washington, 1872.

Compendium of the Seventh Census of the United States. Washington, 1854.

Documents and Records of New Hampshire. Vols. 6, 8, 1776-83.

Documents Relative to the Colonial History of New York, the State of New York, Procured in Holland, England, and France. Vols. 1, 3, 4, 14. Ed. E. B. O'Callaghan. Albany, 1856.

Eaton, John. The Relation of Education to Labor. Washington, 1872.

"Education and the Prevention of Crime." Twelfth Annual Report of the Inspectors of the Eastern Penitentiary, Pennsylvania. Pennsylvania, 1840.

Historical Statistics of the United States. Series Z, p. 8; Series P, pp. 43-72; Series A, pp. 119-34; Series B, pp. 163-75.
Honaker, Dewey. "1860 Census of Pike County." Mimeographed. Pikesville, Kentucky, 1974.
Hull, John T. York Deeds. Vols. 1-13. Portland, Me., 1887.
"The Indentures of Managers of the House of Employment in Philadelphia County in 1798. Administered under the Form of the Act of Assembly for the Relief of the Poor." Book 13 folio, Microfilm 980136, Indentures, Loose Papers, Almshouses, Guardians of the Poor, Philadelphia County, 1795-1806. Genealogical Society of Salt Lake City.
James, Uriah P. Papers. "Catalog" (1852), "Catalog" (1840). Collection no. 198. Ohio Historical Society.
Kerr, John. Papers. "Catalog of Books in the Chillicothe Library," 1804, Container 3. Western Reserve Historical Society.
King, Sarah Worthington. Family Papers. Ohio Historical Society.
Massachusetts Bureau of Statistics of Labor, Sixth Annual Report. March, 1875. Public Document no. 31.
"Memorial of a Number of Citizens of Boston to the Senate and House of Representatives," 13 Feb. 1832. American State Papers. Class VII. Washington: GPO, 1834.
National Archives. Record Groups 36, 94, various boxes.
National Center for Education Statistics. The Condition of Education, 1976. Washington: GPO, 1976.
Norris, Geal Grover. "Autobiographical Account," 1855. Western Reserve Historical Society.
Ohio Journal of Education. Columbus, 1853-70.
"Packet Book" and "Mail Book." Ashtabula Sentinel. Ashtabula County Records, Ohio Historical Society.
Payne, John. "Diary." Ohio Historical Society.
"Probate Records," 1813-59. Athens County, Ohio.
Probate Records of the Province of New Hampshire. Vols. 1-6. Ed. Albert Batchellor, Henry Metcalf, and Otis Hammond. Concord 1907-38.
"Probate Records," 1790-1859. Washington County, Ohio.
Records of the Colony of New Plymouth in New England. Ed. Nathaniel B. Shurtleff. Boston, 1855.
Records of the Colony of Rhode Island and Providence Plantations. Vol. 1. Providence, 1856.
Ross County and Meigs County Collections. Special Collections, Ohio University.
Seward, William Henry. Special Collections, University of Rochester, Rochester, New York.
State Commissioner of Common Schools, Ohio. Annual Reports, 1853-75. Columbus, 1853-75.
State Commissioner of Common Schools, Ohio. Annual Report, 1886. Columbus, 1887.
Subscription books for the Mansfield Gazette. In James Purdy Collection, Ohio Historical Society.
Superintendent of Public Instruction, Pennsylvania. Annual Reports, 1860-80. Harrisburg, 1860-80.
Teacher Records. Districts 3 and 5, Perry Township, Columbiana Co., Ohio, 1840-52; District 5, Butler Township, Columbiana Co., Ohio, 1846-60; District 1, Sullivan Township, Ashland Co., Ohio, 1847-53; Districts 1, 2, 3, 4, 6, 8, 9, and 10, Bainbridge Township, Geauga Co., Ohio, 1875-76; District 6, Springfield Township, Hamilton Co., Ohio, 1844-45; District 5, Twinsburg, Summit Co., Ohio, 1847-56; Greenfield Union School, Highland Co., Ohio, 1859-67.
Tenth Annual Report. Eastern State Penitentiary, Pennsylvania. Philadelphia, 1839.
"Testimony." Journal of the Senate of the Commonwealth of Pennsylvania. Vol. 2, 5 Dec. 1837.
Statistics of the Population of the United States, Ninth Census. Vol. 1. Washington: GPO, 1872.
United States Census Manuscripts, 1840-70.
United States Census of 1890, Miscellaneous. Vol. 2, part 2.
United States Commissioner of Education. Report, 1875, 1880. Washington.

United States Statutes at Large, 1789-99. Fourth Congress, Session I, chap.
        36, 1796.
Williams, Samuel. "Papers." Box 15, Folder 1, Collection no. 148. Ohio
        Historical Society.

Judicial Decisions

Nathaniel Atwood v. James Cobb (1834), 15 Mass., 227.
Bauer and others v. Roth and another (1833), Pa. Reports, 4 Rawle, 83.
Thomas Hemphill et al. v. James Hemphill et al. (1830), 13 N.C., 251.
Clifton v. Murray (1849), 7 Ga., 564.
Helton v. Burdette (1918), 180 Ky., 492.
Lee's Estate (1887), 5 Pa. Co., 396.
Shank v. Butsch (1867), 28 Ind., 19.
Shulter's Case (1655), 12 Rep., 90, 1366.
Suffern and Galloway v. Butler and Butler (1868), 19 N.J. Eq., 202.
State of Louisiana v. Albert Push (1871), 23 La. Ann., 14.
State, ex rel. Bateman v. Bode (1896), 224 Ohio St., 230-31.
State, ex rel. v. Miller (1912), 87 Ohio St., 43, 44.
State, ex rel. v. Sweeney (1950), 154 Ohio St., 229, 230.
State, ex rel. Weinberger, A. Taxpayer v. Miller et al. (1912), 87 Ohio St., 12.
Taylor v. Atchison (1870), 54 Ill., 196.
Thoroughgood's Case (1582), 2 Rep., 9, 408.
Walker v. Ebert (1871), 29 Wis., 194.
Yeagley v. Webb (1882), 86 Ind., 424.
Zacharie v. Franklin (1838), 37 U. S. (12 Pet.), 151.

Newspapers

Annals of Cleveland, vols. 1-48 (1818-1865), Cleveland, 1938.
Athens Messenger and Hocking Valley Gazette, Athens, Ohio, 1850-65.
Athens Mirror and Literary Register, Athens, Ohio, 1825-30.
Centinel of the North-Western Territory, Cincinnati, Ohio, 1793-96.
Chenango Weekly Advertiser, Norwich, New York, 1811-13.
Cleveland Plain Dealer, Cleveland, Ohio, 1860.
Daily Cincinnati Enquirer, Cincinnati, Ohio, 1842-52.
Daily Dayton Journal, Dayton, Ohio, 1852-56.
Delaware Patron and Franklin Chronicle, Steubenville, Ohio, 1821.
Franklin Chronicle, Steubenville, Ohio, 1820.
Hocking Valley Gazette and Athens Journal, Athens, Ohio, 1838-40.
Huran Reflector, Norwalk, Ohio, 1830-51.
Ohio Argus, Lebanon, Ohio, 1831-33.
Scioto Gazette, Chillicothe, Ohio, 1828-32.
Patriot (Broome County), Binghamton, New York, 1812-13.
Summit Beacon and Summit County Beacon, Akron, Ohio, 1841-70.
Western Herald, Steubenville, Ohio, 1806-19.
Western Spectator and Athens Chronicle, Athens, Ohio, 1831.
Western Spy and Hamilton Gazette, Cincinnati, Ohio, 1800-1821.
Zanesville Aurora, Zanesville, Ohio, 1838-41.
Zanesville City Times, Zanesville, Ohio, 1855-60.
Zanesville Express and Republican Standard, Zanesville, Ohio, 1812-16.
Zanesville Gazette, Zanesville, Ohio, 1831-51.
Zanesville Muskingum Messenger, Zanesville, Ohio, 1816-22.
[The Zanesville] Ohio Republican, Zanesville, Ohio, 1823-42.
Zanesville Triweekly Courier, Zanesville, Ohio, 1846-64.

Textbooks, Children's Literature, and Children's Newspapers

1740-99

Barbauld, Mrs. Anna Letitia. Lessons for Children from Two to Four Years Old.
        Philadelphia, 1788.
Benezet, Anthony. The Pennsylvania Spelling Book; or, Youth's Friendly
        Instructor and Monitor. Philadelphia, 1799.
Bingham, Caleb. The Child's Companion Being a Concise Spelling Book. Sixth
        edition. Boston, 1798.

[Dunlap, W.]. The Child's New Play-Thing: Being a Spelling-Book Intended to Make the Learning to Read, a Diversion instead of a Task Consisting of a New-Invented Alphabet for Children. Philadelphia, 1763.

Fox, [George]. Instructions for Right Spelling and Plain Directions for Reading and Writing True English, with Several Delightful Things, Very Useful and Necessary, Both for Young and Old, to Read and Learn. Boston, 1743.

The Good Child's Delight; or, The Road to Knowledge in Short, Entertaining Lessons of One and Two Syllables. Philadelphia, 1795.

The Juvenile Biographer Containing the Lives of Little Masters and Misses Including a Variety of Good and Bad Characters. Worcester, Mass., 1787.

The Mother's Gift; or, a Present for All Little Boys Who Wish to Be Good. Philadelphia, 1791.

Perry, W[illiam]. The Only Sure Guide to the English Tongue. Brookfield, Mass., 1798.

A Present to Children. Norwich, 1794.

[Thomas, Isaiah]. Tom Thumb's Playbook: To Teach Children Their Letters as Soon as They Can Speak Being a New and Pleasant Method to Allure Little Ones in the First Principles of Learning. Boston, 1761.

Watts, I[saac]. The First Set of Catechisms and Prayers; or, The Religion of Little Children, under Seven or Eight Years of Age. Twelfth edition. Boston, 1762.

Webster, Noah. The American Spelling Book: Containing an Easy Standard of Pronunciation Being the First Part of a Grammatical Institute of the English Language. Second edition. Boston, 1790.

Winchester, Elhanan. A Plain Political Catechism Intended for the Use of Schools in the United States of America. Greenfield, Mass., 1796.

The Youth's Instructor in the English Tongue; or, The Art of Spelling Improved. Boston, 1767.

1800-1809

The American Primer Calculated for the Instruction of Young Children. Norfolk, 1803.

Daggett, Herman. The American Reader. Sag-Harbor, N. Y., 1806.

Dialogue between a Fond Father and His Little Son, Designed to Amuse and Instruct Children. Norwich, 1804.

Edgeworth, Maria. The Little Merchants; or, Honesty and Knavery Contrasted. New Haven, 1808.

Juvenal Poems; or, The Alphabet in Verse, Designed for the Enlightenment of All Good Boys and Girls, and No Others. New Haven, 1807.

Saunders, Samuel H. An Easy First Book for Children. Philadelphia, 1809.

Webster, Noah. The American Spelling Book. Second revised impression. Philadelphia, 1804.

1810-19

The American Primer; or, An Easy Introduction to Spelling and Reading. Philadelphia, 1813.

Barbauld, Mrs. [Anna Letitia]. Lessons for Children. Philadelphia, 1818.

English, Clara. The Children in the Wood; an Instructive Tale. Philadelphia, 1813.

Hays, S. Stories for Little Children. Philadelphia, 1812.

Horwood, Miss. The Deserted Boy; or, Cruel Parents. Philadelphia, 1817.

Hubbard, John. The American Reader. Walpole, N. H., 1811.

Johnson's Philadelphia Primer. Philadelphia, 1810.

The Juvenile Budget; or, Entertaining Stories for Little Children. Boston, 1810.

Lyman, Asa. The American Reader: Containing Elegant Selections in Prose and Poetry. Second edition. Portland, Me., 1811.

The Present: A First Book for Children. Boston, 1811.

Remarks on Children's Play. New York, 1818.

Richmond, Leigh. The Dairyman's Daughter. Newark, 1815.

Wood, Samuel. The New York Reader, Adapted to the Capacities of the Younger Class of Learners. No. 1, New York, 1812.

1820-29

Babcock, Sidney. The Poetic Gift, or, Alphabet in Rhyme. New Haven, c.
      1825.
Blackbird's Nest. New Haven, 1824.
Cardell, William S. Story of Jack Halyard, the Sailor Boy; or, The Virtuous
      Family. Philadelphia, 1827.
Colburn, Warren. Intellectual Arithmetic upon the Inductive Method of In-
      struction. Boston, 1826.
Crandall, Daniel. The Columbian Spelling-Book: Containing the Elements of the
      English Language. Cooperstown, 1820.
Hyll, Joseph. A Guide to the English Language. Utica, N. Y., 1820.
Keagy, John M. The Pestalozzian Primer; or, First Step in Teaching Children the
      Art of Reading and Thinking. Harrisburg, Pa., 1827.
Little Emma and Her Father; or, The Effects of Pride. Philadelphia, 1820.
The New England Primer, Containing the Shorter Catechism; with a brief
      Introduction to Spelling and Reading. Cincinnati, 1827.
The New England Primer Improved; or, An Easy and Pleasant Guide to the Art
      of Reading. Hartford, 1820.
The Ohio Primer; or, An Introduction to Spelling and Reading. Pittsburgh,
      1826.
Phoebe, the Cottage Maid. New York, 1824.
Rural Scenes; or, A Peep into the Country for Children. New York, 1823.
Stockton, J. The Western Spelling Book. Pittsburgh, 1822.
The United States Primer. Salem, Ohio, 1825.
Webster, Noah. The Elementary Spelling Book. Medina, Ohio, 1829.
The Western Preceptor: A Spelling Book in Two Parts. Part 2. Mountpleasant,
      Ohio, 1821.

1830-39

The American Primer. Cincinnati, 1830.
The Children in the Wood. Cooperstown, 1837.
The Children's Magazine. New York, 1830, various issues.
The Child's Newspaper. Cincinnati, 1834, various issues.
[Darby, William]. The United States Reader or Juvenile Instructor, No. 2.
      Baltimore, 1832.
Ells, B. F. The Dialogue Arithmetic or Book Instructor. Dayton, 1836.
Emerson, Frederick.   The North American Arithmetic. Philadelphia, 1835.
[Goodrich, Samuel G.]. Peter Parley's Short Stories for Long Nights.
      Boston, 1834.
Guilford, Nathan. The Western Spelling Book, Designed for the Use of Common
      Schools. Cincinnati, 1831.
Jones, Mrs. Elizabeth C. Infantine Ditties. Providence, 1830.
Kip, John D. W. The Union Speller, an English Spelling Book for the Use of
      Schools in the United States. Washington Court House, Ohio, 1830.
[A Lady]. Poems for Children. New York, 1837.
McGuffey, William H. McGuffey's Eclectic First Reader. Cincinnati, 1836.
McGuffey, William H. McGuffey's Eclectic Second Reader. Cincinnati, 1836.
Pickett, A., and John W. Pickett. The New Juvenile Spelling Book and Rudi-
      mental Reader. Cincinnati, 1837.
Pickett, A., and John W. Pickett. Pickett's Primer; or, First Book for Children
      Designed to Precede the Spelling Book. Cincinnati, 1836.
The Union Spelling Book. Philadelphia, 1838.
The Visiter. Cincinnati, 1835, various issues.
The Western Primer; or, Introduction to Webster's Spelling Book. Columbus,
      Ohio, 1837.

1840-49

[Abbot, Anne W.]. Doctor Busby and His Neighbors. Salem, 1844.
Cobb, Lyman. Cobb's New Spelling Book in Six Parts. New York, 1843.
Colamn, Miss. How to Be Happy, a Love Gift for Little Folks. Boston, 1847.
Ells, B. F. The Pleasing Speller and Definer. Dayton, 1841.
Hazen, E. The Speller and Definer. Philadelphia, 1845.
The History of Goody Two Shoes. Cleveland, 1841.

McGuffey, William H. The Eclectic First Reader for Young Children. Cincinnati, 1840.
McGuffey, William H. McGuffey's Eclectic Third Reader. Cincinnati, 1848.
McGuffey, William H. McGuffey's Newly Revised Eclectic Spelling Book. Cincinnati, 1846.
Sanders, Charles W. Sanders' Spelling Book Containing a Minute and Comprehensive System of Introductory Orthography. Cleveland, 1844.
The School Friend. Cincinnati, 1846, various issues.
Talbott, John L. The Scholar's Guide to the Science of Numbers. Cincinnati, 1848.
The Western Primer Ornamented with Engravings. Columbus, 1843.

1850-59

Abbott, Jacob. Rollo's Correspondence. Philadelphia, 1850.
The Boy of Spirit, a Story for the Young. Tenth edition. Boston, 1855.
Comly, John. John Comly's Spelling and Reading Book. Philadelphia, 1851.
The Friend of Youth. Washington, D. C., 1851, various issues.
Life in the West; or, The Moreton Family. Philadelphia, 1851.
McGuffey, William H. McGuffey's New First Eclectic Reader. Cincinnati and New York, 1857.
McGuffey, William H. McGuffey's New Primary Reader. Cincinnati, 1866.
McGuffey, William H. McGuffey's Newly Revised Eclectic Second Reader. Cincinnati, 1853.
McGuffey, William H. McGuffey's Newly Revised First Reader. Cincinnati, 1854.
[Neal, Alice B.]. No Such Word as Fail; or, The Children's Journey. New York, 1852.
Optic, Oliver (pseud). Try Again; or, The Trials and Triumphs of Harry West. Boston, 1859.
Sanders, Charles W. Sanders' Pictorial Primer. Philadelphia, 1858.
Sargent, Epes. The Standard Speller Containing Exercizes for Oral Spelling. Boston, 1856.
Town, Salem. Town's Speller and Definer. Portland, Me., 1855.
Webster, Noah. The Elementary Spelling Book. New York, 1857.

1860-69

Bunbury, Miss Selina. Fanny, the Flower Girl; and the Infant's Prayer. Nashville, Tenn., 1861.
City Sights for Little Folks. New York, 1862.
Leigh, Edward. Leigh's McGuffey's New Primary Reader. Cincinnati, 1866.
Right and About Right; or, The Boy on the Farm. Boston, 1867.
Webster, Noah. The Elementary Spelling-Book. New York, 1866.
Worcester, Joseph E. A Comprehensive Spelling-Book on the Plan of the Pronouncing Spelling-Book. Chicago, 1864.

No Date

Book of Riddles. New York.
Dogwood, Edward. Little Boy Eight Years Old, a History of the Big Letters: Intended for the Instruction and Amusement of All Little Children in the Nation. Pittsburgh.
Learning to Read. 18--.

Index

Acculturation, 131-39
American enlightenment, 80
American seamen, illiteracy of. See
     Literacy rates
Anti-intellectualism, 62
Appalachia, 23, 42, 185-88, 195
Apprenticeship, 30-33, 37, 54, 207
Army enlistees, illiteracy of. See
     Literacy rates
Athens County, 69, 73, 79-80

Barnard, Henry, 91
Bell, Andrew, 12
Book ownership, 68-69; and marri-
     age, 69, 196; and wealth, 70

Campaign for literacy, 58
Census enumeration, 5-6, 156, 159
Child labor, 152-53
Children's literature, 65-67
Civil War, 154, 177-79
Clinton, De Witt, 49
Cognitive imperialism, 8
Common school, reform of, 51, 91,
     142, 189
Compulsory school legislation, 29-30,
     51
Contracts, 45, 151-52, 179, 225
Cotton, John, 29
Crime, and illiteracy, 48, 86-87,
     143-44, 153
Crockett, Davy, 62
Cultural pluralism, 94-95, 130-35,
     137-40, 145-47

Daily school schedule, 220
Davies, Charles, 152
Deeds, 149
Dwight, Timothy, 90

Economic mobility, 25-26, 46, 86, 123,
     136, 144, 177-79, 194
Equality of educational opportunity,
     42, 48, 93-94, 115-16, 128, 144,
     153
Estate data, for Ohio, 212-13

First Day Society of Philadelphia, 16
Functional literacy, 3-4
Franklin, Benjamin, 30
Free School Society, 49
Frontier, 42, 77-79

Gini coefficient of inequality, 84, 116,
     167, 169, 178, 195, 226
Grant, Ulysses S., 92-93

Hedge schools, 137

Ideology: and morality, 60, 86; and
     reform, 86, 142; definition of,
     59-61, 211; of common school,
     26; of literacy, 20, 47, 55, 86,
     189, 193; use of, 60, 142-43,
     189
Illiterates, contemporary, 8-9
Income differentials, 123-27
Intellectual elite, 147
Irish immigrants, 137

Jefferson, Thomas, 62, 89-90
Jones, Griffith, 12-13
Jurors, 46

Lancasterian plan of education, 49, 91
Lewis, Samuel, 197
Liancourt, La Rochefoucault, 29

245